J.W. Mackail

The Aeneid of Virgil

J.W. Mackail

The Aeneid of Virgil

ISBN/EAN: 9783741161018

Manufactured in Europe, USA, Canada, Australia, Japa

Cover: Foto ©Thomas Meinert / pixelio.de

Manufactured and distributed by brebook publishing software (www.brebook.com)

J.W. Mackail

The Aeneid of Virgil

THE AENEID OF VIRGIL

THE

AENEID OF VIRGIL

TRANSLATED INTO ENGLISH

BY

J. W. MACKAIL, M.A.

FELLOW OF BALLIOL COLLEGE, OXFORD

London

MACMILLAN AND CO.

1885

PREFACE

THERE is something grotesque in the idea of a
prose translation of a poet, though the practice is
become so common that it has ceased to provoke
a smile or demand an apology. The language of
poetry is language in fusion; that of prose is
language fixed and crystallised; and an attempt
to copy the one material in the other must always
count on failure to convey what is, after all, one of
the most essential things in poetry,—its poetical
quality. And this is so with Virgil more, perhaps,
than with any other poet; for more, perhaps, than
any other poet Virgil depends on his poetical quality
from first to last. Such a translation can only have
the value of a copy of some great painting executed
in mosaic, if indeed a copy in Berlin wool is not a
closer analogy; and even at the best all it can
have to say for itself will be in Virgil's own words,
Experiar sensus; nihil hic nisi carmina desunt.

In this translation I have in the main followed
the text of Conington and Nettleship. The more
important deviations from this text are mentioned
in the notes; but I have not thought it necessary

to give a complete list of various readings, or to mention any change except where it might lead to misapprehension. Their notes have also been used by me throughout.

Beyond this I have made constant use of the mass of ancient commentary going under the name of Servius ; the most valuable, perhaps, of all, as it is in many ways the nearest to the poet himself. The explanation given in it has sometimes been followed against those of the modern editors. To other commentaries only occasional reference has been made. The sense that Virgil is his own best interpreter becomes stronger as one studies him more.

My thanks are due to Mr. EVELYN ABBOTT, Fellow and Tutor of Balliol, and to the Rev. H. C. BEECHING, for much valuable suggestion and criticism.

THE AENEID

BOOK FIRST

THE COMING OF AENEAS TO CARTHAGE

I SING of arms and the man who of old from the coasts of Troy came, an exile of fate, to Italy and the shore of Lavinium; hard driven on land and on the deep by the violence of heaven, for cruel Juno's unforgetful anger, and hard bestead in war also, ere he might found a city and carry his gods into Latium; from whom is the Latin race, the lords of Alba, and the stately city Rome.

Muse, tell me why, for what attaint of her deity, or in what vexation, did the Queen of heaven drive one so excellent in goodness to circle through so many afflictions, to face so many toils? Is anger so fierce in celestial spirits?

There was a city of ancient days that Tyrian settlers dwelt in, Carthage, over against Italy and the Tiber mouths afar; rich of store, and mighty in war's fierce pursuits; wherein, they say, alone beyond all other lands had Juno her seat, and held Samos itself less dear. Here was her armour, here her chariot; even now, if fate permit, the goddess strives to nurture it for queen of the nations. Nevertheless she had heard a race was issuing of the blood of

B

Troy, which sometime should overthrow her Tyrian citadel ; from it should come a people, lord of lands and tyrannous in war, the destroyer of Libya: so rolled the destinies. Fearful of that, the daughter of Saturn, the old war in her remembrance that she fought at Troy for her beloved Argos long ago,—nor had the springs of her anger nor the bitterness of her vexation yet gone out of mind : deep stored in her soul lies the judgment of Paris, the insult of her slighted beauty, the hated race and the dignities of ravished Ganymede ; fired with this also, she tossed all over ocean the Trojan remnant left of the Greek host and merciless Achilles, and held them afar from Latium ; and many a year were they wandering driven of fate around all the seas. Such work was it to found the Roman people.

Hardly out of sight of the land of Sicily did they set their sails to sea, and merrily upturned the salt foam with brazen prow, when Juno, the undying wound still deep in her heart, thus broke out alone :

'Am I then to abandon my baffled purpose, powerless to keep the Teucrian king from Italy ? and because fate forbids me ? Could Pallas lay the Argive fleet in ashes, and sink the Argives in the sea, for one man's guilt, mad Oïlean Ajax ? Her hand darted Jove's flying fire from the clouds, scattered their ships, upturned the seas in tempest ; him, his pierced breast yet breathing forth the flame, she caught in a whirlwind and impaled on a spike of rock. But I, who move queen among immortals, I sister and wife of Jove, wage warfare all these years with a single people ; and is there any who still adores Juno's divinity, or will kneel to lay sacrifice on her altars ?'

Such thoughts inly revolving in her kindled bosom, the goddess reaches Aeolia, the home of storm-clouds, the land laden with furious southern gales. Here in a desolate cavern Aeolus keeps under royal dominion and yokes in

dungeon fetters the struggling winds and loud storms.
They with mighty moan rage indignant round their
mountain barriers. In his lofty citadel Aeolus sits
sceptred, assuages their temper and soothes their rage;
else would they carry with them seas and lands, and the
depth of heaven, and sweep them through space in their
flying course. But, fearful of this, the lord omnipotent
hath hidden them in caverned gloom, and laid a mountain
mass high over them, and appointed them a ruler, who
should know by certain law to strain and slacken the reins
at command. To him now Juno spoke thus in suppliant
accents : '

'Aeolus—for to thee hath the father of gods and king
of men given the wind that lulls and that lifts the waves—
a people mine enemy sails the Tyrrhene sea, carrying into
Italy the conquered gods of their Ilian home. Rouse thy
winds to fury, and overwhelm their sinking vessels, or drive
them asunder and strew ocean with their bodies. Mine
are twice seven nymphs of passing loveliness ; her who of
them all is most excellent in beauty, Deïopea, I will unite
to thee in wedlock to be thine for ever ; that for this thy
service she may fulfil all her years at thy side, and make
thee father of a beautiful race.'

Aeolus thus returned : 'Thine, O queen, the task to
search whereto thou hast desire ; for me it is right to do
thy bidding. From thee have I this poor kingdom, from
thee my sceptre and Jove's grace ; thou dost grant me to
take my seat at the feasts of the gods, and makest me
sovereign over clouds and storms.'

Even with these words, turning his spear, he struck the
side of the hollow hill, and the winds, as in banded array,
pour where passage is given them, and cover earth with
eddying blasts. East wind and west wind together, and
the gusty south-wester, falling prone on the sea, stir it up

from its lowest chambers, and roll vast billows to the shore. Behind rises shouting of men and whistling of cordage. In a moment clouds blot sky and daylight from the Teucrians' eyes; black night broods over the deep. Pole thunders to pole, and the air quivers with incessant flashes; all menaces them with instant death. Straightway Aeneas' frame grows unnerved and chill, and stretching either hand to heaven, he cries thus aloud: 'Ah, thrice and four times happy they who found their doom under high Troy town before their fathers' faces! Ah, son of Tydeus, bravest of the Grecian race, that I could not have fallen on the Ilian plains, and gasped out this my life beneath thine hand! where under the spear of Aeacides lies fierce Hector, lies mighty Sarpedon; where Simoïs so often bore beneath his whirling wave shields and helmets and brave bodies of men.'

As the cry leaves his lips, a gust of the shrill north strikes full on the sail and raises the waves up to heaven. The oars are snapped; the prow swings away and gives her side to the waves; down in a heap comes a broken mountain of water. These hang on the wave's ridge; to these the yawning billow shows ground amid the surge, where the sea churns with sand. Three ships the south wind catches and hurls on hidden rocks, rocks amid the waves which Italians call the Altars, a vast reef banking the sea. Three the east forces from the deep into shallows and quicksands, piteous to see, dashes on shoals and girdles with a sandbank. One, wherein loyal Orontes and his Lycians rode, before their lord's eyes a vast sea descending strikes astern. The helmsman is dashed away and rolled forward headlong; her as she lies the billow sends spinning thrice round with it, and engulfs in the swift whirl. Scattered swimmers appear in the vast eddy, armour of men, timbers and Trojan treasure amid the water. Ere now the stout ship of Ilioneus, ere now of brave Achates, and she wherein

Abas rode, and she wherein aged Aletes, have yielded to
the storm ; through the shaken fastenings of their sides
they all draw in the deadly water, and their opening seams
give way.

Meanwhile Neptune discerned with astonishment the
loud roaring of the vexed sea, the tempest let loose from
prison, and the still water boiling up from its depths, and
lifting his head calm above the waves, looked forth across
the deep. He sees all ocean strewn with Aeneas' fleet,
the Trojans overwhelmed by the waves and the ruining
heaven. Juno's guile and wrath lay clear to her brother's
eye ; east wind and west he calls before him, and thereon
speaks thus :

'Stand you then so sure in your confidence of birth ?
Careless, O winds, of my deity, dare you confound sky and
earth, and raise so huge a coil ? you whom I—   But
better to still the aroused waves ; for a second sin you
shall pay me another penalty. Speed your flight, and say
this to your king : not to him but to me was allotted the
stern trident of ocean empire. His fastness is, on the
monstrous rocks where thou and thine, east wind, dwell :
there let Aeolus glory in his palace and reign over the
barred prison of his winds.'

Thus he speaks, and ere the words are done he soothes
the swollen seas, chases away the gathered clouds, and
restores the sunlight. Cymothoë and Triton together push
the ships strongly off the sharp reef ; himself he eases them
with his trident, channels the vast quicksands, and assuages
the sea, gliding on light wheels along the water. Even as
when oft in a throng of people strife hath risen, and the
base multitude rage in their minds, and now brands and
stones are flying ; madness lends arms ; then if perchance
they catch sight of one reverend for goodness and service,
they are silent and stand by with attentive ear ; he with

speech sways their temper and soothes their breasts; even so hath fallen all the thunder of ocean, when riding forward beneath a cloudless sky the lord of the sea wheels his coursers and lets his gliding chariot fly with loosened rein.

The outworn Aeneadae hasten to run for the nearest shore, and turn to the coast of Libya. There lies a spot deep withdrawn; an island forms a harbour with out-stretched sides, whereon all the waves break from the open sea and part into the hollows of the bay. On this side and that enormous cliffs rise threatening heaven, and twin crags beneath whose crest the sheltered water lies wide and calm; above hangs a background of flickering forest, and the dark shade of rustling groves. Beneath the seaward brow is a rock-hung cavern, within it fresh springs and seats in the living stone, a haunt of nymphs; where tired ships need no fetters to hold nor anchor to fasten them with crooked bite. Here with seven sail gathered of all his company Aeneas enters; and disembarking on the land of their desire the Trojans gain the chosen beach, and set their feet dripping with brine upon the shore. At once Achates struck a spark from the flint and caught the fire on leaves, and laying dry fuel round kindled it into flame. Then, weary of fortune, they fetch out corn spoiled by the sea and weapons of corn-dressing, and begin to parch over the fire and bruise in stones the grain they had rescued.

Meanwhile Aeneas scales the crag, and seeks the whole view wide over ocean, if he may see aught of Antheus storm-tossed with his Phrygian galleys, aught of Capys or of Caïcus' armour high astern. Ship in sight is none; three stags he espies straying on the shore; behind whole herds follow, and graze in long train across the valley. Stopping short, he snatched up a bow and swift arrows, the arms trusty Achates was carrying; and first the leaders, their stately heads high with branching antlers, then the common

herd fall to his hand, as he drives them with his shafts in
a broken crowd through the leafy woods. Nor stays he
till seven great victims are stretched on the sod, fulfilling
the number of his ships. Thence he seeks the harbour
and parts them among all his company. The casks of
wine that good Acestes had filled on the Trinacrian beach,
the hero's gift at their departure, he thereafter shares, and
calms with speech their sorrowing hearts :

'O comrades, for not now nor aforetime are we ignorant
of ill, O tried by heavier fortunes, unto this last likewise will
God appoint an end. The fury of Scylla and the roaring
recesses of her crags you have been anigh ; the rocks of the
Cyclops you have trodden. Recall your courage, put dull
fear away. This too sometime we shall haply remember
with delight. Through chequered fortunes, through many
perilous ways, we steer for Latium, where destiny points us
a quiet home. There the realm of Troy may rise again
unforbidden. Keep heart, and endure till prosperous fortune come.'

Such words he utters, and sick with deep distress he
feigns hope on his face, and keeps his anguish hidden deep
in his breast. The others set to the spoil they are to feast
upon, tear chine from ribs and lay bare the flesh ; some cut
it into pieces and pierce it still quivering with spits ; others
plant cauldrons on the beach and feed them with flame.
Then they repair their strength with food, and lying along
the grass take their fill of old wine and fat venison. After
hunger is driven from the banquet, and the board cleared,
they talk with lingering regret of their lost companions,
swaying between hope and fear, whether they may believe
them yet alive, or now in their last agony and deaf to
mortal call. Most does good Aeneas inly wail the loss
now of valiant Orontes, now of Amycus, the cruel doom of
Lycus, of brave Gyas, and brave Cloanthus.

And now they ceased; when from the height of air Jupiter looked down on the sail-winged sea and outspread lands, the shores and broad countries, and looking stood on the cope of heaven, and cast down his eyes on the realm of Libya. To him thus troubled at heart Venus, her bright eyes brimming with tears, sorrowfully speaks :

'O thou who dost sway mortal and immortal things with eternal command and the terror of thy thunderbolt, how can my Aeneas have transgressed so grievously against thee? how his Trojans? on whom, after so many deaths outgone, all the world is barred for Italy's sake. From them sometime in the rolling years the Romans were to arise indeed; from them were to be rulers who, renewing the blood of Teucer, should hold sea and land in universal lordship. This thou didst promise: why, O father, is thy decree reversed? This was my solace for the wretched ruin of sunken Troy, doom balanced against doom. Now so many woes are spent, and the same fortune still pursues them ; Lord and King, what limit dost thou set to their agony? Antenor could elude the en-circling Achaeans, could thread in safety the Illyrian bays and inmost realms of the Liburnians, could climb Timavus' source, whence through nine mouths pours the bursting tide amid dreary moans of the mountain, and covers the fields with hoarse waters. Yet here did he set Patavium town, a dwelling-place for his Teucrians, gave his name to a nation and hung up the armour of Troy; now settled in peace, he rests and is in quiet. We, thy children, we whom thou beckonest to the heights of heaven, our fleet miserably cast away for a single enemy's anger, are be-trayed and severed far from the Italian coasts. Is this the reward of goodness? Is it thus thou dost restore our throne?'

Smiling on her with that look which clears sky and

storms, the parent of men and gods lightly kissed his daughter's lips ; then answered thus :

'Spare thy fear, Cytherean ; thy people's destiny abides unshaken. Thine eyes shall see the city Lavinium, their promised home ; thou shalt exalt to the starry heaven thy noble Aeneas ; nor is my decree reversed. He thou lovest (for I will speak, since this care keeps torturing thee, and will unroll further the secret records of fate) shall wage a great war in Italy, and crush warrior nations ; he shall appoint his people a law and a city ; till the third summer see him reigning in Latium, and three winters' camps pass over the conquered Rutulians. But the boy Ascanius, whose surname is now Iülus—Ilus he was while the Ilian state stood sovereign—thirty great circles of rolling months shall he fulfil in government ; he shall carry the kingdom from its fastness in Lavinium, and make a strong fortress of Alba the Long. Here the full space of thrice an hundred years shall the kingdom endure under the race of Hector's kin, till the royal priestess Ilia from Mars' embrace shall give birth to a twin progeny. Thence shall Romulus, gay in the tawny hide of the she-wolf that nursed him, take up their line, and name them Romans after his own name. I appoint to these neither period nor boundary of empire : I have given them dominion without end. Nay, harsh Juno, who in her fear now troubles earth and sea and sky, shall change to better counsels, and with me shall cherish the lords of the world, the gowned race of Rome. Thus is it willed. A day will come in the lapse of cycles, when the house of Assaracus shall lay Phthia and famed Mycenae in bondage, and reign over conquered Argos. From the fair line of Troy a Caesar shall arise, who shall limit his empire with ocean, his glory with the firmament, Julius, inheritor of great Iülus' name. Him one day, thy care done, thou shalt welcome to heaven loaded

with Eastern spoils; to him too shall vows be addressed.
Then shall war cease, and the iron ages soften. Hoar
Faith and Vesta, Quirinus and Remus brothers again, shall
deliver statutes. The dreadful steel-riveted gates of war
shall be shut fast; on murderous weapons the inhuman
Fury, his hands bound behind him with an hundred fetters
of brass, shall sit within, shrieking with terrible blood-
stained lips.'

So speaking, he sends Maia's son down from above,
that the land and towers of Carthage, the new town, may
receive the Trojans with open welcome; lest Dido, ignorant
of doom, might debar them her land. Flying through the
depth of air on winged oarage, the fleet messenger alights
on the Libyan coasts. At once he does his bidding; at
once, for a god willed it, the Phoenicians allay their haughty
temper; the queen above all takes to herself grace and compassion towards the Teucrians.

But good Aeneas, nightlong revolving many and many
a thing, issues forth, so soon as bountiful light is given, to
explore the strange country; to what coasts the wind has
borne him, who are their habitants, men or wild beasts, for
all he sees is wilderness; this he resolves to search, and
bring back the certainty to his comrades. The fleet he
hides close in embosoming groves beneath a caverned rock,
amid shivering shadow of the woodland; himself, Achates
alone following, he strides forward, clenching in his hand
two broad-headed spears. And amid the forest his mother
crossed his way, wearing the face and raiment of a maiden,
the arms of a maiden of Sparta, or like Harpalyce of Thrace
when she tires her coursers and outstrips the winged speed
of Hebrus in her flight. For huntress fashion had she slung
the ready bow from her shoulder, and left her blown tresses
free, bared her knee, and knotted together her garments'
flowing folds. 'Ha! my men,' she begins, 'shew me if

haply you have seen a sister of mine straying here girt with quiver and a lynx's dappled fell, or pressing with shouts on the track of a foaming boar.'

Thus Venus, and Venus' son answering thus began :

'Sound nor sight have I had of sister of thine, O maiden unnamed ; for thy face is not mortal, nor thy voice of human tone ; O goddess assuredly I sister of Phœbus perchance, or one of the nymphs' blood ? Be thou gracious, whoso thou art, and lighten this toil of ours; deign to instruct us beneath what skies, on what coast of the world, we are thrown. Driven hither by wind and desolate waves, we wander in a strange land among unknown men. Many a sacrifice shall fall by our hand before thine altars.'

Then Venus : ' Nay, to no such offerings do I aspire. Tyrian maidens are wont ever to wear the quiver, to tie the purple buskin high above their ankle. Punic is the realm thou seest, Tyrian the people, and the city of Agenor's kin; but their borders are Libyan, a race unassailable in war. Dido sways the sceptre, who flying her brother set sail from the Tyrian town. Long is the tale of crime, long and intricate; but I will briefly follow its argument. Her husband was Sychaeus, wealthiest in lands of the Phoenicians, and loved of her with ill-fated passion ; to whom with virgin rites her father had given her maidenhood in wedlock. But the kingdom of Tyre was in her brother Pygmalion's hands, a monster of guilt unparalleled. Between these madness came ; the unnatural brother, blind with lust of gold, and reckless of his sister's love, lays Sychaeus low before the altars with stealthy unsuspected weapon; and for long he hid the deed, and by many a crafty pretence cheated her love-sickness with hollow hope. But in slumber came the very ghost of her unburied husband ; lifting up a face pale in wonderful wise, he exposed the merciless altars and his breast stabbed through with steel, and unwove all the blind web of household guilt. Then he counsels hasty flight out of the country, and to aid her passage discloses treasures long hidden underground, an untold mass of silver and gold. Stirred thereby, Dido gathered a company for flight. All assemble in whom hatred of the tyrant was relentless or fear keen; they seize on ships that chanced to lie ready, and load them with the gold. Pygmalion's hoarded wealth is borne overseas; a woman leads the work. They came at last to the land where thou wilt descry a city now great, New Carthage, and her rising citadel, and bought ground, called thence Byrsa, as much as a bull's hide would encircle. But who, I pray, are you, or from what coasts come, or whither hold you your way?'

At her question he, sighing and drawing speech deep from his breast, thus replied:

'Ah goddess, should I go on retracing from the fountain head, were time free to hear the history of our woes, sooner would the evening star lay day asleep in the closed gates of heaven. Us, as from ancient Troy (if the name of Troy hath haply passed through your ears) we sailed over alien seas, the tempest at his own wild will hath driven on the Libyan coast. I am Aeneas the good, who carry in my fleet the household gods I rescued from the enemy; my fame is known high in heaven. I seek Italy my country, my kin of Jove's supreme blood. With twenty sail did I climb the Phrygian sea; oracular tokens led me on; my goddess mother pointed the way; scarce seven survive the shattering of wave and wind. Myself unknown, destitute, driven from Europe and Asia, I wander over the Libyan wilderness.'

But staying longer complaint, Venus thus broke in on his half-told sorrows:

'Whoso thou art, not hated I think of the immortals

dost thou draw the breath of life, who hast reached the
Tyrian city.   Only go on, and betake thee hence to the
courts of the queen.   For I declare to thee thy comrades
are restored, thy fleet driven back into safety by the shifted
northern gales, except my parents were pretenders, and unavailing the augury they taught me.   Behold these twelve
swans in joyous line, whom, stooping from the tract of
heaven, the bird of Jove fluttered over the open sky ;
now in long train they seem either to take the ground or
already to look down on the ground they took.   As they
again disport with clapping wings, and utter their notes
as they circle the sky in company, even so do these ships
and crews of thine either lie fast in harbour or glide under
full sail into the harbour mouth.   Only go on, and turn thy
steps where the pathway leads thee.'

Speaking she turned away, and her neck shone roseate,
her immortal tresses breathed the fragrance of deity ; her
raiment fell flowing down to her feet, and the godhead was
manifest in her tread.   He knew her for his mother, and
with this cry pursued her flight : ' Thou also merciless !
Why mockest thou thy son so often in feigned likeness ?
Why is it forbidden to clasp hand in hand, to hear and
utter true speech ? '   Thus reproaching her he bends his
steps towards the city.   But Venus girt them in their going
with dull mist, and shed round them a deep divine clothing
of cloud, that none might see them, none touch them, or
work delay, or ask wherefore they came.   Herself she speeds
through the sky to Paphos, and joyfully revisits her habitation, where the temple and its hundred altars steam with
Sabaean incense, and are fresh with fragrance of chaplets
in her worship.

They meantime have hasted along where the pathway
points, and now were climbing the hill which hangs enormous over the city, and looks down on its facing towers.

Aeneas marvels at the mass of building, pastoral huts once
of old, marvels at the gateways and clatter of the pavements.
The Tyrians are hot at work to trace the walls, to rear the
citadel, and roll up great stones by hand, or to choose a
spot for their dwelling and enclose it with a furrow.   They
ordain justice and magistrates, and the august senate.   Here
some are digging harbours, here others lay the deep foundations of their theatre, and hew out of the cliff vast columns,
the lofty ornaments of the stage to be : even as bees when
summer is fresh over the flowery country ply their task
beneath the sun, when they lead forth their nation's grown
brood, or when they press the liquid honey and strain their
cells with nectarous sweets, or relieve the loaded incomers,
or in banded array drive the idle herd of drones far from
their folds ; they swarm over their work, and the odorous
honey smells sweet of thyme.   'Happy they whose city
already rises !' cries Aeneas, looking on the town roofs
below.   Girt in the cloud he passes amid them, wonderful
to tell, and mingling with the throng is descried of none.

In the heart of the town was a grove deep with luxuriant
shade, wherein first the Phoenicians, buffeted by wave and
whirlwind, dug up the token Queen Juno had appointed,
the head of a war horse : thereby was their race to be
through all ages illustrious in war and opulent in living.
Here to Juno was Sidonian Dido founding a vast temple,
rich with offerings and the sanctity of her godhead : brazen
steps rose on the threshold, brass clamped the pilasters,
doors of brass swung on grating hinges.   First in this grove
did a strange chance meet his steps and allay his fears ;
first here did Aeneas dare to hope for safety and have fairer
trust in his shattered fortunes.   For while he closely scans
the temple that towers above him, while, awaiting the queen,
he admires the fortunate city, the emulous hands and elabo-
rate work of her craftsmen, he sees ranged in order the

battles of Ilium, that war whose fame was already rumoured
through all the world, the sons of Atreus and Priam, and
Achilles whom both found pitiless. He stopped and cried
weeping, 'What land is left, Achates, what tract on earth
that is not full of our agony? Behold Priam I Here too
is the meed of honour, here mortal estate touches the soul
to tears. Dismiss thy fears ; the fame of this will somehow
bring thee salvation.'

So speaks he, and fills his soul with the painted show,
sighing often the while, and his face wet with a full river of
tears. For he saw, how warring round the Trojan citadel
here the Greeks fled, the men of Troy hard on their rear;
here the Phrygians, plumed Achilles in his chariot pressing
their flight. Not far away he knows the snowy canvas of
Rhesus' tents, which, betrayed in their first sleep, the blood-
stained son of Tydeus laid desolate in heaped slaughter, and
turns the ruddy steeds away to the camp ere ever they tasted
Trojan fodder or drunk of Xanthus. Elsewhere Troïlus, his
armour flung away in flight—luckless boy, no match for
Achilles to meet I—is borne along by his horses, and thrown
back entangled with his empty chariot, still clutching the
reins; his neck and hair are dragged over the ground, and
his reversed spear scores the dust. Meanwhile the Ilian
women went with disordered tresses to unfriendly Pallas'
temple, and bore the votive garment, sadly beating breast
with palm : the goddess turning away held her eyes fast on
the ground. Thrice had Achilles whirled Hector round the
walls of Troy, and was selling the lifeless body for gold ;
then at last he heaves a loud and heart-deep groan, as the
spoils, as the chariot, as the dear body met his gaze, and
Priam outstretching unarmed hands. Himself too he knew
joining battle with the foremost Achaeans, knew the Eastern
ranks and swart Memnon's armour. Penthesilea leads her
crescent-shielded Amazonian columns in furious heat with

thousands around her; clasping a golden belt under her naked breast, the warrior maiden clashes boldly with men.

While these marvels meet Dardanian Aeneas' eyes, while he dizzily hangs rapt in one long gaze, Dido the queen entered the precinct, beautiful exceedingly, a youthful train thronging round her. Even as on Eurotas' banks or along the Cynthian ridges Diana wheels the dance, while behind her a thousand mountain nymphs crowd to left and right; she carries quiver on shoulder, and as she moves outshines them all in deity; Latona's heart is thrilled with silent joy; such was Dido, so she joyously advanced amid the throng, urging on the business of her rising empire. Then in the gates of the goddess, beneath the central vault of the temple roof, she took her seat girt with arms and high enthroned. And now she gave justice and laws to her people, and adjusted or allotted their taskwork in due portion; when suddenly Aeneas sees advancing with a great crowd about them Antheus and Sergestus and brave Cloanthus, and other of his Trojans, whom the black squall had sundered at sea and borne far away on the coast. Dizzy with the shock of joy and fear he and Achates together were on fire with eagerness to clasp their hands; but in confused uncertainty they keep hidden, and clothed in the sheltering cloud wait to espy what fortune befalls them, where they are leaving their fleet ashore, why they now come; for they advanced, chosen men from all the ships, praying for grace, and held on with loud cries towards the temple.

After they entered in, and free speech was granted, aged Ilioneus with placid mien thus began:

'Queen, to whom Jupiter hath given to found this new city, and lay the yoke of justice upon haughty tribes, we beseech thee, we wretched Trojans storm-driven over all

the seas, stay the dreadful flames from our ships; spare
a guiltless race, and bend a gracious regard on our
fortunes. We are not come to deal slaughter through
Libyan homes, or to drive plundered spoils to the coast.
Such violence sits not in our mind, nor is a conquered
people so insolent. There is a place Greeks name Hesperia, an ancient land, mighty in arms and foison of the
clod; Oenotrian men dwelt therein; now rumour is that a
younger race from their captain's name have called it Italy.
Thither lay our course . . . when Orion rising on us
through the cloudrack with sudden surf bore us on blind
shoals, and scattered us afar with his boisterous gales and
whelming brine over waves and trackless reefs. To these
your coasts we a scanty remnant floated up. What race of
men, what land how barbarous soever, allows such a
custom for its own? We are debarred the shelter of the
beach; they rise in war, and forbid us to set foot on the
brink of their land. If you slight human kinship and
mortal arms, yet look for gods unforgetful of innocence and
guilt. Aeneas was our king, foremost of men in righteousness, incomparable in goodness as in warlike arms; whom
if fate still preserves, if he draws the breath of heaven and
lies not yet low in dispiteous gloom, fear we have none;
nor mayest thou repent of challenging the contest of service.
In Sicilian territory too is tilth and town, and famed
Acestes himself of Trojan blood. Grant us to draw ashore
our storm-shattered fleet, to shape forest trees into beams
and strip them for oars; so, if to Italy we may steer with our
king and comrades found, Italy and Latium shall we gladly
seek; but if salvation is clean gone, if the Libyan gulf
holds thee, dear lord of thy Trojans, and Iülus our hope
survives no more, seek we then at least the straits of Sicily,
the open homes whence we sailed hither, and Acestes for
our king.' Thus Ilioneus, and all the Dardanian company

c

murmured assent. . . . Then Dido, with downcast face,
briefly speaks :

'Cheer your anxious hearts, O Teucrians; put by your
care.   Hard fortune in a strange realm forces me to this
task, to keep watch and ward on my wide frontiers.   Who
can be ignorant of the race of Aeneas' people, who of Troy
town and her men and deeds, or of the great war's con-
suming fire?   Not so dull are the hearts of our Punic
wearing, not so far doth the sun yoke his steeds from our
Tyrian town.   Whether your choice be broad Hesperia,
the fields of Saturn's dominion, or Eryx for your country
and Acestes for your king, my escort shall speed you in
safety, my arsenals supply your need.   Or will you even
find rest here with me and share my kingdom?   The city
I establish is yours; draw your ships ashore ; Trojan and
Tyrian shall be held by me in even balance.   And would
that he your king, that Aeneas were here, storm-driven to
this same haven!   But I will send messengers along the
coast, and bid them trace Libya to its limits, if haply he
strays shipwrecked in forest or town.'

Stirred by these words brave Achates and lord Aeneas
both ere now burned to break through the cloud.   Achates
first accosts Aeneas : 'Goddess-born, what purpose now
rises in thy spirit?   Thou seest all is safe, our fleet and
comrades are restored.   One only is wanting, whom our
eyes saw whelmed amid the waves; all else is answerable
to thy mother's words.'

Scarce had he spoken when the encircling cloud suddenly parts and melts into clear air.   Aeneas stood discovered in sheen of brilliant light, like a god in face and
shoulders; for his mother's self had shed on her son the
grace of clustered locks, the radiant light of youth, and the
lustre of joyous eyes ; as when ivory takes beauty under the
artist's hand, or when silver or Parian stone is inlaid in gold.

Then breaking in on all with unexpected speech he thus addresses the queen :

'I whom you seek am here before you, Aeneas of Troy, snatched from the Libyan waves. O thou who alone hast pitied Troy's untold agonies, thou who with us the rem- nant of the Grecian foe, worn out ere now by every suffer- ing land and sea can bring, with us in our utter want dost share thy city and home! to render meet recompense is not possible for us, O Dido, nor for all who scattered over the wide world are left of our Dardanian race. The gods grant thee worthy reward, if their deity turn any regard on goodness, if aught avails justice and conscious purity of soul. What happy ages bore thee? what mighty parents gave thy virtue birth? While rivers run into the sea, while the mountain shadows move across their slopes, while the stars have pasturage in heaven, ever shall thine honour, thy name and praises endure in the unknown lands that summon me.' With these words he advances his right hand to dear Ilioneus, his left to Serestus ; then to the rest, brave Gyas and brave Cloanthus.

Dido the Sidonian stood astonished, first at the sight of him, then at his strange fortunes ; and these words left her lips :

'What fate follows thee, goddess-born, through perilous ways? what violence lands thee on this monstrous coast ? Art thou that Aeneas whom Venus the bountiful bore to Dardanian Anchises by the wave of Phrygian Simoïs ? And well I remember how Teucer came to Sidon, when exiled from his native land he sought Belus' aid to gain new realms ; Belus my father even then ravaged rich Cyprus and held it under his conquering sway. From that time forth have I known the fall of the Trojan city, known thy name and the Pelasgian princes. Their very foe would extol the Teucrians with highest praises, and boasted himself a branch of the ancient Teucrian stem. Come therefore, O men, and enter our house. Me too hath a like fortune driven through many a woe, and willed at last to find my rest in this land. Not ignorant of ill do I learn to succour the afflicted.'

With such speech she leads Aeneas into the royal house, and orders sacrifice in the gods' temples. Therewith she sends his company on the shore twenty bulls, an hundred great bristly-backed swine, an hundred fat lambs and their mothers with them, gifts of the day's gladness. . . . But the palace within is decked with splendour of royal state, and a banquet made ready amid the halls. The coverings are curiously wrought in splendid purple ; on the tables is massy silver and deeds of ancestral valour graven in gold, all the long course of history drawn through many a heroic name from the nation's primal antiquity.

Aeneas—for a father's affection denied his spirit rest— sends Achates speeding to his ships, to carry this news to Ascanius, and lead him to the town : in Ascanius is fixed all the parent's loving care. Presents likewise he bids him bring saved from the wreck of Ilium, a mantle stiff with gold embroidery, and a veil with woven border of yellow acanthus-flower, that once decked Helen of Argos, the marvel of her mother Leda's giving ; Helen had borne them from Mycenae, when she sought Troy towers and a lawless bridal ; the sceptre too that Ilione, Priam's eldest daughter, once had worn, a beaded necklace, and a double circlet of jewelled gold. Achates, hasting on his message, bent his way towards the ships.

But in the Cytherean's breast new arts, new schemes revolve ; if Cupid, changed in form and feature, may come in sweet Ascanius' room, and his gifts kindle the queen to madness and set her inmost sense aflame. Verily she fears the uncertain house, the double-tongued race of Tyre ;

cruel Juno frets her, and at nightfall her care floods back.
Therefore to winged Love she speaks these words :

'Son, who art alone my strength and sovereignty, son,
who scornest the mighty father's Typhoïan shafts, to thee I
fly for succour, and sue humbly to thy deity.   How Aeneas
thy brother is driven about all the sea-coasts by bitter Juno's
malignity, this thou knowest, and hast often grieved in our
grief.   Now Dido the Phoenician holds him stayed with soft
words, and I tremble to think how the welcome of Juno's
house may issue ; she will not be idle in this supreme turn
of fortune.   Wherefore I counsel to prevent her wiles and
circle the queen with flame, that, unalterable by any deity,
she may be held fast to me by passionate love for Aeneas.
Take now my thought how to do this.   The boy prince, my
chiefest care, makes ready at his dear father's summons to
go to the Sidonian city, carrying gifts that survive the sea
and the flames of Troy.   Him will I hide deep asleep in
my holy habitation, high on Cythera's hills or in Idalium,
that he may not know nor cross our wiles.   Do thou but
for one night feign his form, and, boy as thou art, put on
the familiar face of a boy ; so when in festal cheer, amid
royal dainties and Bacchic juice, Dido shall take thee to
her lap, shall fold thee in her clasp and kiss thee close and
sweet, thou mayest imbreathe a hidden fire and unsuspected
poison.'

Love obeys his dear mother's words, lays by his wings,
and walks rejoicingly with Iülus' tread.   But Venus pours
gentle dew of slumber on Ascanius' limbs, and lifts him
lulled in her lap to the tall Idalian groves of her deity,
where soft amaracus folds him round with the shadowed
sweetness of its odorous blossoms.   And now, obedient to
her words, Cupid went merrily in Achates' guiding, with
the royal gifts for the Tyrians.   Already at his coming the
queen hath sate her down in the midmost on her golden

throne under the splendid tapestries; now lord Aeneas,
now too the men of Troy gather, and all recline on the
strewn purple. Servants pour water on their hands, serve
corn from baskets, and bring napkins with close-cut pile.
Fifty handmaids are within, whose task is in their course to
keep unfailing store and kindle the household fire. An
hundred others, and as many pages all of like age, load the
board with food and array the wine cups. Therewithal the
Tyrians are gathered full in the wide feasting chamber, and
take their appointed places on the broidered cushions.
They marvel at Aeneas' gifts, marvel at Iülus, at the god's
face aflame and forged speech, at the mantle and veil
wrought with yellow acanthus-flower. Above all the hapless Phoenician, victim to coming doom, cannot satiate her
soul, but, stirred alike by the boy and the gifts, she gazes
and takes fire. He, when hanging clasped on Aeneas'
neck he had satisfied all the deluded parent's love, makes
his way to the queen; the queen clings to him with her
eyes and all her soul, and ever and anon fondles him in
her lap, ah, poor Dido! witless how mighty a deity sinks
into her breast; but he, mindful of his mother the Acida-
lian, begins touch by touch to efface Sychaeus, and sows the
surprise of a living love in the long-since-unstirred spirit and
disaccustomed heart. Soon as the noise of banquet ceased
and the board was cleared, they set down great bowls and
enwreathe the wine. The house is filled with hum of voices
eddying through the spacious chambers; lit lamps hang
down by golden chainwork, and flaming tapers expel the
night. Now the queen called for a heavy cup of jewelled
gold, and filled it with pure wine; therewith was the use of
Belus and all of Belus' race: then the hall was silenced.
'Jupiter,' she cries, 'for thou art reputed lawgiver of hospitality, grant that this be a joyful day to the Tyrians and the
voyagers from Troy, a day to live in our children's memory.

Bacchus the giver of gladness, be with us, and Juno the
bountiful; and you, O Tyrians, be favourable to our assembly.' She spoke, and poured liquid libation on the board,
which done, she first herself touched it lightly with her lips,
then handed it to Bitias and bade him speed; he valiantly
drained the foaming cup, and flooded him with the brimming gold. The other princes followed. Long-haired
Iopas on his gilded lyre fills the chamber with songs ancient
Atlas taught; he sings of the wandering moon and the
sun's travails; whence is the human race and the brute,
whence water and fire; of Arcturus, the rainy Hyades, and
the twin Oxen; why wintry suns make such haste to dip
in ocean, or what delay makes the nights drag lingeringly.
Tyrians and Trojans after them redouble applause. Therewithal Dido wore the night in changing talk, alas! and
drank long draughts of love, asking many a thing of Priam,
many a thing of Hector; now in what armour the son of
the Morning came; now of what fashion were Diomede's
horses; now of mighty Achilles. 'Nay, come,' she cries,
'tell to us, O guest, from their first beginning the treachery
of the Grecians, thy people's woes, and thine own wanderings; for this is now the seventh summer that bears thee a
wanderer over all the earth and sea.'

BOOK SECOND

THE STORY OF THE SACK OF TROY

ALL were hushed, and sate with steadfast countenance;
thereon, high from his cushioned seat, lord Aeneas thus
began :

. 'Dreadful, O Queen, is the woe thou bidst me recall,
how the Grecians pitiably overthrew the wealth and lordship
of Troy; and I myself saw these things in all their horror,
and I bore great part in them. What Myrmidon or Dolopian, or soldier of stern Ulysses, could in such a tale restrain
his tears ! and now night falls dewy from the steep of heaven,
and the setting stars counsel to slumber. Yet if thy desire
be such to know our calamities, and briefly to hear Troy's
last agony, though my spirit shudders at the remembrance
and recoils in pain, I will essay.

'Broken in war and beaten back by fate, and so many
years now slid away, the Grecian captains build by Pallas'
divine craft a horse of mountainous build, ribbed with
sawn fir; they feign it vowed for their return, and this
rumour goes about. Within the blind sides they stealthily
imprison chosen men picked out one by one, and fill the
vast cavern of its womb full with armed soldiery.

'There lies in sight an island well known in fame,
Tenedos, rich of store while the realm of Priam endured,

now but a bay and roadstead treacherous to ships. Hither
they launch forth, and hide on the solitary shore : we fancied
they were gone, and had run down the wind for Mycenae.
So all the Teucrian land put her long grief away. The gates
are flung open ; men go rejoicingly to see the Doric camp,
the deserted stations and abandoned shore. Here the Dolopian troops were tented, here cruel Achilles ; here their
squadrons lay ; here the lines were wont to meet in battle.
Some gaze astonished at the deadly gift of Minerva the
Virgin, and wonder at the horse's bulk ; and Thymoetes
begins to advise that it be drawn within our walls and set
in the citadel, whether in guile, or that the doom of Troy
was even now setting thus. But Capys and they whose
mind was of better counsel, bid us either hurl sheer into the
sea the guileful and sinister gift of Greece, or heap flames
beneath to consume it, or pierce and explore the hollow
hiding-place of its womb. The wavering crowd is torn
apart in high dispute.

' At that, foremost of all and with a great throng about
him, Laocoön runs hotly down from the high citadel, and
cries from far : "Ah, wretched citizens, what height of madness is this ? Believe you the foe is gone ? or think you
any Grecian gift is free of treachery ? is it thus we know
Ulysses ? Either Achaeans are hid in this cage of wood, or
the engine is fashioned against our walls to overlook the
houses and descend upon the city ; some delusion lurks
there: trust not the horse, O Trojans. Be it what it may, I
fear the Grecians even when they offer gifts." Thus speaking, he hurled his mighty spear with great strength at the
creature's side and the curved framework of the belly : the
spear stood quivering, and the jarred cavern of the womb
sounded hollow and uttered a groan. And had divine
ordinance, had a soul not infatuate been with us, he had
moved us to lay violent steel on the Argolic hiding place ;

and Troy would now stand, and you, tall towers of Priam,
yet abide.

'Lo, Dardanian shepherds meanwhile dragged clamorously before the King a man with hands tied behind his
back, who to compass this very thing, to lay Troy open to
the Achaeans, had gone to meet their ignorant approach,
confident in spirit and doubly prepared to spin his snares
or to meet assured death. From all sides, in eagerness to
see, the people of Troy run streaming in, and vie in jeers at
their prisoner. Know now the treachery of the Grecians,
and from a single crime learn all. . . . For as he stood
amid our gaze confounded, disarmed, and cast his eyes
around the Phrygian columns, "Alas!" he cried, "what
land now, what seas may receive me? or what is the last
doom that yet awaits my misery? who have neither any
place among the Grecians, and likewise the Dardanians
clamour in wrath for the forfeit of my blood." At that
lament our spirit was changed, and all assault stayed: we
encourage him to speak, and tell of what blood he is sprung,
or what assurance he brings his captors.

'"In all things assuredly," says he, "O King, befall
what may, I will confess to thee the truth; nor will I deny
myself of Argolic birth—this first—nor, if Fortune hath
made Sinon unhappy, shall her malice mould him to a
cheat and a liar. Hath a tale of the name of Palamedes,
son of Belus, haply reached thine ears, and of his glorious
rumour and renown; whom under false evidence the Pelasgians, because he forbade the war, sent innocent to death
by wicked witness; now they bewail him when he hath left
the light;—in his company, being near of blood, my father,
poor as he was, sent me hither to arms from mine earliest
years. While he stood unshaken in royalty and potent in
the councils of the kings, we too wore a name and honour.
When by subtle Ulysses' malice (no unknown tale do I tell)

he left the upper regions, my shattered life crept on in
darkness and grief, inly indignant at the fate of my innocent
friend.   Nor in my madness was I silent : and, should any
chance offer, did I ever return a conqueror to my native
Argos, I vowed myself his avenger, and with my words I
stirred his bitter hatred.   From this came the first taint of
ill ; from this did Ulysses ever threaten me with fresh
charges, from this flung dark sayings among the crowd and
sought confederate arms.   Nay, nor did he rest, till by
Calchas' service—but yet why do I vainly unroll the unavailing tale, or why hold you in delay, if all Achaeans are
ranked together in your mind, and it is enough that I bear
the name ?   Take the vengeance deferred ; this the Ithacan
would desire, and the sons of Atreus buy at a great ransom."

  'Then indeed we press on to ask and inquire the cause,
witless of wickedness so great and Pelasgian craft.   Trem-
blingly the false-hearted one pursues his speech :

  ' " Often would the Grecians have taken to flight, leaving
Troy behind, and disbanded in weariness of the long war :
and would God they had I as often the fierce sea-tempest -
barred their way, and the gale frightened them from going.
Most of all when this horse already stood framed with
beams of maple, storm clouds roared over all the sky.   In
perplexity we send Eurypylus to inquire of Phoebus' oracle ;
and he brings back from the sanctuary these words of terror :
*With blood of a slain maiden, O Grecians, you appeased the
winds when first you came to the Ilian coasts; with blood
must you seek your return, and an Argive life be the accepted
sacrifice.*   When that utterance reached the ears of the crowd,
their hearts stood still, and a cold shudder ran through their
inmost sense : for whom is doom purposed? who is claimed
of Apollo?   At this the Ithacan with loud clamour drags
Calchas the soothsayer forth amidst them, and demands of
him what is this the gods signify.   And now many an one

foretold me the villain's craft and cruelty, and silently saw what was to come. Twice five days he is speechless in his tent, and will not have any one denounced by his lips, or given up to death. Scarcely at last, at the loud urgence of the Ithacan, he breaks into speech as was planned, and appoints me for the altar. All consented; and each one's particular fear was turned, ah me! to my single destruction. And now the dreadful day was at hand; the rites were being ordered for me, the salted corn, and the chaplets to wreathe my temples. I broke away, I confess it, from death; I burst my bonds, and lurked all night darkling in the sedge of the marshy pool, till they might set their sails, if haply they should set them. Nor have I any hope more of seeing my old home nor my sweet children and the father whom I desire. Of them will they even haply claim vengeance for my flight, and wash away this crime in their wretched death. By the heavenly powers I beseech thee, the deities to whom truth is known, by all the faith yet unsullied that is anywhere left among mortals; pity woes so great; pity an undeserving sufferer."

'At these his tears we grant him life, and accord our pity. Priam himself at once commands his shackles and strait bonds to be undone, and thus speaks with kindly words: "Whoso thou art, now and henceforth dismiss and forget the Greeks: thou shalt be ours. And unfold the truth to this my question: wherefore have they reared this vast size of horse? who is their counsellor? or what their aim? what propitiation, or what engine of war is this?" He ended; the other, stored with the treacherous craft of Pelasgia, lifts to heaven his freed hands. "You, everlasting fires," he cries, "and your inviolable sanctity be my witness; you, O altars and accursed swords I fled, and chaplets of the gods I wore as victim! unblamed may I break the oath of Greek allegiance, unblamed hate them and bring all to light that they

conceal; nor am I bound by any laws of country. Do
thou only keep by thy promise, O Troy, and preserve faith
with thy preserver, as my news shall be true, as my recompense great.

‘ “ All the hope of Greece, and the confidence in which
the war began, ever centred in Pallas' aid. But since the
wicked son of Tydeus, and Ulysses, forger of crime, made
bold to tear the fated Palladium from her sanctuary, and
cut down the sentries on the towered height; since they
grasped the holy image, and dared with bloody hands to
touch the maiden chaplets of the goddess; since then the
hope of Greece ebbed and slid away backwards, their
strength was broken, and the mind of the goddess estranged.
Whereof the Tritonian gave token by no uncertain signs.
Scarcely was the image set in the camp; flame shot sparkling from its lifted eyes, and salt sweat started over its body;
thrice, wonderful to tell, it leapt from the ground with shield
and spear quivering. Immediately Calchas prophesies that
the seas must be explored in flight, nor may Troy towers be
overthrown by Argive weapons, except they repeat their auspices at Argos, and bring back that divine presence they have
borne away with them in the curved ships overseas. And
now they have run down the wind for their native Mycenae,
to gather arms and gods to attend them; they will remea-
sure ocean and be on you unawares. So Calchas expounds
the omens. This image at his warning they reared in recompense for the Palladium and the injured deity, to expiate
the horror of sacrilege. Yet Calchas bade them raise it to
this vast size with oaken crossbeams, and build it up to
heaven, that it may not find entry at the gates nor be drawn
within the city, nor protect your people beneath the consecration of old. For if hand of yours should violate Minerva's
offering, then utter destruction (the gods turn rather on
himself his augury !) should be upon Priam's empire and

the Phrygian people. But if under your hands it climbed
into your city, Asia should advance in mighty war to the
walls of Pelops, and a like fate awaited our children's
children."

'So by Sinon's wiles and craft and perjury the thing
gained belief; and we were ensnared by treachery and
forced tears, we whom neither the son of Tydeus nor
Achilles of Larissa, whom not ten years nor a thousand
ships brought down.

'Here another sight, greater, alas! and far more terrible meets us, and alarms our thoughtless senses. Laocoön,
allotted priest of Neptune, was slaying a great bull at the
accustomed altars. And lo! from Tenedos, over the placid
depths (I shudder as I recall) two snakes in enormous
coils press down the sea and advance together to the shore;
their breasts rise through the surge, and their blood-red
crests overtop the waves; the rest trails through the main
behind and wreathes back in voluminous curves; the brine
gurgles and foams. And now they gained the fields, while
their bloodshot eyes blazed with fire, and their tongues
lapped and flickered in their hissing mouths. We scatter,
pallid at the sight. They in unfaltering train make towards
Laocoön. And first the serpents twine in their double embrace his two little children, and bite deep in their wretched
limbs; then him likewise, as he comes up to help with
arms in his hand, they seize and fasten in their enormous
coils; and now twice clasping his waist, twice encircling
his neck with their scaly bodies, they tower head and neck
above him. He at once strains his hands to tear their
knots apart, his fillets spattered with foul black venom; at
once raises to heaven awful cries; as when, bellowing, a
bull shakes the wavering axe from his neck and runs
wounded from the altar. But the two snakes glide away
to the high sanctuary and seek the fierce Tritonian's cita-

del, and take shelter under the goddess' feet beneath the
circle of her shield. Then indeed a strange terror thrills
in all our amazed breasts; and Laocoön, men say, hath
fulfilled his crime's desert, in piercing the consecrated wood
and hurling his guilty spear into its body. All cry out that
the image must be drawn to its home and supplication made
to her deity. . . . We sunder the walls, and lay open the
inner city. All set to the work; they fix rolling wheels
under its feet, and tie hempen bands on its neck. The
fated engine climbs our walls, big with arms. Around it
boys and unwedded girls chant hymns and joyfully lay
their hand on the rope. It moves up, and glides menacing
into the middle of the town. O native land! O Ilium,
house of gods, and Dardanian city renowned in war! four
times in the very gateway did it come to a stand, and four
times armour rang in its womb. Yet we urge it on, mindless and infatuate, and plant the ill-ominous thing in our
hallowed citadel. Even then Cassandra opens her lips to
the coming doom, lips at a god's bidding never believed by
the Trojans. We, the wretched people, to whom that day
was our last, hang the shrines of the gods with festal
boughs throughout the city. /Meanwhile the heavens wheel
on, and night rises from the sea, wrapping in her vast
shadow earth and sky and the wiles of the Myrmidons;
about the town the Teucrians are stretched in silence;
slumber laps their tired limbs.

'And now the Argive squadron was sailing in order
from Tenedos, and in the favouring stillness of the quiet
moon sought the shores it knew; when the royal galley
ran out a flame, and, protected by the gods' malign decrees,
Sinon stealthily lets loose the imprisoned Grecians from
their barriers of pine; the horse opens and restores them
to the air; and joyfully issuing from the hollow wood,
Thessander and Sthenelus the captains, and terrible Ulysses,

slide down the dangling rope, with Acamas and Thoas and
Neoptolemus son of Peleus, and Machaon first of all, and
Menelaus, and Epeüs himself the artificer of the treachery.
They sweep down the city buried in drunken sleep; the
watchmen are cut down, and at the open gates they wel-
come all their comrades, and unite their confederate bands.

'It was the time when by the gift of God rest comes
stealing first and sweetest on unhappy men. In slumber,
lo! before mine eyes Hector seemed to stand by, deep in
grief and shedding abundant tears; torn by the chariot, as
once of old, and black with gory dust, his swoln feet
pierced with the thongs. Ah me! in what guise was he!
how changed from the Hector who returns from putting
on Achilles' spoils, or launching the fires of Phrygia on the
Grecian ships! with ragged beard and tresses clotted with
blood, and all the many wounds upon him that he received
around his ancestral walls. Myself too weeping I seemed
to accost him ere he spoke, and utter forth mournful
accents: "O light of Dardania, O surest hope of the
Trojans, what long delay is this hath held thee? from what
borders comest thou, Hector our desire? with what weary
eyes we see thee, after many deaths of thy kin, after
divers woes of people and city! What indignity hath
marred thy serene visage? or why discern I these wounds?"
He replies naught, nor regards my idle questioning; but
heavily drawing a heart-deep groan, "Ah, fly, goddess-
born," he says, "and rescue thyself from these flames.
The foe holds our walls; from her high ridges Troy is
toppling down. Thy country and Priam ask no more. If
Troy towers might be defended by strength of hand, this
hand too had been their defence. Troy commends to thee
her holy things and household gods; take them to accompany thy fate; seek for them a city, which, after all the seas
have known thy wanderings, thou shalt at last establish in

might." So speaks he, and carries forth in his hands from
their inner shrine the chaplets and strength of Vesta, and
the everlasting fire.

'Meanwhile the city is stirred with mingled agony ; and
more and more, though my father Anchises' house lay deep
withdrawn and screened by trees, the noises grow clearer
and the clash of armour swells. I shake myself from sleep
and mount over the sloping roof, and stand there with ears
attent : even as when flame catches a corn-field while south
winds are furious, or the racing torrent of a mountain
stream sweeps the fields, sweeps the smiling crops and
labours of the oxen, and hurls the forest with it headlong ;
the shepherd in witless amaze hears the roar from the cliff-
top. Then indeed proof is clear, and the treachery of the
Grecians opens out. Already the house of Deïphobus
hath crashed down in wide ruin amid the overpowering
flames ; already our neighbour Ucalegon is ablaze : the
broad Sigean bay is lit with the fire. Cries of men and
blare of trumpets rise up. Madly I seize my arms, nor is
there so much purpose in arms ; but my spirit is on fire to
gather a band for fighting and charge for the citadel with
my comrades. Fury and wrath drive me headlong, and I
think how noble is death in arms.

'And lo ! Panthus, eluding the Achaean weapons,
Panthus son of Othrys, priest of Phoebus in the citadel,
comes hurrying with the sacred vessels and conquered gods
and his little grandchild in his hand, and runs distractedly
towards my gates. "How stands the state, O Panthus ?
what stronghold are we to occupy ?" Scarcely had I said
so, when groaning he thus returns : "The crowning day is
come, the irreversible time of the Dardanian land. No
more are we a Trojan people ; Ilium and the great glory of
the Teucrians is no more. Angry Jupiter hath cast all into
the scale of Argos. The Grecians are lords of the burning

town. The horse, standing high amid the city, pours forth armed men, and Sinon scatters fire, insolent in victory. Some are at the wide-flung gates, all the thousands that ever came from populous Mycenae. Others have beset the narrow streets with lowered weapons; edge and glittering point of steel stand drawn, ready for the slaughter; scarcely at the entry do the guards of the gates essay battle, and hold out in the blind fight.",⸍

'Heaven's will thus declared by the son of Othrys drives me amid flames and arms, where the baleful Fury calls, and tumult of shouting rises up. Rhipeus and Epytus, most mighty in arms, join company with me; Hypanis and Dymas meet us in the moonlight and attach themselves to our side, and young Corœbus son of Mygdon. In those days it was he had come to Troy, fired with mad passion for Cassandra, and bore a son's aid to Priam and the Phrygians: hapless, that he listened not to his raving bride's counsels. . . . Seeing them close-ranked and daring for battle, I therewith began thus: " Men, hearts of supreme and useless bravery, if your desire be fixed to follow one who dares the utmost; you see what is the fortune of our state: all the gods by whom this empire was upheld have gone forth, abandoning shrine and altar; your aid comes to a burning city. Let us die, and rush on their encircling weapons. The conquered have one safety, to hope for none."

'So their spirit is heightened to fury. Then, like wolves ravening in a black fog, whom mad malice of hunger hath driven blindly forth, and their cubs left behind await with throats unslaked; through the weapons of the enemy we march to certain death, and hold our way straight into the town. Night's sheltering shadow flutters dark around us. Who may unfold in speech that night's horror and death-agony, or measure its woes in weeping? The

ancient city falls with her long years of sovereignty; corpses
lie stretched stiff all about the streets and houses and
awful courts of the gods. Nor do Teucrians alone pay
forfeit of their blood; once and again valour returns even
in conquered hearts, and the victorious Grecians fall.
Everywhere is cruel agony, everywhere terror, and the sight
of death at every turn.

'First, with a great troop of Grecians attending him,
Androgeus meets us, taking us in ignorance for an allied
band, and opens on us with friendly words: " Hasten, my
men; why idly linger so late? others plunder and harry
the burning citadel; are you but now on your march from
the tall ships?"   He spoke, and immediately (for no
answer of any assurance was offered) knew he was fallen
among the foe.   In amazement, he checked foot and
voice; even as one who struggling through rough briers
hath trodden a snake on the ground unwarned, and suddenly shrinks fluttering back as it rises in anger and puffs
its green throat out; even thus Androgeus drew away,
startled at the sight.   We rush in and encircle them with
serried arms, and cut them down dispersedly in their
ignorance of the ground and seizure of panic.   Fortune
speeds our first labour.   And here Coroebus, flushed with
success and spirit, cries: " O comrades, follow me where
fortune points before us the path of safety, and shews
her favour.   Let us exchange shields, and accoutre ourselves in Grecian suits; whether craft or courage, who will
ask of an enemy? the foe shall arm our hands."   Thus
speaking, he next dons the plumed helmet and beautifully
blazoned shield of Androgeus, and fits the Argive sword
to his side.   So does Rhipeus, so Dymas in like wise, and
all our men in delight arm themselves one by one in the
fresh spoils.   We advance, mingling with the Grecians,
under a protection not our own, and join many a battle

with those we meet amid the blind night; many a Greek
we send down to hell. Some scatter to the ships and run
for the safety of the shore; some in craven fear again
climb the huge horse, and hide in the belly they knew.
Alas that none may trust at all to estranged gods!

'Lo! Cassandra, maiden daughter of Priam, was being
dragged with disordered tresses from the temple and
sanctuary of Minerva, straining to heaven her blazing eyes
in vain; her eyes, for fetters locked her delicate hands. At
this sight Coroebus burst forth infuriate, and flung himself
on death amid their columns. We all follow him up, and
charge with massed arms. Here first from the high temple
roof we are overwhelmed with our own people's weapons,
and a most pitiful slaughter begins through the fashion of
our armour and the mistaken Greek crests; then the
Grecians, with angry cries at the maiden's rescue, gather
from every side and fall on us; Ajax in all his valour, and
the two sons of Atreus, and the whole Dolopian army: as
oft when bursting in whirlwind West and South clash with
adverse blasts, and the East wind exultant on the coursers
of the Dawn; the forests cry, and fierce in foam Nereus
with his trident stirs the seas from their lowest depth.
Those too appear, whom our stratagem routed through the
darkness of dim night and drove all about the town; at
once they know the shields and lying weapons, and mark
the alien tone on our lips. We go down, overwhelmed by
numbers. First Coroebus is stretched by Peneleus' hand at
the altar of the goddess armipotent; and Rhipeus falls,
the one man who was most righteous and steadfast in
justice among the Teucrians: the gods' ways are not as
ours: Hypanis and Dymas perish, pierced by friendly hands;
nor did all thy goodness, O Panthus, nor Apollo's fillet
protect thy fall. O ashes of Ilium and death flames of
my people! you I call to witness that in your ruin I

shunned no Grecian weapon or encounter, and my hand
earned my fall, had destiny been thus. We tear ourselves
away, I and Iphitus and Pelias, Iphitus now stricken in
age, Pelias halting too under the wound of Ulysses, called
forward by the clamour to Priam's house.

'Here indeed the battle is fiercest, as if all the rest of
the fighting were nowhere, and no slaughter but here
throughout the city, so do we descry the war in full fury,
the Grecians rushing on the building, and their shielded
column driving up against the beleaguered threshold.
Ladders cling to the walls ; and hard by the doors and
planted on the rungs they hold up their shields in the left
hand to ward off our weapons, and with their right clutch
the battlements. The Dardanians tear down turrets and
the covering of the house roof against them ; with these
for weapons, since they see the end is come, they prepare
to defend themselves even in death's extremity : and hurl
down gilded beams, the stately decorations of their fathers
of old.   Others with drawn swords have beset the doorway
below and keep it in crowded column.   We renew our
courage, to aid the royal dwelling, to support them with
our succour, and swell the force of the conquered.

'There was a blind doorway giving passage through the
range of Priam's halls by a solitary postern, whereby, while
our realm endured, hapless Andromache would often and
often glide unattended to her father-in-law's house, and carry
the boy Astyanax to his grandsire.   I issue out on the sloping height of the ridge, whence wretched Teucrian hands
were hurling their ineffectual weapons.   A tower stood on
the sheer brink, its roof ascending high into heaven, whence
was wont to be seen all Troy and the Grecian ships and
Achaean camp : attacking it with iron round about, where
the joints of the lofty flooring yielded, we wrench it from
its deep foundations and shake it free ; it gives way, and

suddenly falls thundering in ruin, crashing wide over the
Grecian ranks. But others swarm up; nor meanwhile do
stones nor any sort of missile slacken. . . . . Right before
the vestibule and in the front doorway Pyrrhus moves rejoicingly in the sparkle of arms and gleaming brass: like as
when a snake fed on poisonous herbs, whom chill winter kept
hid and swollen underground, now fresh from his weeds outworn and shining in youth, wreathes his slippery body into
the daylight, his upreared breast meets the sun, and his
triple-cloven tongue flickers in his mouth. With him huge
Periphas, and Automedon the armour-bearer, driver of
Achilles' horses, with him all his Scyrian men climb the
roof and hurl flames on the housetop. Himself among
the foremost he grasps a poleaxe, bursts through the hard
doorway, and wrenches the brazen-plated doors from the
hinge; and now he hath cut out a plank from the solid
oak and pierced a vast gaping hole. The house within is
open to sight, and the long halls lie plain; open to sight
are the secret chambers of Priam and the kings of old, and
they see armed men standing in front of the doorway.

'But the inner house is stirred with shrieks and misery
and confusion, and the court echoes deep with women's
wailing; the golden stars are smitten with the din.
Affrighted mothers stray about the vast house, and cling
fast to the doors and print them with kisses. With his
father's might Pyrrhus presses on; nor guards nor barriers
can hold out. The gate totters under the hard driven
ram, and the doors fall flat, rent from the hinge. Force
makes way; the Greeks burst through the entrance and
pour in, slaughtering the foremost, and filling the space
with a wide stream of soldiers. Not so furiously when
a foaming river bursts his banks and overflows, beating down the opposing dykes with whirling water, is he
borne mounded over the fields, and sweeps herds and

pens all about the plains. Myself I saw in the gateway
Neoptolemus mad in slaughter, and the two sons of
Atreus, saw Hecuba and the hundred daughters of her
house, and Priam polluting with his blood the altar fires
of his own consecration. The fifty bridal chambers—so
great was the hope of his children's children—their doors
magnificent with spoils of barbaric gold, have sunk in ruin ;
where the fire fails the Greeks are in possession.

'Perchance too thou mayest inquire what was Priam's
fate. When he saw the ruin of his captured city, the
gates of his house burst open, and the enemy amid his
innermost chambers, the old man idly fastens round his
aged trembling shoulders his long disused armour, girds on
the unavailing sword, and advances on his death among
the thronging foe.

'Within the palace and under the bare cope of sky
was a massive altar, and hard on the altar an ancient
bay tree leaned clasping the household gods in its shadow.
Here Hecuba and her daughters crowded vainly about
the altar-stones, like doves driven headlong by a black
tempest, and crouched clasping the gods' images. And
when she saw Priam her lord with the armour of youth on
him; "What spirit of madness, my poor husband," she
cries, "hath stirred thee to gird on these weapons? or
whither dost thou run? Not such the succour nor these
the defenders the time requires : no, were mine own
Hector now beside us. Retire, I beseech thee, hither ;
this altar will protect us all, or thou wilt share our death."
With these words on her lips she drew the aged man to
her, and set him on the holy seat.

'And lo, escaped from slaughtering Pyrrhus through
the weapons of the enemy, Polites, one of Priam's children,
flies wounded down the long colonnades and circles the
empty halls. Pyrrhus pursues him fiercely with aimed

wound, just catching at him, and follows hard on him
with his spear. As at last he issued before his parents'
eyes and faces, he fell, and shed his life in a pool of blood.
At this Priam, although even now fast in the toils of death,
yet withheld not nor spared a wrathful cry: " Ah, for thy
crime, for this thy hardihood, may the gods, if there is
goodness in heaven to care for aught such, pay thee in full
thy worthy meed, and return thee the reward that is due !
who hast made me look face to face on my child's murder,
and polluted a father's countenance with death. Ah, not
such to a foe was the Achilles whose parentage thou beliest ;
but he revered a suppliant's right and trust, restored to the
tomb Hector's pallid corpse, and sent me back to my realm."
Thus the old man spoke, and launched his weak and un-
wounding spear, which, recoiling straight from the jarring
brass, hung idly from his shield above the boss. Thereat
Pyrrhus: " Thou then shalt tell this, and go with the
message to my sire the son of Peleus: remember to tell
him of my baleful deeds, and the degeneracy of Neoptolemus. Now die." So saying, he drew him quivering
to the very altar, slipping in the pool of his child's blood,
and wound his left hand in his hair, while in his right the
sword flashed out and plunged to the hilt in his side. · This
was the end of Priam's fortunes ; thus did allotted fate find
him, with burning Troy and her sunken towers before his
eyes, once magnificent lord over so many peoples and
lands of Asia. The great corpse lies along the shore, a
head severed from the shoulders and a body without a
name.

' But then an awful terror began to encircle me ; I
stood in amaze ; there rose before me the likeness of my
loved father, as I saw the king, old as he, sobbing out his
life under the ghastly wound ; there rose Creüsa forlorn,
my plundered house, and little Iülus' peril. I look back

and survey what force is around me. All, outwearied,
have given up and leapt headlong to the ground, or flung
themselves wretchedly into the fire:

['Yes, and now I only was left; when I espy the
daughter of Tyndarus close in the courts of Vesta, crouching silently in the fane's recesses; the bright glow of the
fires lights my wandering, as my eyes stray all about. Fearing the Teucrians' anger for the overthrown towers of Troy,
and the Grecians' vengeance and the wrath of the husband
she had abandoned, she, the common Fury of Troy and her
native country, had hidden herself and cowered unseen by
the altars.   My spirit kindles to fire, and rises in wrath to
avenge my dying land and take repayment for her crimes.
Shall she verily see Sparta and her native Mycenae unscathed, and depart a queen and triumphant?   Shall she
see her spousal and her home, her parents and children,
attended by a crowd of Trojan women and Phrygians to
serve her? and Priam have fallen under the sword?   Troy
blazed in fire? the shore of Dardania so often soaked
with blood?   Not so.   For though there is no name or
fame in a woman's punishment, nor honour in the victory,
yet shall I have praise in quenching a guilty life and exacting a just recompense; and it will be good to fill my soul
with the flame of vengeance, and satisfy the ashes of my
people.   Thus broke I forth, and advanced infuriate;]

'—— When my mother came visibly before me, clear
to sight as never till then, and shone forth in pure radiance
through the night, gracious, evident in godhead, in shape
and stature such as she is wont to appear to the heavenly
people; she caught me by the hand and stayed me, and
pursued thus with roseate lips:

'"Son, what overmastering pain thus wakes thy wrath?
Why ravest thou? or whither is thy care for us fled?   Wilt
thou not first look to it, where thou hast left Anchises,

thine aged worn father; or if Creüsa thy wife and the child Ascanius survive? round about whom all the Greek battalions range; and without my preventing care, the flames ere this had made them their portion, and the hostile sword drunk their blood. Not the hated face of the Laconian woman, Tyndarus' daughter; not Paris is to blame; the gods, the gods in anger overturn this magnificence, and make Troy topple down. Look, for all the cloud that now veils thy gaze and dulls mortal vision with damp encircling mist, I will rend from before thee. Fear thou no commands of thy mother, nor refuse to obey her counsels. Here, where thou seest sundered piles of masonry and rocks violently torn from rocks, and smoke eddying mixed with dust, Neptune with his great trident shakes wall and foundation out of their places, and upturns all the city from her base. Here Juno in all her terror holds the Scaean gates at the entry, and, girt with steel, calls her allied army furiously from their ships. . . . Even now on the citadel's height, look back! Tritonian Pallas is planted in glittering halo and Gorgonian terror. Their lord himself pours courage and prosperous strength on the Grecians, himself stirs the gods against the arms of Dardania. Haste away, O son, and put an end to the struggle. I will never desert thee; I will set thee safe in the courts of thy father's house."

'She ended, and plunged in the dense blackness of the night. Awful faces shine forth, and, set against Troy, divine majesties . . .

'Then indeed I saw all Ilium sinking in flame, and Neptunian Troy uprooted from her base: even as an ancient ash on the mountain heights, hacked all about with steel and fast-falling axes, when husbandmen emulously strain to cut it down: it hangs threateningly, with shaken top and quivering tresses asway; till gradually, overmastered with

wounds, it utters one last groan, and rending itself away,
falls in ruin along the ridge. I descend, and under a god's
guidance clear my way between foe and flame; weapons
give ground before me, and flames retire.

'And now, when I have reached the courts of my
ancestral dwelling, our home of old, my father, whom it
was my first desire to carry high into the hills, and whom
first I sought, declines, now Troy is rooted out, to prolong
his life through the pains of exile.

' " Ah, you," he cries, " whose blood is at the prime,
whose strength stands firm in native vigour, do you take your
flight. . . . Had the lords of heaven willed to prolong life
for me, they should have preserved this my home. Enough
and more is the one desolation we have seen, survivors
of a captured city. Thus, oh thus salute me and depart,
as a body laid out for burial. Mine own hand shall find
me death: the foe will be merciful and seek my spoils:
light is the loss of a tomb. This long time hated of heaven,
I uselessly delay the years, since the father of gods and
king of men blasted me with wind of thunder and scathe
of flame."

' Thus held he on in utterance, and remained obstinate.
We press him, dissolved in tears, my wife Creüsa, Ascanius,
all our household, that our father involve us not all in his
ruin, and add his weight to the sinking scale of doom. He
refuses, and keeps seated steadfast in his purpose. Again
I rush to battle, and choose death in my misery. For what
had counsel or chance yet to give? Thoughtest thou my
feet, O father, could retire and abandon thee? and fell so
unnatural words from a parent's lips? " If heaven wills that
naught be left of our mighty city, if this be thy planted
purpose, thy pleasure to cast in thyself and thine to the
doom of Troy; for this death indeed the gate is wide, and
even now Pyrrhus will be here newly bathed in Priam's

blood, Pyrrhus who slaughters the son before the father's face, the father upon his altars. For this was it, bountiful mother, thou dost rescue me amid fire and sword, to see the foe in my inmost chambers, and Ascanius and my father, Creüsa by their side, hewn down in one another's blood? My arms, men, bring my arms! the last day calls on the conquered. Return me to the Greeks; let me revisit and renew the fight. Never to-day shall we all perish unavenged."

'Thereat I again gird on my sword, and fitting my left arm into the clasps of the shield, strode forth of the palace. And lo! my wife clung round my feet on the threshold, and held little Iülus up to his father's sight. "If thou goest to die, let us too hurry with thee to the end. But if thou knowest any hope to place in arms, be this household thy first defence. To what is little Iülus and thy father, to what am I left who once was called thy wife?"

'So she shrieked, and filled all the house with her weeping; when a sign arises sudden and marvellous to tell. For, between the hands and before the faces of his sorrowing parents, lo! above Iülus' head there seemed to stream a light luminous cone, and a flame whose touch hurt not to flicker in his soft hair and play round his brows. We in a flutter of affright shook out the blazing hair and quenched the holy fires with spring water. But lord Anchises joyfully upraised his eyes; and stretching his hands to heaven: "Jupiter omnipotent," he cries, "if thou dost relent at any prayers, look on us this once alone; and if our goodness deserve it, give thine aid hereafter, O lord, and confirm this thine omen."

'Scarcely had the aged man spoken thus, when with sudden crash it thundered on the left, and a star gliding through the dusk shot from heaven drawing a bright trail of light. We watch it slide over the palace roof, leaving

the mark of its pathway, and bury its brilliance in the wood
of Ida; the long drawn track shines, and the region all
about fumes with sulphur.   Then conquered indeed my
father rises to address the gods and worship the holy star.
"Now, now delay is done with: I follow, and where you
lead, I come.   Gods of my fathers, save my house, save my
grandchild.   Yours is this omen, and in your deity Troy
stands.   I yield, O my son, and refuse not to go in thy
company."

   ' He ended; and now more loudly the fire roars along
the city, and the burning tides roll nearer.   " Up then,
beloved father, and lean on my neck ; these shoulders of
mine will sustain thee, nor will so dear a burden weigh me
down.   Howsoever fortune fall, one and undivided shall be
our peril, one the escape of us twain.   Little Iülus shall go
along with me, and my wife follow our steps afar.   You
of my household, give heed to what I say.   As you leave
the city there is a mound and ancient temple of Ceres
lonely on it, and hard by an aged cypress, guarded many
years in ancestral awe : to this resting-place let us gather
from diverse quarters.   Thou, O father, take the sacred
things and the household gods of our ancestors in thine
hand.   For me, just parted from the desperate ·battle,
with slaughter fresh upon me, to handle them were guilt,
until I wash away in a living stream the soilure. . . ."   So
spoke I, and spread over my neck and broad shoulders a
tawny lion-skin for covering, and stoop to my burden.
Little Iülus, with his hand fast in mine, keeps uneven pace
after his father.   Behind my wife follows.   We pass on in
the shadows.   And I, lately moved by no weapons launched
against me, nor by the thronging bands of my Grecian foes,
am now terrified at every breath, startled by every noise,
thrilling with fear alike for my companion and my burden.

   ' And now I was nearing the gates, and thought I had

outsped all the way; when suddenly the crowded trampling
of feet came to our ears, and my father, looking forth into
the darkness, cries: "My son, my son, fly; they draw near.
I espy the gleaming shields and the flicker of brass."
At this, in my flurry and confusion, some hostile god
bereft me of my senses. For while I plunge down by-
ways, and swerve from where the familiar streets ran,
Creüsa, alas! whether, torn by fate from her unhappy husband, she stood still, or did she mistake the way, or sink
down outwearied? I know not; and never again was she
given back to our eyes; nor did I turn to look for my lost
one, or cast back a thought, ere we were come to ancient
Ceres' mound and hallowed seat; here at last, when all
gathered, one was missing, vanished from her child's and
her husband's company. What man or god did I spare in
frantic reproaches? or what crueller sight met me in our
city's overthrow? I charge my comrades with Ascanius
and lord Anchises, and the gods of Teucria, hiding them in
the winding vale. Myself I regain the city, girding on my
shining armour; fixed to renew every danger, to retrace my
way throughout Troy, and fling myself again on its perils.
First of all I regain the walls and the dim gateway whence
my steps had issued; I scan and follow back my footprints
with searching gaze in the night. Everywhere my spirit
shudders, dismayed at the very silence. Thence I pass
on home, if haply her feet (if haply!) had led her thither.
The Grecians had poured in, and filled the palace. The
devouring fire goes rolling before the wind high as the
roof; the flames tower over it, and the heat surges up into
the air. I move on, and revisit the citadel and Priam's
dwelling; where now in the spacious porticoes of Juno's
sanctuary, Phoenix and accursed Ulysses, chosen sentries,
were guarding the spoil. Hither from all quarters is flung
in masses the treasure of Troy torn from burning shrines,

tables of the gods, bowls of solid gold, and raiment of the
captives. Boys and cowering mothers in long file stand
round. . . . Yes, and I dared to cry abroad through the
darkness; I filled the streets with calling, and again and
yet again with vain reiterance cried piteously on Creüsa.
As I stormed and sought her endlessly among the houses of
the town, there rose before mine eyes a melancholy phantom,
the ghost of very Creüsa, in likeness larger than her wont.
I was motionless; my hair stood up, and the accents faltered
on my tongue.   Then she thus addressed me, and with this
speech allayed my distresses: "What help is there in this
mad passion of grief, sweet my husband? not without divine
influence does this come to pass: nor may it be, nor does
the high lord of Olympus allow, that thou shouldest carry
Creüsa hence in thy company.   Long shall be thine exile,
and weary spaces of sea must thou furrow through; and
thou shalt come to the land Hesperia, where Lydian Tiber
flows with soft current through rich and populous fields.
There prosperity awaits thee, and a kingdom, and a king's
daughter for thy wife.   Dispel these tears for thy beloved
Creüsa. Never will I look on the proud homes of the
Myrmidons or Dolopians, or go to be the slave of Greek
matrons, I a daughter of Dardania, a daughter-in-law of
Venus the goddess. . . . But the mighty mother of the
gods keeps me in these her borders. And now farewell,
and still love thy child and mine."   This speech uttered,
while I wept and would have said many a thing, she
left me and retreated into thin air.   Thrice there was I
fain to lay mine arms round her neck; thrice the vision I
vainly clasped fled out of my hands, even as the light
breezes, or most like to fluttering sleep.   So at last, when
night is spent, I revisit my comrades.

' And here I find a marvellous great company, newly
flocked in, mothers and men, a people gathered for exile,

a pitiable crowd.   From all quarters they are assembled, ready in heart and fortune, to whatsoever land I will conduct them overseas.   And now the morning star rose over the high ridges of Ida, and led on the day ; and the Grecians held the gateways in leaguer, nor was any hope of help given. I withdrew, and raising my father up, I sought the mountain.'

BOOK THIRD

'AFTER heaven's lords pleased to overthrow the state of
Asia and Priam's guiltless people, and proud Ilium fell, and
Neptunian Troy smokes all along the ground, we are driven
by divine omens to seek distant places of exile in waste lands.
Right under Antandros and the mountains of Phrygian Ida
we build a fleet, uncertain whither the fates carry us or
where a resting-place is given, and gather the people together. Scarcely had the first summer set in, when lord
Anchises bids us spread our sails to fortune, and weeping
I leave the shores and havens of my country, and the plains
where once was Troy. I sail to sea an exile, with my comrades and son and the gods of household and state.

'A land of vast plains lies apart, the home of Mavors,
in Thracian tillage, and sometime under warrior Lycurgus'
reign; friendly of old to Troy, and their gods in alliance
while our fortune lasted. Hither I pass, and on the
winding shore I lay under thwarting fates the first foundations of a city, and from my own name fashion its name,
Aeneadae.

'I was paying sacrifice to my mother, daughter of
Dione, and to all the gods, so to favour the work begun,
and slew a shining bull on the shore to the high lord of

E

the heavenly people. Haply there lay a mound hard at
hand, crowned with cornel thickets and bristling dense with
shafts of myrtle. I drew near; and essaying to tear up the
green wood from the soil, that I might cover the altar with
leafy boughs, I see a portent ominous and wonderful to
tell. For from the first tree whose roots are rent away
and broken from the ground, drops of black blood trickle,
and gore stains the earth. An icy shudder shakes my
limbs, and my blood curdles chill with terror. Yet from
another I go on again to tear away a tough shoot, fully to
fathom its secret; yet from another black blood follows
out of the bark. With many searchings of heart I
prayed the woodland nymphs, and lord Gradivus, who
rules in the Getic fields, to make the sight propitious
as was meet and lighten the omen. But when I assail
a third spearshaft with a stronger effort, pulling with
knees pressed against the sand; shall I speak or be silent?
from beneath the mound is heard a pitiable moan, and
a voice is uttered to my ears: "Woe's me, why rendest
thou me, Aeneas? spare me at last in the tomb, spare
pollution to thine innocent hands. Troy bore me; not
alien to thee am I, nor this blood that oozes from the
stem. Ah, fly the cruel land, fly the greedy shore! For I
am Polydorus; here the iron harvest of weapons hath
covered my pierced body, and shot up in sharp javelins."
Then indeed, borne down with dubious terror, I was
motionless, my hair stood up, and the accents faltered on
my tongue.

'This Polydorus once with great weight of gold had
hapless Priam sent in secret to the nurture of the Thracian
king, when now he was losing trust in the arms of Dardania, and saw his city leaguered round about. The king,
when the Teucrian power was broken and fortune withdrew, following Agamemnon's estate and triumphant arms,

severs every bond of duty; murders Polydorus, and lays
strong hands on the gold. O accursed hunger of gold, to
what dost thou not compel human hearts! When the
terror left my senses, I lay the divine tokens before the
chosen princes of the people, with my father at their head,
and demand their judgment. All are of one mind, to leave
the guilty land, and abandoning a polluted home, to let the
gales waft our fleets. So we bury Polydorus anew, and
the earth is heaped high over his mound; altars are reared
to his ghost, sad with dusky chaplets and black cypress;
and around are the Ilian women with hair unbound in their
fashion. We offer bubbling bowls of warm milk and cups
of consecrated blood, and lay the spirit to rest in her tomb,
and with loud voice utter the last call.

'Thereupon, so soon as ocean may be trusted, and the
winds leave the seas in quiet, and the soft whispering south
wind calls seaward, my comrades launch their ships and
crowd the shores. We put out from harbour, and lands and
towns sink away. There lies in mid sea a holy land, most
dear to the mother of the Nereids and Neptune of Aegae,
which strayed about coast and strand till the Archer god in
his affection chained it fast from high Myconos and Gyaros,
and made it lie immoveable and slight the winds. Hither
I steer; and it welcomes my weary crew to the quiet shelter
of a safe haven. We disembark and worship Apollo's
town. Anius the king, king at once of the people and
priest of Phoebus, his brows garlanded with fillets and consecrated laurel, comes to meet us; he knows Anchises, his
friend of old; we clasp hands in welcome, and enter his
palace. I worshipped the god's temple, an ancient pile of
stone. "Lord of Thymbra, give us an enduring dwelling-
place; grant a house and family to thy weary servants, and
a city to abide: keep Troy's second fortress, the remnant
left of the Grecians and merciless Achilles. Whom follow

we ? or whither dost thou bid us go, where fix our seat ?
Grant an omen, O lord, and inspire our minds."

'Scarcely had I spoken thus ; suddenly all seemed to
shake, all the courts and laurels of the god, the whole hill
to be stirred round about, and the cauldron to moan in the
opening sanctuary. We sink low on the ground, and a
voice is borne to our ears : "Stubborn race of Dardanus,
the same land that bore you by parentage of old shall
receive you again on her bountiful breast. Seek out your
ancient mother ; hence shall the house of Aeneas sway all
regions, his children's children and they who shall be born
of them." Thus Phoebus ; and mingled outcries of great
gladness uprose ; all ask, what is that city ? whither calls
Phoebus our wandering, and bids us return ? Then my
father, unrolling the records of men of old, "Hear, O
princes," says he, "and learn your hopes. In mid ocean
lies Crete, the island of high Jove, wherein is mount Ida, the
cradle of our race. An hundred great towns are inhabited
in that opulent realm ; from it our forefather Teucer of old,
if I recall the tale aright, sailed to the Rhoetean coasts and
chose a place for his kingdom. Not yet was Ilium nor the
towers of Pergama reared ; they dwelt in the valley bottoms.
Hence came our Lady, haunter of Cybele, the Corybantic
cymbals and the grove of Ida ; hence the rites of inviolate
secrecy, and the lions yoked under the chariot of their
mistress. Up then, and let us follow where divine com-
mandments lead ; let us appease the winds, and seek the
realm of Gnosus. Nor is it a far journey away. Only be
Jupiter favourable, the third day shall bring our fleet to
anchor on the Cretan coast." So spoke he, and slew fit
sacrifice on the altars, a bull to Neptune, a bull to thee,
fair Apollo, a black sheep to Tempest, a white to the prosperous West winds.

'Rumour flies that Idomeneus the captain is driven

forth of his father's realm, and the shores of Crete are abandoned, that the houses are void of foes and the dwellings
lie empty to our hand.   We leave the harbour of Ortygia,
and fly along the main, by the revel-trod ridges of Naxos,
by green Donusa, Olearos and snow-white Paros, and
the sea-strewn Cyclades, threading the racing channels
among the crowded lands.   The seamen's clamour rises
in emulous dissonance; each cheers his comrade: *Seek we
Crete and our forefathers.*   A wind rising astern follows us
forth on our way, and we glide at last to the ancient
Curetean coast.   So I set eagerly to work on the walls of
my chosen town, and call it Pergamea, and exhort my
people, joyful at the name, to cherish their homes and rear
the castle buildings.   And even now the ships were drawn
up on the dry beach; the people were busy in marriages and
among their new fields; I was giving statutes and homesteads; when suddenly from a tainted space of sky came,
noisome on men's bodies and pitiable on trees and crops,
pestilence and a year of death.   They left their sweet lives
or dragged themselves on in misery; Sirius scorched the
fields into barrenness; the herbage grew dry, and the sickly
harvest denied sustenance.   My father counsels to remea-
sure the sea and go again to Phoebus in his Ortygian oracle,
to pray for grace and ask what issue he ordains to our exhausted state; whence he bids us search for aid to our
woes, whither bend our course.

  ' Night fell, and sleep held all things living on the earth.
The sacred images of the gods and the household deities of
Phrygia, that I had borne with me from Troy out of the
midst of the burning city, seemed to stand before mine
eyes as I lay sleepless, clear in the broad light where the
full moon poured through the latticed windows; then
thus addressed me, and with this speech allayed my distresses : "What Apollo hath to tell thee when thou dost

reach Ortygia, he utters here, and sends us unsought to
thy threshold. We who followed thee and thine arms when
Dardania went down in fire; we who under thee have
traversed on shipboard the swelling sea; we in like wise
will exalt to heaven thy children to be, and give empire to
their city. Do thou prepare a mighty town for a mighty
people, nor draw back from the long wearisome chase.
Thou must change thy dwelling. Not to these shores did
the god at Delos counsel thee, or Apollo bid thee find rest
in Crete. There is a region Greeks name Hesperia, an
ancient land, mighty in arms and foison of the clod; Oenotrian men dwell therein; now rumour is that a younger
race have called it Italy after their captain's name. This
is our true dwelling place; hence is Dardanus sprung, and
lord Iasius, the first source of our race. Up, arise, and
tell with good cheer to thine aged parent this plain tale, to
seek Corythus and the lands of Ausonia. Jupiter denies
thee the Dictaean fields."

'Astonished at this vision and divine utterance (nor
was that slumber; but openly I seemed to know their
countenances, their veiled hair and gracious faces, and
therewith a cold sweat broke out all over me) I spring
from my bed and raise my voice and upturned hands sky-
ward and pay pure offering on the hearth. The sacrifice done, I joyfully tell Anchises, and relate all in order.
He recognises the double descent and twofold parentage,
and the later wanderings that had deceived him among
ancient lands. Then he speaks: "O son, hard wrought
by the destinies of Ilium, Cassandra only foretold me this
fortune. Now I recall how she prophesied this was fated
to our race, and often cried of Hesperia, often of an Italian
realm. But who was to believe that Teucrians should come
to Hesperian shores? or whom might Cassandra then move
by prophecy? Yield we to Phoebus, and follow the better

way he counsels." So says he, and we all rejoicingly obey
his speech. This dwelling likewise we abandon ; and leaving some few behind, spread our sails and run over the
waste sea in our hollow wood.

'After our ships held the high seas, nor any land yet
appears, the sky all round us and all round us the deep, a
dusky shower drew up overhead carrying night and tempest,
and the wave shuddered and gloomed. Straightway the
winds upturn the main, and great seas rise ; we are tossed
asunder over the dreary gulf. Stormclouds enwrap the
day, and rainy gloom blots out the sky; out of the
clouds bursts fire fast upon fire. Driven from our course,
we go wandering on the blind waves. Palinurus himself
professes he cannot tell day from night on the sky, nor
remember the way amid the waters. Three dubious days
of blind darkness we wander on the deep, as many nights
without a star. Not till the fourth day was land at last
seen to rise, discovering distant hills and sending up wreaths
of smoke. The sails drop; we swing back to the oars ;
without delay the sailors strongly toss up the foam, and
sweep through the green water. The shores of the Stro-
phades first receive me thus won from the waves, Stro-
phades the Greek name they bear, islands lying in the
great Ionian sea, which boding Celaeno and the other
Harpies inhabit since Phineus' house was shut on them,
and they fled in terror from the board of old. Than these
no deadlier portent nor any fiercer plague of divine wrath
hath issued from the Stygian waters; winged things with
maidens' countenance, bellies dropping filth, and clawed
hands and faces ever wan with hunger. . . .

'When borne hitherward we enter the haven, lo ! we
see goodly herds of oxen scattered on the plains, and goats
flocking untended over the grass. We attack them with
the sword, and call the gods and Jove himself to share our

spoil. Then we build seats on the winding shore and banquet on the dainty food. But suddenly the Harpies are upon us, swooping awfully from the mountains, and shaking their wings with loud clangour, plunder the feast, and defile everything with unclean touch, spreading a foul smell, and uttering dreadful cries. Again, in a deep recess under a caverned rock, shut in with waving shadows of woodland, we array the board and renew the altar fires; again, from their blind ambush in diverse quarters of the sky, the noisy crowd flutter with clawed feet around their prey, defiling the feast with their lips. Then I bid my comrades take up arms, and proclaim war on the accursed race. Even as I bade they do, range their swords in cover among the grass, and hide their shields out of sight. So when they swooped clamorously down along the winding shore, Misenus from his watch-tower on high signals on the hollow brass; my comrades rush in and essay the strange battle, to set the stain of steel on the winged horrors of the sea. But they take no violence on their plumage, nor wounds on their bodies; and soaring into the firmament with rapid flight, leave their foul traces on the spoil they had half consumed. Celaeno alone, prophetess of ill, alights on a towering cliff, and thus breaks forth in deep accents:

' "War is it for your slaughtered oxen and steers cut down, O children of Laomedon, war is it you would declare, and drive the guiltless Harpies from their ancestral kingdom? Take then to heart and fix fast these words of mine; which the Lord omnipotent foretold to Phoebus, Phoebus Apollo to me, I eldest born of the Furies reveal to you. Italy is your goal; wooing the winds you shall go to Italy, and enter her harbours unhindered. Yet shall you not wall round your ordained city, ere this murderous outrage on us compel you, in portentous hunger, to eat your tables with gnawing teeth."

' She spoke, and winged her way back to the shelter of

the wood. But my comrades' blood froze chill with sudden
affright ; their spirits fell ; and no longer with arms, nay
with vows and prayers they bid me entreat favour, whether
these be goddesses, or winged things ill-ominous and foul.
And lord Anchises from the beach calls with outspread
hands on the mighty gods, ordering fit sacrifices : " Gods,
avert their menaces ! Gods, turn this woe away, and graciously save the righteous !" Then he bids pluck the cable
from the shore and shake loose the sheets. Southern winds
stretch the sails ; we scud over the foam-flecked waters,
whither wind and pilot called our course. Now wooded
Zacynthos appears amid the waves, and Dulichium and
Same and Neritos' sheer rocks. We fly past the cliffs of
Ithaca, Laërtes' realm, and curse the land, fostress of cruel
Ulysses. Soon too Mount Leucata's cloudy peaks are
sighted, and Apollo dreaded of sailors. Hither we steer
wearily, and stand in to the little town. The anchor is cast
from the prow ; the sterns are grounded on the beach.

   ' So at last having attained to land beyond our hopes,
we purify ourselves in Jove's worship, and kindle altars of
offering, and make the Actian shore gay with the games of
Ilium. My comrades strip, and, slippery with oil, exercise
their ancestral contests ; glad to have got past so many
Argive towns, and held on their flight through the encircling
foe. Meanwhile the sun rounds the great circle of the year,
and icy winter ruffles the waters with Northern gales. I fix
against the doorway a hollow shield of brass, that tall Abas
had borne, and mark the story with a verse : *These arms
Aeneas from the conquering Greeks.* Then I bid leave the
harbour and sit down at the thwarts ; emulously my comrades
strike the water, and sweep through the seas. Soon we see
the cloud-capped Phaeacian towers sink away, skirt the
shores of Epirus, and enter the Chaonian haven and approach high Buthrotum town.

'Here the rumour of a story beyond belief comes on
our ears; Helenus son of Priam is reigning over Greek
towns, master of the bride and sceptre of Pyrrhus the
Aeacid; and Andromache hath again fallen to a husband
of her people. I stood amazed; and my heart kindled
with marvellous desire to accost him and learn of so strange
a fortune. I advance from the harbour, leaving the fleet
ashore; just when haply Andromache, in a grove before
the town, by the waters of a feigned Simoïs, was pouring
libation to the dust, and calling Hector's ghost to a tomb
with his name, on an empty turfed green with two altars
that she had consecrated, a wellspring of tears. When she
caught sight of me coming, and saw distractedly the encircling
arms of Troy, terror-stricken at the vision marvellously
shewn, her gaze fixed, and the heat left her frame. She
swoons away, and hardly at last speaks after long interval:
"Comest thou then a real face, a real messenger to me,
goddess-born? livest thou? or if sweet light is fled, ah,
where is Hector?" She spoke, and bursting into tears
filled all the place with her crying. Just a few words I force
up, and deeply moved gasp out in broken accents: "I
live indeed, I live on through all extremities; doubt not,
for real are the forms thou seest . . . Alas! after such an
husband, what fate receives thy fall? or what worthier
fortune revisits thee? Dost thou, Hector's Andromache,
keep bonds of marriage with Pyrrhus?" She cast down
her countenance, and spoke with lowered voice:
'"O single in happy eminence that maiden daughter of
Priam, sentenced to die under high Troy town at an enemy's
grave, who never bore the shame of the lot, nor came a captive to her victorious master's bed! We, sailing over alien
seas from our burning land, have endured the haughty youthful pride of Achilles' seed, and borne children in slavery:
he thereafter, wooing Leda's Hermione and a Lacedaemonian

marriage, passed me over to Helenus' keeping, a bondwoman to a bondman. But him Orestes, aflame with passionate desire for his stolen bride, and driven by the furies of crime, catches unguarded and murders at his ancestral altars. At Neoptolemus' death a share of his realm fell to Helenus' hands, who named the plains Chaonian, and called all the land Chaonia after Chaon of Troy, and built withal a Pergama and this Ilian citadel on the hills. But to thee how did winds, how fates give passage? or whose divinity landed thee all unwitting on our coasts? what of the boy Ascanius? lives he yet, and draws breath, thy darling, whom Troy's . . . Yet hath the child affection for his lost mother? is he roused to the valour of old and the spirit of manhood by his father Aeneas, by his uncle Hector?"

'Such words she poured forth weeping, and prolonged the vain wail; when the hero Helenus son of Priam approaches from the town with a great company, knows us for his kin, and leads us joyfully to his gates, shedding a many tears at every word. I advance and recognise a little Troy, and a copy of the great Pergama, and a dry brook with the name of Xanthus, and clasp a Scaean gateway. Therewithal my Teucrians make holiday in the friendly town. The king entertained them in his spacious colonnades; in the central hall they poured goblets of wine in libation, and held the cups while the feast was served on gold.

'And now a day and another day hath sped; the breezes woo our sails, and the canvas blows out to the swelling south. With these words I accost the prophet, and thus make request:

'"Son of Troy, interpreter of the gods, whose sense is open to Phoebus' influences, his tripods and laurels, to stars and tongues of birds and auguries of prosperous flight, tell me now,—for the voice of revelation was all favourable to my course, and all divine influence counselled me to seek Italy and explore remote lands; only Celaeno the Harpy prophesies of strange portents, a horror to tell, and cries out of wrath and bale and foul hunger,—what perils are the first to shun? or in what guidance may I overcome these sore labours?"

'Hereat Helenus, first suing for divine favour with fit sacrifice of steers, and unbinding from his head the chaplets of consecration, leads me in his hand to thy courts, O Phoebus, thrilled with the fulness of the deity, and then utters these prophetic words from his augural lips:

'"Goddess-born: since there is clear assurance that under high omens thou dost voyage through the deep; so the king of the gods allots destiny and unfolds change; this is the circle of ordinance; a few things out of many I will unfold to thee in speech, that so thou mayest more safely traverse the seas of thy sojourn, and find rest in the Ausonian haven; for Helenus is forbidden by the destinies to know, and by Juno daughter of Saturn to utter more: first of all, the Italy thou deemest now nigh, and close at hand, unwitting! the harbours thou wouldst enter, far are they sundered by a long and trackless track through length of lands. First must the Trinacrian wave clog thine oar, and thy ships traverse the salt Ausonian plain, by the infernal pools and Aeaean Circe's isle, ere thou mayest build thy city in safety on a peaceful land. I will tell thee the token, and do thou keep it close in thine heart. When in thy perplexity, beside the wave of a sequestered river, a great sow shall be discovered lying under the oaks on the brink, with her newborn litter of thirty, couched white on the ground, her white brood about her teats; that shall be the place of the city, that the appointed rest from thy toils. Neither shrink thou at the gnawn tables that await thee; the fates will find a way, and Apollo aid thy call. These lands moreover, on this nearest border of the Italian shore

that our own sea's tide washes, flee thou : evil Greeks dwell
in all their towns. Here the Locrians of Narycos have
set their city, and here Lyctian Idomeneus beset the
Sallentine plains with soldiery ; here is the town of the
Meliboean captain, Philoctetes' little Petelia fenced by her
wall. Nay, when thy fleets have crossed overseas and lie
at anchor, when now thou rearest altars and payest vows on
the beach, veil thine hair with a purple garment for covering, that no hostile face at thy divine worship may meet
thee amid the holy fires and make void the omens.
This fashion of sacrifice keep thou, thyself and thy comrades, and let thy children abide in this pure observance.
But when at thy departure the wind hath borne thee to the
Sicilian coast, and the barred straits of Pelorus open out,
steer for the left-hand country and the long circuit of the
seas on the left hand ; shun the shore and water on thy
right. These lands, they say, of old broke asunder, torn
and upheaved by vast force, when either country was one
and undivided ; the ocean burst in between, cutting off
with its waves the Hesperian from the Sicilian coast, and
with narrow tide washes tilth and town along the severance
of shore. On the right Scylla keeps guard, on the left
unassuaged Charybdis, who thrice swallows the vast flood
sheer down her swirling gulf, and ever again hurls it
upward, lashing the sky with water. But Scylla lies
prisoned in her cavern's blind recesses, thrusting forth
her mouth and drawing ships upon the rocks. In front
her face is human, and her breast fair as a maiden's to the
waist down ; behind she is a sea-dragon of monstrous frame,
with dolphins' tails joined on her wolf-girt belly. Better to
track the goal of Trinacrian Pachynus, lingering and wheeling round through long spaces, than once catch sight of
misshapen Scylla deep in her dreary cavern, and of the
rocks that ring to her sea-coloured hounds. Moreover, if

Helenus hath aught of foresight or his prophecy of assurance, if Apollo fills his spirit with the truth, this one thing, goddess-born, one thing for all will I foretell thee, and again and again repeat my counsel : to great Juno's deity be thy first prayer and worship; to Juno utter thy willing vows, and overcome thy mighty mistress with gifts and supplications; so at last thou shalt leave Trinacria behind, and be sped in triumph to the Italian borders. When borne hither thou drawest nigh the Cymaean city, the haunted lakes and rustling woods of Avernus, thou shalt behold the raving prophetess who deep in the rock chants of fate, and marks down her words on leaves. What verses she writes down on them, the maiden sorts into order and shuts behind her in the cave ; they stay in their places unstirred and quit not their rank.   But when at the turn of the hinge the light wind from the doorway stirs them, and disarranges the delicate foliage, never after does she trouble to capture them as they flutter about the hollow rock, nor restore their places or join the verses ; men depart without counsel, and hate the Sibyl's dwelling.   Here let no waste in delay be of such account to thee (though thy company chide, and the passage call thy sails strongly to the deep, and thou mayest fill out their folds to thy desire) that thou do not approach the prophetess, and plead with prayers that she herself utter her oracles and deign to loose the accents from her lips.   The nations of Italy and the wars to come, and the fashion whereby every toil may be avoided or endured, she shall unfold to thee, and grant her worshipper prosperous passage.   Thus far is our voice allowed to counsel thee : go thy way, and exalt Troy to heaven by thy deeds."

   ' This the seer uttered with friendly lips ; then orders gifts to be carried to my ships, of heavy gold and sawn ivory, and loads the hulls with massy silver and cauldrons

of Dodona, a mail coat triple-woven with hooks of gold,
and a helmet splendid with spike and tressed plumes, the
armour of Neoptolemus. My father too hath his gifts.
Horses besides he brings, and grooms . . . fills up the
tale of our oarsmen, and equips my crews with arms.

' Meanwhile Anchises bade the fleet set their sails, that
the fair wind might meet no delay. Him Phoebus' interpreter accosts with high courtesy : "Anchises, honoured
with the splendour of Venus' espousal, the gods' charge,
twice rescued from the fallen towers of Troy, lo ! the land
of Ausonia is before thee : sail thou and seize it. And yet
needs must thou float past it on the sea ; far away lies
the quarter of Ausonia that is revealed of Apollo. Go,"
he continues, "happy in thy son's affection : why do I
run on further, and delay the rising winds in talk?"
Andromache too, sad at this last parting, brings figured
raiment with woof of gold, and a Phrygian scarf for
Ascanius, and wearies not in courtesy, loading him with
gifts from the loom. "Take these too," so says she, " my
child, to be memorials to thee of my hands, and testify long
hence the love of Andromache wife of Hector. Take
these last gifts of thy kinsfolk, O sole surviving likeness to
me of my own Astyanax ! Such was he, in eyes and hands
and features ; and now his equal age were growing into
manhood like thine."

' To them as I departed I spoke with starting tears :
" Live happily, as they do whose fortunes are perfected !
We are summoned ever from fate to fate. For you there
is rest in store, and no ocean floor to furrow, no ever-
retreating Ausonian fields to pursue. You see a pictured
Xanthus, and a Troy your own hands have built ; with
better omens, I pray, and to be less open to the Greeks.
If ever I enter Tiber and Tiber's bordering fields, and see
a city granted to my nation, then of these kindred towns

and allied peoples in Epirus and Hesperia, which have the same Dardanus for founder, and whose story is one, of both will our hearts make a single Troy.   Let that charge await our posterity."

'We put out to sea, keeping the Ceraunian mountains close at hand, whence is the shortest passage and seaway to Italy.   The sun sets meanwhile, and the dusky hills grow dim.   We choose a place, and fling ourselves on the lap of earth at the water's edge, and, allotting the oars, spread ourselves on the dry beach for refreshment : the dew of slumber falls on our weary limbs.   Not yet had Night driven of the Hours climbed her mid arch ; Palinurus rises lightly from his couch, explores all the winds, and listens to catch a breeze ; he marks the constellations gliding together through the silent sky, Arcturus, the rainy Hyades and the twin Oxen, and scans Orion in his armour of gold.   When he sees the clear sky quite unbroken, he gives from the stern his shrill signal ; we disencamp and explore the way, and spread the wings of our sails.   And now reddening Dawn had chased away the stars, when we descry afar dim hills and the low line of Italy.   Achates first raises the cry of *Italy;* and with joyous shouts my comrades salute Italy. Then lord Anchises enwreathed a great bowl and filled it up with wine ; and called on the gods, standing high astern . . . "Gods sovereign over sea and land and weather ! bring wind to ease our way, and breathe favourably."   The breezes freshen at his prayer, and now the harbour opens out nearer at hand, and a temple appears on the Fort of Minerva.   My comrades furl the sails and swing the prows to shore.   The harbour is scooped into an arch by the Eastern flood ; reefs run out and foam with the salt spray ; itself it lies concealed ; turreted walls of rock let down their arms on either hand, and the temple retreats from the beach.   Here, an inaugural sight, four horses of snowy whiteness are grazing abroad on the grassy plain. And lord Anchises : " War dost thou carry, land of our sojourn ; horses are armed in war, and menace of war is in this herd. But yet these same beasts are wont in time to enter harness, and carry yoke and bit in concord ; there is hope of peace too," says he. Then we pray to the holy deity, Pallas of the clangorous arms, the first to welcome our cheers. And before the altars we veil our heads in Phrygian garments, and duly, after the counsel Helenus had urged deepest on us, pay the bidden burnt-sacrifice to Juno of Argos.

'Without delay, once our vows are fully paid, we round to the arms of our sailyards and leave the dwellings and menacing fields of the Grecian people. Next is descried the bay of Tarentum, town, if rumour is true, of Hercules. Over against it the goddess of Lacinium rears her head, with the towers of Caulon, and Scylaceum wrecker of ships. Then Trinacrian Aetna is descried in the distance rising from the waves, and we hear from afar a great roaring of the sea on beaten rocks, and broken noises by the shore : the channels boil up, and the surge churns with sand. And lord Anchises : " Of a surety this is that Charybdis ; of these cliffs, these awful rocks did Helenus prophesy. Out, O comrades, and rise together to the oars." Even as bidden they do ; and first Palinurus swung the gurgling prow leftward through the water ; to the left all our squadron bent with oar and wind. We are lifted skyward on the crescent wave, and again sunk deep into the nether world as the water is sucked away. Thrice amid their rocky caverns the cliffs uttered a cry; thrice we see the foam flung out, and the stars through a dripping veil. Meanwhile the wind falls with sundown; and weary and ignorant of the way we glide on to the Cyclopes' coast.

'There lies a harbour large and unstirred by the winds'

F

entrance ; but nigh it Aetna thunders awfully in wrack, and
ever and again hurls a black cloud into the sky, smoking
with boiling pitch and embers white hot, and heaves balls
of flame flickering up to the stars : ever and again vomits
out on high crags from the torn entrails of the mountain,
tosses up masses of molten rock with a groan, and boils forth
from the bottom.   Rumour is that this mass weighs down
the body of Enceladus, half-consumed by the thunderbolt,
and mighty Aetna laid over him suspires the flame that
bursts from her furnaces ; and so often as he changes his
weary side, all Trinacria shudders and moans, veiling the
sky in smoke.   That night we spend in cover of the forest
among portentous horrors, and see not from what source
the noise comes.   For neither did the stars show their fires,
nor was the vault of constellated sky clear ; but vapours
blotted heaven, and the moon was held in a storm-cloud
through dead of night.

‘ And now the morrow was rising in the early east, and
the dewy darkness rolled away from the sky by Dawn, when
sudden out of the forest advances a human shape strange
and unknown, worn with uttermost hunger and pitiably
attired, and stretches entreating hands towards the shore.
We look back.   Filthy and wretched, with shaggy beard
and a coat pinned together with thorns, he was yet a Greek,
and had been sent of old to Troy in his father’s arms.
And he, when he saw afar the Dardanian habits and armour
of Troy, hung back a little in terror at the sight, and stayed
his steps; then ran headlong to the shore with weeping and
prayers : “ By the heavens I beseech you, by the heavenly
powers and this luminous sky that gives us breath, take me
up, O Trojans, carry me away to any land soever, and it
will be enough.   I know I am one out of the Grecian
fleets, I confess I warred against the household gods of
Ilium ; for that, if our wrong and guilt is so great, throw

me piecemeal on the flood or plunge me in the waste sea.
If I do perish, gladly will I perish at human hands." He
ended ; and clung clasping our knees and grovelling at
them.   We encourage him to tell who he is and of what
blood born, and reveal how Fortune pursues him since
then.   Lord Anchises after little delay gives him his hand,
and strengthens his courage by visible pledge.   At last,
laying aside his terror, he speaks thus :

'" I am from an Ithacan home, Achemenides by name,
set out for Troy in luckless Ulysses' company; poor was
my father Adamastus, and would God fortune had stayed
thus ! Here my comrades abandoned me in the Cyclops'
vast cave, mindless of me while they hurry away from the
barbarous gates.   It is a house of gore and blood-stained
feasts, dim and huge within.   Himself he is great of
stature and knocks at the lofty sky (gods, take away a
curse like this from earth !) to none gracious in aspect or
courteous of speech.   He feeds on the flesh and dark blood
of wretched men.   I myself saw, when he caught the bodies
of two of us with his great hand, and lying back in the
middle of the cave crushed them on the rock, and the
courts splashed and swam with gore ; I saw when he
champed the flesh adrip with dark clots of blood, and the
warm limbs quivered under his teeth.   Yet not unavenged .
Ulysses brooked not this, nor even in such straits did the
Ithacan forget himself.   For so soon as he, gorged with his
feast and buried in wine, lay with bent neck sprawling huge
over the cave, in his sleep vomiting gore and gobbets mixed
with wine and blood, we, praying to the great gods and
with parts allotted, pour at once all round him, and pierce
with a sharp weapon the huge eye that lay sunk single
under his savage brow, in fashion of an Argolic shield or
the lamp of the moon ; and at last we exultingly avenge
the ghosts of our comrades.   But fly, O wretched men, fly

and pluck the cable from the beach. . . . For even in the
shape and stature of Polyphemus, when he shuts his fleeced
flocks and drains their udders in the cave's covert, an
hundred other horrible Cyclopes dwell all about this shore
and stray on the mountain heights. Thrice now does the
horned moon fill out her light, while I linger in life among
desolate lairs and haunts of wild beasts in the woodland,
and from a rock survey the giant Cyclopes and shudder at
their cries and echoing feet. The boughs yield a miserable
sustenance, berries and stony sloes, and plants torn up by
the root feed me. Sweeping all the view, I at last espied
this fleet standing in to shore. On it, whatsoever it were,
I cast myself; it is enough to have escaped the accursed
tribe. Do you rather, by any death you will, destroy this
life of mine."

    'Scarcely had he spoken thus, when on the mountain
top we see shepherding his flocks a vast moving mass,
Polyphemus himself seeking the shores he knew, a horror
ominous, shapeless, huge, bereft of sight. A pine lopped
by his hand guides and steadies his footsteps. His fleeced
sheep attend him, this his single delight and solace in ill.
. . . After he hath touched the deep flood and come to the
sea, he washes in it the blood that oozes from his eye-
socket, grinding his teeth with groans ; and now he strides
through the sea up to his middle, nor yet does the wave
wet his towering sides. We hurry far away in precipitate
flight, with the suppliant who had so well merited rescue ;
and silently cut the cable, and bending forward sweep the
sea with emulous oars. He heard, and turned his steps
towards the echoing sound. But when he may in no wise
lay hands on us, nor can fathom the Ionian waves in
pursuit, he raises a vast cry, at which the sea and all his
waves shuddered, and the deep land of Italy was startled,
and Aetna's vaulted caverns moaned. But the tribe of the

Cyclopes, roused from the high wooded hills, run to the
harbour and fill the shore. We descry the Aetnean
brotherhood standing impotent with scowling eye, their
stately heads up to heaven, a dreadful consistory; even
as on a mountain summit stand oaks high in air or coned
cypresses, a high forest of Jove or covert of Diana. Sharp
fear urges us to shake out the sheets in reckless haste, and
spread our sails to the favouring wind. Yet Helenus'
commands counsel that our course keep not the way
between Scylla and Charybdis, the very edge of death on
either hand. We are resolved to turn our canvas back.
And lo! from the narrow fastness of Pelorus the North
wind comes down and reaches us. I sail past Pantagias'
mouth with its living stone, the Megarian bay, and low-
lying Thapsus. Such names did Achemenides, of luckless
Ulysses' company, point out as he retraced his wanderings
along the returning shores.

'Stretched in front of a bay of Sicily lies an islet over
against wavebeat Plemyrium ; they of old called it Ortygia.
Hither Alpheus the river of Elis, so rumour runs, hath
cloven a secret passage beneath the sea, and now through
thy well-head, Arethusa, mingles with the Sicilian waves.
We adore as bidden the great deities of the ground ; and
thence I cross the fertile soil of Helorus in the marsh.
Next we graze the high reefs and jutting rocks of Pachynus;
and far off appears Camarina, forbidden for ever by oracles
to move, and the Geloan plains, and vast Gela named after
its river. Then Acragas on the steep, once the breeder of
noble horses, displays its massive walls in the distance ; and
with granted breeze I leave thee behind, palm-girt Selinus,
and thread the difficult shoals and blind reefs of Lilybaeum.
Thereon Drepanum receives me in its haven and joyless
border. Here, so many tempestuous seas outgone, alas !
my father, the solace of every care and chance, Anchises is

lost to me. Here thou, dear lord, abandonest me in weariness, alas! rescued in vain from peril and doom. Not Helenus the prophet, though he counselled of many a terror, not boding Celaeno foretold me of this grief. This was the last agony, this the goal of the long ways; thence it was I had departed when God landed me on your coasts.'

Thus lord Aeneas with all attent retold alone the divine doom and the history of his goings. At last he was hushed, and here in silence made an end.

BOOK FOURTH

THE LOVE OF DIDO, AND HER END

But the Queen, long ere now pierced with sore distress,
feeds the wound with her life-blood, and catches the fire
unseen. Again and again his own valiance and his line's
renown flood back upon her spirit; look and accent cling
fast in her bosom, and the pain allows not rest or calm to
her limbs. The morrow's dawn bore the torch of Phoebus
across the earth, and had rolled away the dewy darkness
from the sky, when, scarce herself, she thus opens her confidence to her sister:

'Anna, my sister, such dreams of terror thrill me
through! What guest unknown is this who hath entered
our dwelling? How high his mien! how brave in heart
as in arms! I believe it well, with no vain assurance, his
blood is divine. Fear proves the vulgar spirit. Alas, by what
destinies is he driven! what wars outgone he chronicled!
Were my mind not planted, fixed and immoveable, to ally
myself to none in wedlock since my love of old was false
to me in the treachery of death; were I not sick to the
heart of bridal torch and chamber, to this temptation
alone I might haply yield. Anna, I will confess it; since
Sychaeus mine husband met his piteous doom, and our
household was shattered by a brother's murder, he only hath

touched mine heart and stirred the balance of my soul   I
know the prints of the ancient flame.   But rather, I pray,
may earth first yawn deep for me, or the Lord omnipotent
hurl me with his thunderbolt into gloom, the pallid gloom
and profound night of Erebus, ere I soil thee, mine honour,
or unloose thy laws.   He took my love away who made me
one with him long ago; he shall keep it with him, and
guard it in the tomb.'   She spoke, and welling tears filled
the bosom of her gown.

Anna replies: 'O dearer than the daylight to thy
sister, wilt thou waste, sad and alone, all thy length of
youth, and know not the sweetness of motherhood, nor
love's bounty?   Deemest thou the ashes care for that, or the
ghost within the tomb?   Be it so: in days gone by no wooers
bent thy sorrow, not in Libya, not ere then in Tyre; Iarbas
was slighted, and other princes nurtured by the triumphal
land of Africa; wilt thou contend so with a love to thy
liking?   nor does it cross thy mind whose are these fields
about thy dwelling?   On this side are the Gaetulian towns,
a race unconquerable in war; the reinless Numidian riders
and the grim Syrtis hem thee in; on this lies a thirsty
tract of desert, swept by the raiders of Barca.   Why speak
of the war gathering from Tyre, and thy brother's menaces?
. . . With gods' auspices to my thinking, and with Juno's
favour, hath the Ilian fleet held on hither before the gale.
What a city wilt thou discern here, O sister! what a realm
will rise on such a union! the arms of Troy ranged with
ours, what glory will exalt the Punic state!   Do thou only,
asking divine favour with peace-offerings, be bounteous in
welcome and draw out reasons for delay, while the storm
rages at sea and Orion is wet, and his ships are shattered
and the sky unvoyageable.'   With these words she made
the fire of love flame up in her spirit, put hope in her
wavering soul, and let honour slip away.

First they visit the shrines, and desire grace from altar
to altar; they sacrifice sheep fitly chosen to Ceres the Lawgiver, to Phoebus and lord Lyaeus, to Juno before all,
guardian of the marriage bond. Dido herself, excellent in
beauty, holds the cup in her hand, and pours libation
between the horns of a milk-white cow, or moves in state
to the rich altars before the gods' presences, day by day
renewing her gifts, and gazing athirst into the breasts of
cattle laid open to take counsel from the throbbing entrails. Ah, witless souls of soothsayers! how may vows or
shrines help her madness? all the while the subtle flame
consumes her inly, and deep in her breast the wound is
silent and alive. Stung to misery, Dido wanders in frenzy
all down the city, even as an arrow-stricken deer, whom,
far and heedless amid the Cretan woodland, a shepherd
archer hath pierced and left the flying steel in her unaware;
she ranges in flight the Dictaean forest lawns; fast in her
side clings the deadly reed. Now she leads Aeneas with her
through the town, and displays her Sidonian treasure and
ordered city; she essays to speak, and breaks off half-way
in utterance. Now, as day wanes, she seeks the repeated
banquet, and again madly pleads to hear the agonies of
Ilium, and again hangs on the teller's lips. Thereafter, when
all are gone their ways, and the dim moon in turn quenches
her light, and the setting stars counsel to sleep, alone in the
empty house she mourns, and flings herself on the couch
he left: distant she hears and sees him in the distance; or
enthralled by the look he has of his father, she holds
Ascanius on her lap, if so she may steal the love she may not
utter. No more do the unfinished towers rise, no more
do the people exercise in arms, nor work for safety in war
on harbour or bastion; the works hang broken off, vast
looming walls and engines towering into the sky.

So soon as she perceives her thus fast in the toils, and

madly careless of her name, Jove's beloved wife, daughter
of Saturn, accosts Venus thus :

'Noble indeed is the fame and splendid the spoils you
win, thou and that boy of thine, and mighty the renown
of deity, if two gods have vanquished one woman by
treachery. Nor am I so blind to thy terror of our town,
thine old suspicion of the high house of Carthage. But
what shall be the end ? or why all this contest now ? Nay,
rather let us work an enduring peace and a bridal compact.
Thou hast what all thy soul desired ; Dido is on fire with
love, and hath caught the madness through and through.
Then rule we this people jointly in equal lordship; allow
her to be a Phrygian husband's slave, and to lay her Tyrians
for dowry in thine hand.'

To her—for she knew the dissembled purpose of her
words, to turn the Teucrian kingdom away to the coasts of
Libya—Venus thus began in answer: 'Who so mad as to
reject these terms, or choose rather to try the fortune of
war with thee ? if only when done, as thou sayest, fortune
follow. But I move in uncertainty of Jove's ordinance,
whether he will that Tyrians and wanderers from Troy be
one city, or approve the mingling of peoples and the treaty
of union. Thou art his wife, and thy prayers may essay his
soul. Go on ; I will follow.'

Then Queen Juno thus rejoined : 'That task shall be
mine. Now, by what means the present need may be fulfilled, attend and I will explain in brief. Aeneas and
Dido (alas and woe for her !) are to go hunting together in
the woodland when to-morrow's rising sun goes forth and his
rays unveil the world. On them, while the beaters run up
and down, and the lawns are girt with toils, will I pour
down a blackening rain-cloud mingled with hail, and startle
all the sky in thunder. Their company will scatter for
shelter in the dim darkness ; Dido and the Trojan captain

shall take refuge in the same cavern. I will be there, and
if thy goodwill is assured me, I will unite them in wedlock,
and make her wholly his; here shall Hymen be present.'
The Cytherean gave ready assent to her request, and laughed
at the wily invention.

Meanwhile Dawn rises forth of ocean. A chosen company issue from the gates while the morning star is high;
they pour forth with meshed nets, toils, broad-headed hunting
spears, Massylian horsemen and sinewy sleuth-hounds. At
her doorway the chief of Carthage await their queen, who
yet lingers in her chamber, and her horse stands splendid in
gold and purple with clattering feet and jaws champing on the
foamy bit. At last she comes forth amid a great thronging
train, girt in a Sidonian mantle, broidered with needlework; her quiver is of gold, her tresses knotted into gold,
a golden buckle clasps up her crimson gown. Therewithal
the Phrygian train advances with joyous Iülus. Himself
first and foremost of all, Aeneas joins her company and
unites his party to hers: even as Apollo, when he leaves
wintry Lycia and the streams of Xanthus to visit his
mother's Delos, and renews the dance, while Cretans and
Dryopes and painted Agathyrsians mingle clamorous about
his altars: himself he treads the Cynthian ridges, and plaits
his flowing hair with soft heavy sprays and entwines it with
gold; the arrows rattle on his shoulder: as lightly as he
went Aeneas; such glow and beauty is on his princely face.
When they are come to the mountain heights and pathless
coverts, lo, wild goats driven from the cliff-tops run down the
ridge; in another quarter stags speed over the open plain and
gather their flying column in a cloud of dust as they leave
the hills. But the boy Ascanius is in the valleys, exultant
on his fiery horse, and gallops past one and another, praying that among the unwarlike herds a foaming boar may
issue or a tawny lion descend the hill.

Meanwhile the sky begins to thicken and roar aloud.
A rain-cloud comes down mingled with hail; the Tyrian
train and the men of Troy, and the Dardanian boy of
Venus' son scatter in fear, and seek shelter far over the
fields. Streams pour from the hills. Dido and the Trojan
captain take refuge in the same cavern. Primeval Earth
and Juno the bridesmaid give the sign; fires flash out high
in air, witnessing the union, and Nymphs cry aloud on the
mountain-top. That day opened the gate of death and
the springs of ill. For now Dido recks not of eye or
tongue, nor sets her heart on love in secret: she calls it
marriage, and with this name veils her fall.

Straightway Rumour runs through the great cities of
Libya,—Rumour, than whom none other is more swift to
mischief; she thrives on restlessness and gains strength by
going: at first small and timorous; soon she lifts herself on
high and paces the ground with head hidden among the
clouds. Her, one saith, Mother Earth, when stung by
wrath against the gods, bore last sister to Coeus and
Enceladus, fleet-footed and swift of wing, ominous, awful,
vast; for every feather on her body is a waking eye
beneath, wonderful to tell, and a tongue, and as many loud
lips and straining ears. By night she flits between sky and
land, shrilling through the dusk, and droops not her lids in
sweet slumber; in daylight she sits on guard upon tall
towers or the ridge of the house-roof, and makes great
cities afraid; obstinate in perverseness and forgery no less
than messenger of truth. She then exultingly filled the
countries with manifold talk, and blazoned alike what was
done and undone: one Aeneas is come, born of Trojan
blood; on him beautiful Dido thinks no shame to fling
herself; now they hold their winter, long-drawn through
mutual caresses, regardless of their realms and enthralled
by passionate dishonour. This the pestilent goddess

spreads abroad in the mouths of men, and bends her course right on to King Iarbas, and with her words fires his spirit and swells his wrath.

He, the seed of Ammon by a ravished Garamantian Nymph, had built to Jove in his wide realms an hundred great temples, an hundred altars, and consecrated the wakeful fire that keeps watch by night before the gods perpetually, where the soil is fat with blood of beasts and the courts blossom with pied garlands. And he, distracted and on fire at the bitter tidings, before his altars, amid the divine presences, often, it is said, bowed in prayer to Jove with uplifted hands :

'Jupiter omnipotent, to whom from the broidered cushions of their banqueting halls the Maurusian people now pour Lenaean offering, lookest thou on this? or do we shudder vainly when our father hurls the thunderbolt, and do blind fires in the clouds and idle rumblings appal our soul? The woman who, wandering in our coasts, planted a small town on purchased ground, to whom we gave fields by the shore and laws of settlement, she hath spurned our alliance and taken Aeneas for lord of her realm. And now that Paris, with his effeminate crew, his chin and oozy hair swathed in the turban of Maeonia, takes and keeps her; since to thy temples we bear oblation, and hallow an empty name.'

In such words he pleaded, clasping the altars ; the Lord omnipotent heard, and cast his eye on the royal city and the lovers forgetful of their fairer fame. Then he addresses this charge to Mercury :

'Up and away, O son I call the breezes and slide down them on thy wings : accost the Dardanian captain who now loiters in Tyrian Carthage and casts not a look on destined cities ; carry down my words through the fleet air. Not such an one did his mother most beautiful vouch him to us, nor for this twice rescue him from Grecian arms; but he was to rule an Italy teeming with empire and loud with war, to transmit the line of Teucer's royal blood, and lay all the world beneath his law. If such glories kindle him in nowise, and he take no trouble for his own honour, does a father grudge his Ascanius the towers of Rome? with what device or in what hope loiters he among a hostile race, and casts not a glance on his Ausonian children and the fields of Lavinium? Let him set sail: this is the sum: thereof be thou our messenger.'

He ended: his son made ready to obey his high command. And first he laces to his feet the shoes of gold that bear him high winging over seas or land as fleet as the gale; then takes the rod wherewith he calls wan souls forth of Orcus, or sends them again to the sad depth of hell, gives sleep and takes it away and unseals dead eyes; in whose strength he courses the winds and swims across the tossing clouds. And now in flight he descries the peak and steep sides of toiling Atlas, whose crest sustains the sky; Atlas, whose pine-clad head is girt alway with black clouds and beaten by wind and rain; snow is shed over his shoulders for covering; rivers tumble over his aged chin; and his rough beard is stiff with ice. Here the Cyllenian, poised evenly on his wings, made a first stay; hence he shot himself sheer to the water. Like a bird that flies low, skirting the sea about the craggy shores of its fishery, even thus the brood of Cyllene left his mother's father, and flew, cutting the winds between sky and land, along the sandy Libyan shore. So soon as his winged feet reached the settlement, he espies Aeneas founding towers and ordering new dwellings; his sword twinkled with yellow jasper, and a cloak hung from his shoulders ablaze with Tyrian sea-purple, a gift that Dido had made costly and shot the warp with thin gold. Straight-

way he breaks in : ' Layest thou now the foundations of tall
Carthage, and buildest up a fair city in dalliance? ah,
forgetful of thine own kingdom and state I From bright
Olympus I descend to thee at express command of heaven's
sovereign, whose deity sways sky and earth ; expressly he
bids me carry this charge through the fleet air : with what
device or in what hope dost thou loiter idly on Libyan
lands? if such glories kindle thee in nowise, yet cast an
eye on growing Ascanius, on Iülus thine hope and heir, to
whom the kingdom of Italy and the Roman land are due.'
As these words left his lips the Cyllenian, yet speaking,
quitted mortal sight and vanished into thin air away out of
his eyes.

But Aeneas in truth gazed in dumb amazement, his
hair thrilled up, and the accents faltered on his tongue.
He burns to flee away and leave the pleasant land, aghast
at the high warning and divine ordinance. Alas, what
shall he do? how venture to smooth the tale to the
frenzied queen? what prologue shall he find? and this
way and that he rapidly throws his mind, and turns
it on all hands in swift change of thought. In his
perplexity this seemed the better counsel ; he calls Mnestheus and Sergestus, and brave Serestus, and bids them
silently equip the fleet, gather their crews on shore, and
order their armament, keeping the cause of the commo-
tion hid ; himself meanwhile, since Dido the gracious
knows not nor looks for severance to so strong a love, will
essay to approach her when she may be told most gently,
and the way for it be fair. All at once gladly do as bidden,
and obey his command.

But the Queen—who may delude a lover?—foreknew
his devices, and at once caught the presaging stir. Safety's
self was fear ; to her likewise had evil Rumour borne
the maddening news that they equip the fleet and prepare

for passage. Helpless at heart, she reels aflame with rage throughout the city, even as the startled Thyiad in her frenzied triennial orgies, when the holy vessels move forth and the cry of Bacchus re-echoes, and Cithaeron calls her with nightlong din. Thus at last she opens out upon Aeneas :

'And thou didst hope, traitor, to mask the crime, and slip away in silence from my land? Our love holds thee not, nor the hand thou once gavest, nor the bitter death that is left for Dido's portion? Nay, under the wintry star thou labourest on thy fleet, and hastenest to launch into the deep amid northern gales; ah, cruel! Why, were thy quest not of alien fields and unknown dwellings, did thine ancient Troy remain, should Troy be sought in voyages over tossing seas? Fliest thou from me? me who by these tears and thine own hand beseech thee, since naught else, alas! have I kept mine own—by our union and the marriage rites preparing; if I have done thee any grace, or aught of mine hath once been sweet in thy sight,—pity our sinking house, and if there yet be room for prayers, put off this purpose of thine. For thy sake Libyan tribes and Nomad kings are hostile; my Tyrians are estranged; for thy sake, thine, is mine honour perished, and the former fame, my one title to the skies. How leavest thou me to die, O my guest? since to this the name of husband is dwindled down. For what do I wait? till Pygmalion overthrow his sister's city, or Gaetulian Iarbas lead me to captivity? At least if before thy flight a child of thine had been clasped in my arms,—if a tiny Aeneas were playing in my hall, whose face might yet image thine,—I would not think myself ensnared and deserted utterly.'

She ended; he by counsel of Jove held his gaze unstirred, and kept his distress hard down in his heart. At last he briefly answers:

'Never, O Queen, will I deny that thy goodness hath

gone high as thy words can swell the reckoning; nor will
my memory of Elissa be ungracious while I remember myself, and breath sways this body. Little will I say in this.
I never hoped to slip away in stealthy flight; fancy not
that; nor did I ever hold out the marriage torch or enter
thus into alliance. Did fate allow me to guide my life by
mine own government, and calm my sorrows as I would,
my first duty were to the Trojan city and the dear remnant
of my kindred; the high house of Priam should abide, and
my hand had set up Troy towers anew for a conquered
people. But now for broad Italy hath Apollo of Grynos
bidden me steer, for Italy the oracles of Lycia. Here is
my desire; this is my native country. If thy Phoenician
eyes are stayed on Carthage towers and thy Libyan city,
what wrong is it, I pray, that we Trojans find our rest on
Ausonian land? We too may seek a foreign realm unforbidden. In my sleep, often as the dank shades of night
veil the earth, often as the stars lift their fires, the troubled
phantom of my father Anchises comes in warning and dread;
my boy Ascanius, how I wrong one so dear in cheating him
of an Hesperian kingdom and destined fields. Now even
the gods' interpreter, sent straight from Jove—I call both
to witness—hath borne down his commands through the
fleet air. Myself in broad daylight I saw the deity passing
within the walls, and these ears drank his utterance. Cease
to madden me and thyself alike with plaints. Not of my
will do I follow Italy. . . .'

Long ere he ended she gazes on him askance, turning
her eyes from side to side and perusing him with silent
glances; then thus wrathfully speaks:

'No goddess was thy mother, nor Dardanus founder of
thy line, traitor! but rough Caucasus bore thee on his iron
crags, and Hyrcanian tigresses gave thee suck. For why
do I conceal it? For what further outrage do I wait?

G

Hath our weeping cost him a sigh, or a lowered glance?
Hath he broken into tears, or had pity on his lover?
Where, where shall I begin? Now neither doth Queen
Juno nor our Saturnian lord regard us with righteous eyes.
Nowhere is trust safe. Cast ashore and destitute I wel-
comed him, and madly gave him place and portion in my
kingdom; I found him his lost fleet and drew his crews
from death. Alas, the fire of madness speeds me on. Now
prophetic Apollo, now oracles of Lycia, now the very gods'
interpreter sent straight from Jove through the air carries
these rude commands! Truly that is work for the gods,
that a care to vex their peace! I detain thee not, nor
gainsay thy words: go, follow thine Italy down the wind;
seek thy realm overseas. Yet midway my hope is, if righteous gods can do aught at all, thou wilt drain the cup of
vengeance on the rocks, and re-echo calls on Dido's name.
In murky fires I will follow far away, and when chill death
hath severed body from soul, my ghost will haunt thee in
every region. Wretch, thou shalt repay! I will hear; and
the rumour of it shall reach me deep in the under world.'

Even on these words she breaks off her speech unfinished, and, sick at heart, escapes out of the air and
sweeps round and away out of sight, leaving him in fear
and much hesitance, and with much on his mind to say.
Her women catch her in their arms, and carry her swooning
to her marble chamber and lay her on her bed.

But good Aeneas, though he would fain soothe and
comfort her grief, and talk away her distress, with many a
sigh, and melted in soul by his great love, yet fulfils the
divine commands and returns to his fleet. Then indeed the
Teucrians set to work, and haul down their tall ships all along
the shore. The hulls are oiled and afloat; they carry from
the woodland green boughs for oars and massy logs unhewn,
in hot haste to go. . . . One might descry them shifting

their quarters and pouring out of all the town: even as
ants, mindful of winter, plunder a great heap of wheat and
store it in their house; a black column advances on the
plain as they carry home their spoil on a narrow track
through the grass. Some shove and strain with their
shoulders at big grains, some marshal the ranks and
chastise delay; all the path is aswarm with work. What
then were thy thoughts, O Dido, as thou sawest it? What
sighs didst thou utter, viewing from the fortress roof the
broad beach aswarm, and seeing before thine eyes the
whole sea stirred with their noisy din? Injurious Love,
to what dost thou not compel mortal hearts! Again she
must needs break into tears, again essay entreaty, and bow
her spirit down to love, not to leave aught untried and go
to death in vain.

'Anna, thou seest the bustle that fills the shore. They
have gathered round from every quarter; already their
canvas woos the breezes, and the merry sailors have
garlanded the sterns. This great pain, my sister, I shall
have strength to bear, as I have had strength to foresee.
Yet this one thing, Anna, for love and pity's sake—for of
thee alone was the traitor fain, to thee even his secret
thoughts were confided, alone thou knewest his moods
and tender fits—go, my sister, and humbly accost the
haughty stranger: I did not take the Grecian oath in
Aulis to root out the race of Troy; I sent no fleet against
her fortresses; neither have I disentombed his father
Anchises' ashes and ghost, that he should refuse my words
entrance to his stubborn ears. Whither does he run? let
him grant this grace—alas, the last!—to his lover, and
await fair winds and an easy passage. No more do I
pray for the old delusive marriage, nor that he give up
fair Latium and abandon a kingdom. A breathing-space
I ask, to give my madness rest and room, till my very

fortune teach my grief submission. This last favour I
implore : sister, be pitiful ; grant this to me, and I will
restore it in full measure when I die.'

So she pleaded, and so her sister carries and recarries
the piteous tale of weeping. But by no weeping is he
stirred, inflexible to all the words he hears. Fate withstands, and lays divine bars on unmoved mortal ears. Even
as when the eddying blasts of northern Alpine winds are
emulous to uproot the secular strength of a mighty oak,
it wails on, and the trunk quivers and the high foliage
strews the ground ; the tree clings fast on the rocks, and
high as her top soars into heaven, so deep strike her roots
to hell ; even thus is the hero buffeted with changeful
perpetual accents, and distress thrills his mighty breast,
while his purpose stays unstirred, and tears fall in vain.

Then indeed, hapless and dismayed by doom, Dido
prays for death, and is weary of gazing on the arch of
heaven. The more to make her fulfil her purpose and
quit the light, she saw, when she laid her gifts on the
altars alight with incense, awful to tell, the holy streams
blacken, and the wine turn as it poured into ghastly
blood. Of this sight she spoke to none—no, not to
her sister. Likewise there was within the house a marble
temple of her ancient lord, kept of her in marvellous
honour, and fastened with snowy fleeces and festal boughs.
Forth of it she seemed to hear her husband's voice crying
and calling when night was dim upon earth, and alone
on the house-tops the screech-owl often made moan with
funeral note and long-drawn sobbing cry. Therewithal
many a warning of wizards of old terrifies her with appalling presage. In her sleep fierce Aeneas drives her wildly,
and ever she seems being left by herself alone, ever going
uncompanioned on a weary way, and seeking her Tyrians
in a solitary land : even as frantic Pentheus sees the

arrayed Furies and a double sun, and Thebes shows
herself twofold to his eyes : or Agamemnonian Orestes,
renowned in tragedy, when his mother pursues him armed
with torches and dark serpents, and the Fatal Sisters crouch
avenging in the doorway.

So when, overcome by her pangs, she caught the madness and resolved to die, she works out secretly the time
and fashion, and accosts her sorrowing sister with mien
hiding her design and hope calm on her brow.

'I have found a way, mine own—wish me joy, sisterlike
—to restore him to me or release me of my love for him.
Hard by the ocean limit and the set of sun is the extreme
Aethiopian land, where ancient Atlas turns on his shoulders
the starred burning axletree of heaven.   Out of it hath
been shown to me a priestess of Massylian race, warder of
the temple of the Hesperides, even she who gave the
dragon his food, and kept the holy boughs on the tree,
sprinkling clammy honey and slumberous poppy-seed.   She
professes with her spells to relax the purposes of whom she
will, but on others to bring passion and pain ; to stay the
river-waters and turn the stars backward : she calls up
ghosts by night ; thou shalt see earth moaning under foot
and mountain-ashes descending from the hills.   I take
heaven, sweet, to witness, and thee, mine own darling
sister, I do not willingly arm myself with the arts of magic.
Do thou secretly raise a pyre in the inner court, and let
them lay on it the arms that the accursed one left hanging
in our chamber, and all the dress he wore, and the bridal
bed where I fell.   It is good to wipe out all the wretch's
traces, and the priestess orders thus.'   So speaks she, and
is silent, while pallor overruns her face.   Yet Anna deems
not her sister veils death behind these strange rites, and
grasps not her wild purpose, nor fears aught deeper than
at Sychaeus' death.   So she makes ready as bidden. . . .

But the Queen, the pyre being built up of piled faggots
and sawn ilex in the inmost of her dwelling, hangs the
room with chaplets and garlands it with funeral boughs :
on the pillow she lays the dress he wore, the sword he left,
and an image of him, knowing what was to come. Altars
are reared around, and the priestess, with hair undone,
thrice peals from her lips the hundred gods of Erebus and
Chaos, and the triform Hecate, the triple-faced maidenhood of Diana. Likewise she had sprinkled pretended waters
of Avernus' spring, and rank herbs are sought mown by
moonlight with brazen sickles, dark with milky venom, and
sought is the talisman torn from a horse's forehead at birth
ere the dam could snatch it. . . . Herself, the holy cake
in her pure hands, hard by the altars, with one foot unshod
and garments flowing loose, she invokes the gods ere she
die, and the stars that know of doom ; then prays to whatsoever deity looks in righteousness and remembrance on
lovers ill allied.

Night fell ; weary creatures took quiet slumber all over
earth, and woodland and wild waters had sunk to rest ;
now the stars wheel midway on their gliding path, now all
the country is silent, and beasts and gay birds that haunt
liquid levels of lake or thorny rustic thicket lay couched
asleep under the still night. But not so the distressed
Phoenician, nor does she ever sink asleep or take the night
upon eyes or breast ; her pain redoubles, and her love swells
to renewed madness, as she tosses on the strong tide of wrath.
Even so she begins, and thus revolves with her heart alone :

'See, what do I ?   Shall I again make trial of mine
old wooers that will scorn me ? and stoop to sue for a
Numidian marriage among those whom already over and
over I have disdained for husbands?   Then shall I follow
the Ilian fleets and the uttermost bidding of the Teucrians?
because it is good to think they were once raised up by my

succour, or the grace of mine old kindness is fresh in their
remembrance ?   And how should they let me, if I would ?
or take the odious woman on their haughty ships ? art
thou ignorant, ah me, even in ruin, and knowest not yet
the forsworn race of Laomedon?   And then ? shall I
accompany the triumphant sailors, a lonely fugitive ? or
plunge forth girt with all my Tyrian train ? so hardly
severed from Sidon city, shall I again drive them seaward,
and bid them spread their sails to the tempest?   Nay die
thou, as thou deservest, and let the steel end thy pain.
With thee it began ; overborne by my tears, thou, O my
sister, dost load me with this madness and agony, and
layest me open to the enemy.   I could not spend a wild
life without stain, far from a bridal chamber, and free from
touch of distress like this !   O faith ill kept, that was
plighted to Sychaeus' ashes !'   Thus her heart broke in
long lamentation.

Now Aeneas was fixed to go, and now, with all set duly
in order, was taking hasty sleep on his high stern.   To
him as he slept the god appeared once again in the same
fashion of countenance, and thus seemed to renew his
warning, in all points like to Mercury, voice and hue and
golden hair and limbs gracious in youth.   'Goddess-born,
canst thou sleep on in such danger? and seest not the
coming perils that hem thee in, madman I nor hearest the
breezes blowing fair?   She, fixed on death, is revolving
craft and crime grimly in her bosom, and swells the changing surge of wrath.   Fliest thou not hence headlong, while
headlong flight is yet possible ?   Even now wilt thou see
ocean weltering with broken timbers, see the fierce glare of
torches and the beach in a riot of flame, if dawn break on
thee yet dallying in this land.   Up ho I linger no more I
Woman is ever a fickle and changing thing.'   So spoke he,
and melted in the black night.

Then indeed Aeneas, startled by the sudden phantom, leaps out of slumber and bestirs his crew. 'Haste and awake, O men, and sit down to the thwarts; shake out sail speedily. A god sent from high heaven, lo! again spurs us to speed our flight and cut the twisted cables. We follow thee, holy one of heaven, whoso thou art, and again joyfully obey thy command. O be favourable; give gracious aid and bring fair sky and weather.' He spoke, and snatching his sword like lightning from the sheath, strikes at the hawser with the drawn steel. The same zeal catches all at once; rushing and tearing they quit the shore; the sea is hidden under their fleets; strongly they toss up the foam and sweep the blue water.

And now Dawn broke, and, leaving the saffron bed of Tithonus, shed her radiance anew over the world; when the Queen saw from her watch-tower the first light whitening, and the fleet standing out under squared sail, and discerned shore and haven empty of all their oarsmen. Thrice and four times she struck her hand on her lovely breast and rent her yellow hair: 'God!' she cries, 'shall he go? shall an alien make mock of our realm? Will they not issue in armed pursuit from all the city, and some launch ships from the dockyards? Go; bring fire in haste, serve weapons, swing out the oars! What do I talk? or where am I? what mad change is on my purpose? Alas, Dido! now thou dost feel thy wickedness; that had graced thee once, when thou gavest away thy crown. Behold the faith and hand of him! who, they say, carries his household's ancestral gods about with him! who stooped his shoulders to a father outworn with age! Could I not have riven his body in sunder and strewn it on the waves? and slain with the sword his comrades and his dear Ascanius, and served him for the banquet at his father's table? But the chance of battle had been dubious. If it had! whom did I fear

with my death upon me? I should have borne firebrands
into his camp and filled his decks with flame, blotted out
father and son and race together, and flung myself atop of
all. Sun, whose fires lighten all the works of the world,
and thou, Juno, mediatress and witness of these my distresses, and Hecate, cried on by night in crossways of cities,
and you, fatal avenging sisters and gods of dying Elissa,
hear me now; bend your just deity to my woes, and listen
to our prayers. If it must needs be that the accursed
one touch his haven and float up to land, if thus Jove's
decrees demand, and this is the appointed term,—yet, distressed in war by an armed and gallant nation, driven
homeless from his borders, rent from Iülus' embrace, let
him sue for succour and see death on death untimely on
his people; nor when he hath yielded him to the terms of
a harsh peace, may he have joy of his kingdom or the
pleasant light; but let him fall before his day and without
burial on a waste of sand. This I pray; this and my blood
with it I pour for the last utterance. And you, O Tyrians,
hunt his seed with your hatred for all ages to come; send
this guerdon to our ashes. Let no kindness nor truce
be between the nations. Arise out of our dust, O unnamed
avenger, to pursue the Dardanian settlement with firebrand
and steel. Now, then, whensoever strength shall be given,
I invoke the enmity of shore to shore, wave to water,
sword to sword; let their battles go down to their children's
children.'

So speaks she as she kept turning her mind round about,
seeking how soonest to break away from the hateful light.
Thereon she speaks briefly to Barce, nurse of Sychaeus;
for a heap of dusky ashes held her own, in her country of
long ago:

'Sweet nurse, bring Anna my sister hither to me. Bid
her haste and sprinkle river water over her body, and bring

with her the beasts ordained for expiation : so let her come: and thou likewise veil thy brows with a pure chaplet. I would fulfil the rites of Stygian Jove that I have fitly ordered and begun, so to set the limit to my distresses and give over to the flames the funeral pyre of the Dardanian.'

So speaks she; the old woman went eagerly with quickened pace. But Dido, fluttered and fierce in her awful purpose, with bloodshot restless gaze, and spots on her quivering cheeks burning through the pallor of imminent death, bursts into the inner courts of the house, and mounts in madness the high funeral pyre, and unsheathes the sword of Dardania, a gift asked for no use like this. Then after her eyes fell on the Ilian raiment and the bed she knew, dallying a little with her purpose through her tears, she sank on the pillow and spoke the last words of all :

' Dress he wore, sweet while doom and deity allowed ! receive my spirit now, and release me from my distresses. I have lived and fulfilled Fortune's allotted course ; and now shall I go a queenly phantom under the earth. I have built a renowned city ; I have seen my ramparts rise ; by my brother's punishment I have avenged my husband of his enemy ; happy, ah me ! and over happy, had but the keels of Dardania never touched our shores !' She spoke ; and burying her face in the pillow, ' Death it will be,' she cries, 'and unavenged ; but death be it. Thus, thus is it good to pass into the dark. Let the pitiless Dardanian's gaze drink in this fire out at sea, and my death be the omen he carries on his way.'

She ceased ; and even as she spoke her people see her sunk on the steel, and blood reeking on the sword and spattered on her hands. A cry rises in the high halls ; Rumour riots down the quaking city. The house resounds with lamentation and sobbing and bitter crying of women ;

heaven echoes their loud wails; even as though all Carthage or ancient Tyre went down as the foe poured in,
and the flames rolled furious over the roofs of house and
temple. Swooning at the sound, her sister runs in a flutter
of dismay, with torn face and smitten bosom, and darts
through them all, and calls the dying woman by her name.
'Was it this, mine own? Was my summons a snare?
Was it this thy pyre, ah me, this thine altar fires meant?
How shall I begin my desolate moan? Didst thou disdain
a sister's company in death? Thou shouldst have called
me to share thy doom; in the self-same hour, the self-same
pang of steel had been our portion. Did these very hands
build it, did my voice call on our father's gods, that with
thee lying thus I should be away as one without pity? Thou
hast destroyed thyself and me together, O my sister, and
the Sidonian lords and people, and this thy city. Give
her wounds water: I will bathe them and catch on my
lips the last breath that haply yet lingers.' So speaking
she had climbed the high steps, and, wailing, clasped and
caressed her half-lifeless sister in her bosom, and stanched
the dark streams of blood with her gown. She, essaying
to lift her heavy eyes, swoons back; the deep-driven
wound gurgles in her breast. Thrice she rose, and
strained to lift herself on her elbow; thrice she rolled
back on the pillow, and with wandering eyes sought the
light of high heaven, and moaned as she found it.

   Then Juno omnipotent, pitying her long pain and
difficult decease, sent Iris down from heaven to unloose
the struggling life from the body where it clung. For since
neither by fate did she perish, nor as one who had earned
her death, but woefully before her day, and fired by sudden
madness, not yet had Proserpine taken her lock from the
golden head, nor sentenced her to the Stygian under world.
So Iris on dewy saffron pinions flits down through the sky

athwart the sun in a trail of a thousand changing dyes, and stopping over her head : 'This hair, sacred to Dis, I take as bidden, and release thee from that body of thine.' So speaks she, and cuts it with her hand. And therewith all the warmth ebbed forth from her, and the life passed away upon the winds.

BOOK FIFTH

THE GAMES OF THE FLEET

MEANWHILE Aeneas and his fleet in unwavering track now held mid passage, and cleft the waves that blackened under the North, looking back on the city that even now gleams with hapless Elissa's funeral flame. Why the broad blaze is lit lies unknown; but the bitter pain of a great love trampled, and the knowledge of what woman can do in madness, draw the Teucrians' hearts to gloomy guesses.

When their ships held the deep, nor any land farther appears, the seas all round, and all round the sky, a dusky shower drew up overhead, carrying night and storm, and the wave shuddered and gloomed. Palinurus, master of the fleet, cries from the high stern: 'Alas, why have these heavy storm-clouds girt the sky? lord Neptune, what wilt thou?' Then he bids clear the rigging and bend strongly to the oars, and brings the sails across the wind, saying thus:

'Noble Aeneas, not did Jupiter give word and warrant would I hope to reach Italy under such a sky. The shifting winds roar athwart our course, and blow stronger out of the black west, and the air thickens into mist: nor are we fit to force our way on and across. Fortune is the stronger; let us follow her, and turn our course whither she calls.

Not far away, I think, are the faithful shores of thy brother
Eryx, and the Sicilian haven, if only my memory retraces
rightly the stars I watched before.'

Then good Aeneas: 'Even I ere now discern the
winds will have it so, and thou urgest against them in
vain. Turn thou the course of our sailing. Could any
land be welcomer to me, or where I would sooner choose
to put in my weary ships, than this that hath Dardanian
Acestes to greet me, and laps in its embrace lord Anchises'
dust?' This said, they steer for harbour, while the following west wind stretches their sails; the fleet runs fast down
the flood, and at last they land joyfully on the familiar
beach. But Acestes high on a hill-top, amazed at the
friendly squadron approaching from afar, hastens towards
them, weaponed and clad in the shaggy skin of a Libyan
she-bear. Him a Trojan mother conceived and bore to
Crimisus river; not forgetful of his parentage, he wishes
them joy of their return, and gladly entertains them on
his rustic treasure and comforts their weariness with his
friendly store. So soon as the morrow's clear daylight
had chased the stars out of the east, Aeneas calls his
comrades along the beach together, and from a mounded
hillock speaks:

'Great people of Dardanus, born of the high blood of
gods, the yearly circle of the months is measured out to
fulfilment since we laid the dust in earth, all that was left
of my divine father, and sadly consecrated our altars.
And now the day is at hand (this, O gods, was your will),
which I will ever keep in grief, ever in honour. Did I
spend it an exile on Gaetulian quicksands, did it surprise me
on the Argolic sea or in Mycenae town, yet would I fulfil
the yearly vows and annual ordinance of festival, and pile the
altars with their due gifts. Now we are led hither, to the
very dust and ashes of our father, not as I deem without

divine purpose and influence, and borne home into the
friendly haven. Up then and let us all gather joyfully
to the sacrifice : pray we for winds, and may he deign
that I pay these rites to him year by year in an established
city and consecrated temple. Two head of oxen Acestes,
the seed of Troy, gives to each of your ships by tale : invite to the feast your own ancestral gods of the household,
and those whom our host Acestes worships. Further, so the
ninth Dawn uplift the gracious day upon men, and her shafts
unveil the world, I will ordain contests for my Trojans ;
first for swift ships ; then whoso excels in the foot-race,
and whoso, confident in strength and skill, comes to shoot
light arrows, or adventures to join battle with gloves of raw
hide ; let all be here, and let merit look for the prize and
palm. Now all be hushed, and twine your temples with
boughs.'

So speaks he, and shrouds his brows with his mother's
myrtle. So Helymus does, so Aletes ripe of years, so
the boy Ascanius, and the rest of the people follow. He
advances from the assembly to the tomb among a throng
of many thousands that crowd about him ; here he pours
on the ground in fit libation two goblets of pure wine,
two of new milk, two of consecrated blood, and flings
bright blossoms, saying thus : 'Hail, holy father, once
again ; hail, ashes of him I saved in vain, and soul and
shade of my sire ! Thou wert not to share the search for
Italian borders and destined fields, nor the dim Ausonian
Tiber.' Thus had he spoken ; when from beneath the
sanctuary a snake slid out in seven vast coils and sevenfold slippery spires, quietly circling the grave and gliding
from altar to altar, his green chequered body and the
spotted lustre of his scales ablaze with gold, as the bow
in the cloud darts a thousand changing dyes athwart the
sun: Aeneas stood amazed at the sight. At last he wound

his long train among the vessels and polished cups, and
tasted the feast, and again leaving the altars where he had
fed, crept harmlessly back beneath the tomb. Doubtful
if he shall think it the Genius of the ground or his
father's ministrant, he slays, as is fit, two sheep of two
years old, as many swine and dark-backed steers, pouring
the while cups of wine, and calling on the soul of great
Anchises and the ghost rearisen from Acheron. Therewithal his comrades, as each hath store, bring gifts to
heap joyfully on the altars, and slay steers in sacrifice:
others set cauldrons arow, and, lying along the grass, heap
live embers under spits and roast the flesh.

The desired day came, and now the ninth Dawn rode
up clear and bright behind Phaëthon's coursers; and the
name and renown of illustrious Acestes had stirred up
all the bordering people; their holiday throng filled the
shore, to see Aeneas' men, and some ready to join in contest. First of all the prizes are laid out to view in the
middle of the racecourse; tripods of sacrifice, green garlands and palms, the reward of the conquerors, armour
and garments dipped in purple, talents of silver and gold :
and from a hillock in the midst the trumpet sounds the
games begun. First is the contest of rowing, and four
ships matched in weight enter, the choice of all the
fleet. Mnestheus' keen oarsmen drive the swift Dragon,
Mnestheus the Italian to be, from whose name is the
Memmian family ; Gyas the huge bulk of the huge
Chimaera, a floating town, whom her triple-tiered Dardanian crew urge on with oars rising in threefold rank ;
Sergestus, from whom the Sergian house holds her name,
sails in the tall Centaur; and in the sea-coloured Scylla
Cloanthus, whence is thy family, Cluentius of Rome.

Apart in the sea and over against the foaming beach, lies
a rock that the swoln waves beat and drown what time the

north-western gales of winter blot out the stars; in calm
it rises silent out of the placid water, flat-topped, and a
haunt where cormorants love best to take the sun. Here
lord Aeneas set up a goal of leafy ilex, a mark for the
sailors to know whence to return, where to wheel their long
course round. Then they choose stations by lot, and on
the sterns their captains glitter afar, beautiful in gold and
purple; the rest of the crews are crowned with poplar
sprays, and their naked shoulders glisten wet with oil.
They sit down at the thwarts, and their arms are tense
on the oars; at full strain they wait the signal, while throbbing fear and heightened ambition drain their riotous
blood. Then, when the clear trumpet-note rang, all in
a moment leap forward from their line; the shouts of
the sailors strike up to heaven, and the channels are
swept into foam by the arms as they swing backward.
They cleave their furrows together, and all the sea is
torn asunder by oars and triple-pointed prows. Not
with speed so headlong do racing pairs whirl the chariots
over the plain, as they rush streaming from the barriers;
not so do their charioteers shake the wavy reins loose over
their team, and hang forward on the whip. All the woodland rings with clapping and shouts of men that cheer
their favourites, and the sheltered beach eddies back their
cries; the noise buffets and re-echoes from the hills.
Gyas shoots out in front of the noisy crowd, and glides
foremost along the water; whom Cloanthus follows next,
rowing better, but held back by his dragging weight of
pine. After them, at equal distance, the Dragon and the
Centaur strive to win the foremost room; and now the
Dragon has it, now the vast Centaur outstrips and passes
her; now they dart on both together, their stems in a line,
and their keels driving long furrows through the salt waterways. And now they drew nigh the rock, and were hard

H

on the goal; when Gyas as he led, winner over half the
flood, cries aloud to Menoetes, the ship's steersman:
'Whither away so far to the right? This way direct her
path; kiss the shore, and let the oarblade graze the leftward reefs. Others may keep to deep water.' He spoke;
but Menoetes, fearing blind rocks, turns the bow away
towards the open sea. 'Whither wanderest thou away?
to the rocks, Menoetes!' again shouts Gyas to bring him
back; and lo! glancing round he sees Cloanthus passing
up behind and keeping nearer. Between Gyas' ship and
the echoing crags he scrapes through inside on his left,
flashes past his leader, and leaving the goal behind is in
safe water. Then indeed grief burned fierce through his
strong frame, and tears sprung out on his cheeks; heedless of his own dignity and his crew's safety, he flings the
too cautious Menoetes sheer into the sea from the high
stern, himself succeeds as guide and master of the helm,
and cheers on his men, and turns his tiller in to shore.
But Menoetes, when at last he rose struggling from the
bottom, heavy with advancing years and wet in his dripping
clothes, makes for the top of the crag, and sits down on
a dry rock. The Teucrians laughed out as he fell and as
he swam, and laugh to see him spitting the salt water
from his chest. At this a joyful hope kindled in the two
behind, Sergestus and Mnestheus, of catching up Gyas'
wavering course. Sergestus slips forward as he nears the
rock, yet not all in front, nor leading with his length of
keel; part is in front, part pressed by the Dragon's jealous
prow. But striding amidships between his comrades,
Mnestheus cheers them on: 'Now, now swing back, oarsmen who were Hector's comrades, whom I chose to
follow me in Troy's extremity; now put forth the might
and courage you showed in Gaetulian quicksands, amid
Ionian seas and Malea's chasing waves. Not the first

place do I now seek for Mnestheus, nor strive for victory;
though ah!—yet let them win, O Neptune, to whom thou
givest it. But the shame of coming in last! Win but
this, fellow-citizens, and avert that disaster!' His men
bend forward, straining every muscle; the brasswork of
the ship quivers to their mighty strokes, and the ground
runs from under her; limbs and parched lips shake with
their rapid panting, and sweat flows in streams all over
them. Mere chance brought the crew the glory they desired.
For while Sergestus drives his prow furiously in towards
the rocks and comes up with too scanty room, alas! he
caught on a rock that ran out; the reef ground, the oars
struck and shivered on the jagged teeth, and the bows
crashed and hung. The sailors leap up and hold her with
loud cries, and get out iron-shod poles and sharp-pointed
boathooks, and pick up their broken oars out of the eddies.
But Mnestheus, rejoicing and flushed by his triumph,
with oars fast-dipping and winds at his call, issues into the
shelving water and runs down the open sea. As a pigeon
whose house and sweet nestlings are in the rock's recesses,
if suddenly startled from her cavern, wings her flight over
the fields and rushes frightened from her house with loud
clapping pinions; then gliding noiselessly through the air,
slides on her liquid way and moves not her rapid wings;
so Mnestheus, so the Dragon under him swiftly cleaves the
last space of sea, so her own speed carries her flying on.
And first Sergestus is left behind, struggling on the steep
rock and shoal water, and shouting in vain for help and
learning to race with broken oars. Next he catches up
Gyas and the vast bulk of the Chimaera; she gives way,
without her steersman. And now on the very goal
Cloanthus alone is left; him he pursues and presses hard,
straining all his strength. Then indeed the shouts
redouble, as all together eagerly cheer on the pursuer, and

the sky echoes their din. These scorn to lose the honour
that is their own, the glory in their grasp, and would sell
life for renown; to these success lends life; power comes
with belief in it. And haply they had carried the prize
with prows abreast, had not Cloanthus, stretching both his
open hands over the sea, poured forth prayers and called
the gods to hear his vows: 'Gods who are sovereign on
the sea, over whose waters I run, to your altars on this
beach will I bring a snow-white bull, my vow's glad
penalty, and will cast his entrails into the salt flood and
pour liquid wine.' He spoke, and far beneath the flood
maiden Panopea heard him, with all Phorcus' choir of
Nereids, and lord Portunus with his own mighty hand
pushed him on his way. The ship flies to land swifter
than the wind or an arrow's flight, and shoots into the deep
harbour. Then the seed of Anchises, summoning all in
order, declares Cloanthus conqueror by herald's outcry,
and dresses his brows in green bay, and gives gifts to each
crew, three bullocks of their choice, and wine, and a large
talent of silver to take away. For their captains he adds
special honours; to the winner a scarf wrought with gold,
encircled by a double border of deep Meliboean purple;
woven in it is the kingly boy on leafy Ida, chasing swift
stags with javelin and racing feet, keen and as one
panting; him Jove's swooping armour-bearer hath caught
up from Ida in his talons; his aged guardians stretch their
hands vainly upwards, and the barking of hounds rings
fierce into the air. But to him who, next in merit, held
the second place, he gives to wear a corslet triple-woven
with hooks of polished gold, stripped by his own conquering hand from Demoleos under tall Troy by the swift
Simoïs, an ornament and safeguard among arms. Scarce
could the straining shoulders of his servants Phegeus and
Sagaris carry its heavy folds; yet with it on, Demoleos at

full speed would chase the scattered Trojans. The third prize he makes twin cauldrons of brass, and bowls wrought in silver and rough with tracery. And now all moved away in the pride and wealth of their prizes, their brows bound with scarlet ribbons; when, hardly torn loose by all his art from the cruel rock, his oars lost, rowing feebly with a single tier, Sergestus brought in his ship jeered at and un-honoured. Even as often a serpent caught on a highway, if a brazen wheel hath gone aslant over him or a wayfarer left him half dead and mangled with the blow of a heavy stone, wreathes himself slowly in vain effort to escape, in part undaunted, his eyes ablaze and his hissing throat lifted high; in part the disabling wound keeps him coiling in knots and twisting back on his own body; so the ship kept rowing slowly on, yet hoists sail and under full sail glides into the harbour mouth. Glad that the ship is saved and the crew brought back, Aeneas presents Sergestus with his promised reward. A slave woman is given him not unskilled in Minerva's labours, Pholoë the Cretan, with twin boys at her breast.

This contest sped, good Aeneas moved to a grassy plain girt all about with winding wooded hills, and amid the valley an amphitheatre, whither, with a concourse of many thousands, the hero advanced and took his seat on a mound. Here he allures with rewards and offer of prizes those who will try their hap in the fleet foot-race. Trojans and Sicilians gather mingling from all sides, Nisus and Euryalus foremost . . . Euryalus in the flower of youth and famed for beauty, Nisus for pure love of the boy. Next follows renowned Diores, of Priam's royal line; after him Salius and Patron together, the one Acarnanian, the other Tegean by family and of Arcadian blood; next two men of Sicily, Helymus and Panopes, foresters and attend-ants on old Acestes; many besides whose fame is hid in

obscurity.   Then among them all Aeneas spoke thus :
' Hearken to this, and attend in good cheer.   None out
of this number will I let go without a gift.   To each will
I give two glittering Gnosian spearheads of polished steel,
and an axe chased with silver to bear away ; one and all
shall be honoured thus.   The three foremost shall receive
prizes, and have pale olive bound about their head.   The
first shall have a caparisoned horse as conqueror ; the
second an Amazonian quiver filled with arrows of Thrace,
girt about by a broad belt of gold, and on the link of the
clasp a polished gem ; let the third depart with this
Argolic helmet for recompense.'   This said, they take
their place, and the signal once heard, dart over the course
and leave the line, pouring forth like a storm-cloud while
they mark the goal.   Nisus gets away first, and shoots out
far in front of the throng, fleeter than the winds or the
winged thunderbolt.   Next to him, but next by a long gap,
Salius follows ; then, left a space behind him, Euryalus
third . . . and Helymus comes after Euryalus ; and close
behind him, lo ! Diores goes flying, just grazing foot with
foot, hard on his shoulder ; and if a longer space were
left, he would creep out past him and win the tie.   And
now almost in the last space, they began to come up
breathless to the goal, when unfortunate Nisus trips on
the slippery blood of the slain steers, where haply it had
spilled over the ground and wetted the green grass.   Here,
just in the flush of victory, he lost his feet ; they slid away
on the ground they pressed, and he fell forward right among
the ordure and blood of the sacrifice.   Yet forgot he not
his darling Euryalus ; for rising, he flung himself over the
slippery ground in front of Salius, and he rolled over and
lay all along on the hard sand.   Euryalus shoots by, wins
and holds the first place his friend gave, and flies on amid
prosperous clapping and cheers.   Behind Helymus comes

up, and Diores, now third for the palm. At this Salius
fills with loud clamour the whole concourse of the vast
theatre, and the lords who looked on in front, demanding
restoration of his defrauded prize. Euryalus is strong in
favour, and beauty in tears, and the merit that gains grace
from so fair a form. Diores supports him, who succeeded
to the palm, so he loudly cries, and bore off the last prize
in vain, if the highest honours be restored to Salius. Then
lord Aeneas speaks: 'For you, O boys, your rewards remain assured, and none alters the prizes' order: let me be
allowed to pity a friend's innocent mischance.' So speaking, he gives to Salius a vast Gaetulian lion-skin, with
shaggy masses of hair and claws of gold. 'If this,' cries
Nisus, 'is the reward of defeat, and thy pity is stirred for
the fallen, what fit recompense wilt thou give to Nisus?
to my excellence the first crown was due, had not I, like
Salius, met Fortune's hostility.' And with the words he
displayed his face and limbs foul with the wet dung. His
lord laughed kindly on him, and bade a shield be brought
forth, the workmanship of Didymaon, torn by him from the
hallowed gates of Neptune's Grecian temple; with this
special prize he rewards his excellence.

Thereafter, when the races are finished and the gifts
fulfilled: 'Now,' he cries, 'come, whoso hath in him
valour and ready heart, and lift up his arms with gaunt-
leted hands.' So speaks he, and sets forth a double
prize of battle; for the conqueror a bullock gilt and garlanded; a sword and beautiful helmet to console the conquered. Straightway without pause Dares issues to view
in his vast strength, rising amid loud murmurs of the
people; he who alone was wont to meet Paris in combat;
he who, at the mound where princely Hector lies, struck
down as he came the vast bulk upborne by conquering
Butes, of Amycus' Debrycian line, and stretched him in

death on the yellow sand. Such was Dares; at once
he raises his head high for battle, displays his broad
shoulders, and stretches and swings his arms right and
left, lashing the air with blows. For him another is
required; but none out of all the train durst approach
or put the gloves on his hands. So he takes his stand
exultant before Aeneas' feet, deeming he excelled all in
victories; and thereon without more delay grasps the
bull's horn with his left hand, and speaks thus: 'Goddess-
born, if no man dare trust himself to battle, to what con-
clusion shall I stand? how long is it seemly to keep me?
bid me carry off thy gifts.' Therewith all the Dardanians
murmured assent, and bade yield him the promised prize.
At this aged Acestes spoke sharply to Entellus, as he sate
next him on the green cushion of grass: 'Entellus, bravest
of heroes once of old in vain, wilt thou thus idly let a gift
so great be borne away uncontested? Where now prithee
is divine Eryx, thy master of fruitless fame? where thy
renown over all Sicily, and those spoils hanging in thine
house?' Thereat he: 'Desire of glory is not gone, nor
ambition checked by fear; but torpid age dulls my chilly
blood, and my strength of limb is numb and outworn. If
I had what once was mine, if I had now that prime
of years, yonder braggart's boast and confidence, it had
taken no prize of goodly bullock to allure me; nor heed
I these gifts.' So he spoke, and on that flung down a
pair of gloves of giant weight, with whose hard hide
bound about his wrists valiant Eryx was wont to come
to battle. They stood amazed; so stiff and grim lay the
vast sevenfold oxhide sewed in with lead and iron. Dares
most of all shrinks far back in horror, and the noble son
of Anchises turns round this way and that their vast
weight and voluminous folds. Then the old man spoke
thus in deep accents: 'How, had they seen the gloves

that were Hercules' own armour, and the fatal fight on
this very beach? These arms thy brother Eryx once
wore; thou seest them yet stained with blood and
spattered brains. In them he stood to face great
Alcides; to them was I used while fuller blood supplied me strength, and envious old age had not yet
strewn her snows on either temple. But if Dares of
Troy will have none of these our arms, and good Aeneas
is resolved on it, and my patron Acestes approves, let us
make the battle even. See, I give up the gauntlets of
Eryx; dismiss thy fears; and do thou put off thy Trojan
gloves.' So spoke he, and throwing back the fold of his
raiment from his shoulders, he bares the massive joints
and limbs, the great bones and muscles, and stands up
huge in the middle of the ground. Then Anchises' lordly
seed brought out equal gloves and bound the hands of
both in matched arms. Straightway each took his stand
on tiptoe, and undauntedly raised his arms high in air.
They lift their heads right back and away out of reach of
blows, and make hand play through hand, inviting attack;
the one nimbler of foot and confident in his youth, the other
mighty in mass of limb, but his knees totter tremulous and
slow, and sick panting shakes his vast frame. Many a
mutual blow they deliver in vain, many an one they redouble on chest and side, sounding hollow and loud:
hands play fast about ear and temple, and jawbones
clash under the hard strokes. Old Entellus stands immoveable and astrain, only parrying hits with body and
watchful eye. The other, as one who casts mounts against
some high city or blockades a hill-fort in arms, tries this
and that entrance, and ranges cunningly over all the
ground, and presses many an attack in vain. Entellus
rose and struck clean out with his right downwards; his
quick opponent saw the descending blow before it came,

and slid his body rapidly out of its way. Entellus hurled
his strength into the air, and all his heavy mass, over-
reaching, fell heavily to the earth; as sometime on Ery-
manthus or mighty Ida a hollow pine falls torn out by the
roots. Teucrians and men of Sicily rise eagerly; a cry goes
up, and Acestes himself runs forward, and pityingly lifts
his friend and birthmate from the ground. But the hero,
not dulled nor dismayed by his mishap, returns the keener
to battle, and grows violent in wrath, while shame and resolved valour kindle his strength. All afire, he hunts
Dares headlong over the lists, and redoubles his blows
now with right hand, now with left; no breath nor pause;
heavy as hailstones rattle on the roof from a storm-cloud,
so thickly shower the blows from both his hands as he
buffets Dares to and fro. Then lord Aeneas allowed not
wrath to swell higher or Entellus to rage out his bitterness,
but stopped the fight and rescued the exhausted Dares,
saying thus in soothing words: 'Unhappy! what height of
madness hath seized thy mind? Knowest thou not the
strength is another's and the gods are changed? Yield
thou to Heaven.' And with the words he proclaimed the
battle over. But him his faithful mates lead to the ships
dragging his knees feebly, swaying his head from side to
side, and spitting from his mouth clotted blood mingled
with teeth. At summons they bear away the helmet and
shield, and leave palm and bull to Entellus. At this the
conqueror, swelling in pride over the bull, cries: 'Goddess-
born, and you, O Trojans! learn thus what my strength of
body was in its prime, and from what a death Dares is
saved by your recall.' He spoke, and stood right opposite
in face of the bullock as it stood by, the prize of battle;
then drew back his hand, and swinging the hard gauntlet
sheer down between the horns, smashed the bones in upon
the shattered brain. The ox rolls over, and quivering and

lifeless lies along the ground. Above it ne utters these deep accents: 'This life, Eryx, I give to thee, a better payment than Dares' death; here I lay down my gloves and unconquered skill.'

Forthwith Aeneas invites all that will to the contest of the swift arrow, and proclaims the prizes. With his strong hand he uprears the mast of Serestus' ship, and on a cord crossing it hangs from the masthead a fluttering pigeon as mark for their steel. They gather, and a helmet of brass takes the lots as they throw them in. First in rank, and before them all, amid prosperous cheers, comes out Hippocoön son of Hyrtacus; and Mnestheus follows on him, but now conqueror in the ship race, Mnestheus with his chaplet of green olive. Third is Eurytion, thy brother, O Pandarus, great in renown, thou who of old, when prompted to shatter the truce, didst hurl the first shaft amid the Achaeans. Last of all, and at the bottom of the helmet, sank Acestes, he too venturing to set hand to the task of youth. Then each and all they strongly bend their bows into a curve and pull shafts from their quivers. And first the arrow of the son of Hyrtacus, flying through heaven from the sounding string, whistles through the fleet breezes, and reaches and sticks fast full in the mast's wood : the mast quivered, and the bird fluttered her feathers in affright, and the whole ground rang with loud clapping. Next valiant Mnestheus took his stand with bow bent, aiming high with levelled eye and arrow ; yet could not, unfortunate ! hit the bird herself with his steel, but cut the knotted hempen bands that tied her foot as she hung from the masthead ; she winged her flight into the dark windy clouds. Then Eurytion, who ere now held the arrow ready on his bended bow, swiftly called in prayer to his brother, marked the pigeon as she now went down the empty sky exultant on clapping wings; and as she passed under a dark cloud,

struck her: she fell breathless, and, leaving her life in the
aery firmament, slid down carrying the arrow that pierced
her. Acestes alone was over, and the prize lost; yet he
sped his arrow up into the air, to display his lordly skill
and resounding bow. At this a sudden sign meets their eyes,
mighty in augural presage, as the high event taught thereafter, and in late days boding seers prophesied of the omen.
For the flying reed blazed out amid the swimming clouds,
traced its path in flame, and burned away on the light
winds; even as often stars shooting from their sphere draw
a train athwart the sky. Trinacrians and Trojans hung in
astonishment, praying to the heavenly powers; neither did
great Aeneas reject the omen, but embraces glad Acestes
and loads him with lavish gifts, speaking thus: 'Take, my
lord: for the high King of heaven by these signs hath
willed thee to draw the lot of peculiar honour. This gift
shalt thou have as from aged Anchises' own hand, a bowl
embossed with figures, that once Cisseus of Thrace gave
my father Anchises to bear, in high token and guerdon of
affection.' So speaking, he twines green bay about his
brows, and proclaims Acestes conqueror first before them
all. Nor did gentle Eurytion, though he alone struck the
bird down from the lofty sky, grudge him to be preferred
in honour. Next comes for his prize he who cut the cord;
he last, who pierced the mast with his winged reed.
    But lord Aeneas, ere yet the contest is sped, calls to
him Epytides, guardian and attendant of ungrown Iülus,
and thus speaks into his faithful ear: 'Up and away, and
tell Ascanius, if he now holds his band of boys ready, and
their horses arrayed for the charge, to defile his squadrons
to his grandsire's honour in bravery of arms.' So says he,
and himself bids all the crowding throng withdraw from the
long racecourse and leave the lists free. The boys move
in before their parents' faces, glittering in rank on their

bitted horses; as they go all the people of Troy and
Trinacria murmur and admire.   On the hair of them all
rests a garland fitly trimmed ; each carries two cornel spear-
shafts tipped with steel; some have polished quivers on
their shoulders ; above their breast and round their neck
goes a flexible circlet of twisted gold.   Three in number
are the troops of riders, and three captains gallop up and
down ; following each in equal command rides a glittering
division of twelve boys.   One youthful line goes rejoicingly
behind little Priam, renewer of his grandsire's name, thy
renowned seed, O Polites, and destined to people Italy ;
he rides a Thracian horse dappled with spots of white,
showing white on his pacing pasterns and white on his
high forehead.   Second is Atys, from whom the Latin Atii
draw their line, little Atys, boy beloved of the boy Iülus.
Last and excellent in beauty before them all, Iülus rode in
on a Sidonian horse that Dido the bright had given him for
token and pledge of love.   The rest of them are mounted
on old Acestes' Sicilian horses. . . . The Dardanians greet
their shy entrance with applause, and rejoice at the view,
and recognise the features of their parents of old.   When
they have ridden merrily round all the concourse of their
gazing friends, Epytides shouts from afar the signal they
await, and sounds his whip.   They gallop apart in equal
numbers, and open their files three and three in deploying
bands, and again at the call wheel about and bear down
with levelled arms.   Next they start on other charges and
other retreats in corresponsive spaces, and interlink circle
with circle, and wage the armed phantom of battle.   And
now they bare their backs in flight, now turn their lances
to the charge, now plight peace and ride on side by side.
As once of old, they say, the labyrinth in high Crete had a
tangled path between blind walls, and a thousand ways of
doubling treachery, where tokens to follow failed in the

maze unmastered and irrecoverable : even in such a track
do the children of Troy entangle their footsteps and weave
the game of flight and battle ; like dolphins who, swimming
through the wet seas, cut Carpathian or Libyan. . . .
This fashion of riding, these games Ascanius first re-
vived, when he girt Alba the Long about with walls, and
taught their celebration to the Old Latins in the way of his
own boyhood, with the youth of Troy about him. The
Albans taught it their children ; on from them mighty
Rome received it and kept the ancestral observance ; and
now it is called Troy, and the boys the Trojan troop.

Thus far sped the sacred contests to their holy lord.
Just at this Fortune broke faith and grew estranged. While
they pay the due rites to the tomb with diverse games,
Juno, daughter of Saturn, sends Iris down the sky to the
Ilian fleet, and breathes a gale to speed her on, revolving
many a thought, and not yet satiate of the ancient pain.
She, speeding her way along the thousand-coloured bow,
runs swiftly, seen of none, down her maiden path. She
discerns the vast concourse, and traverses the shore, and
sees the haven abandoned and the fleet left alone. But
far withdrawn by the solitary verge of the sea the Trojan
women wept their lost Anchises, and as they wept gazed all
together on the fathomless flood. 'Alas ! after all those
weary waterways, that so wide a sea is yet to come !' such
is the single cry of all. They pray for a city, sick of the
burden of their sea-sorrow. So she darts among them, not
witless to harm, and lays by face and raiment of a goddess :
she becomes Deroë, the aged wife of Tmarian Doryclus,
who had once had birth and name and children, and in
this guise goes among the Dardanian matrons. 'Ah,
wretched we,' she cries, 'whom hostile Achaean hands did
not drag to death beneath our native city ! ah hapless race,
for what destruction does Fortune hold thee back ? The

seventh summer now declines since Troy's overthrow, while
we pass measuring out by so many stars the harbourless
rocks over every water and land, pursuing all the while over
the vast sea an Italy that flies us, and tossing on the waves.
Here are our brother Eryx' borders, and Acestes' welcome :
who denies us to cast up walls and give our citizens a city ?
O country, O household gods vainly rescued from the foe I
shall there never be a Trojan town to tell of ? shall I
nowhere see a Xanthus and a Simoïs, the rivers of Hector ?
Nay, up and join me in burning with fire these ill-ominous
ships.   For in sleep the phantom of Cassandra the soothsayer seemed to give me blazing brands : *Here seek your
Troy*, she said ; *here is your home.*   Now is the time to do
it ; nor do these high portents allow delay.   Behold four
altars to Neptune ; the god himself lends the firebrand and
the nerve.'   Speaking thus, at once she strongly seizes the
fiery weapon, and with straining hand whirls it far upreared,
and flings : the souls of the Ilian women are startled and
their wits amazed.   At this one of their multitude, and she
the eldest, Pyrgo, nurse in the palace to all Priam's many
children : 'This is not Beroë, I tell you, O mothers ; this
is not the wife of Doryclus of Rhoeteum.   Mark the lineaments of divine grace and the gleaming eyes, what a
breath is hers, what a countenance, and the sound of her
voice and the steps of her going.   I, I time agone left
Beroë apart, sick and fretting that she alone must have no
part in this our service, nor pay Anchises his due sacrifice.'
So spoke she. . . .   But the matrons at first, dubious and
wavering, gazed on the ships with malignant eyes, between
the wretched longing for the land they trod and the fated
realm that summoned them : when the goddess rose through
the sky on poised wings, and in her flight drew a vast bow
beneath the clouds.   Then indeed, amazed at the tokens and
driven by madness, they raise a cry and snatch fire from the

hearths within ; others plunder the altars, and cast on brushwood boughs and brands. The Fire-god rages with loose
rein over thwarts and oars and hulls of painted fir. Eu-
melus carries the news of the burning ships to the grave of
Anchises and the ranges of the theatre ; and looking back,
their own eyes see the floating cloud of dark ashes. And
in a moment Ascanius, as he rode gaily before his cavalry,
spurred his horse to the disordered camp ; nor can his
breathless guardians hold him back. 'What strange madness is this?' he cries ; 'whither now hasten you, whither,
alas and woe ! O citizens? not on the foe nor on some
hostile Argive camp ; it is your own hopes you burn.
Behold me, your Ascanius !' and he flung before his feet
the empty helmet, put on when he roused the mimicry of
war. Aeneas and the Trojan train together hurry to the
spot. But the women scatter apart in fear all over the
beach, and stealthily seek the woods and the hollow rocks
they find : they loathe their deed and the daylight, and
with changed eyes know their people, and Juno is startled
out of their breast. But not thereby do the flames of the
burning lay down their unconquered strength ; under the
wet oak the seams are alive, spouting slow coils of smoke ;
the creeping heat devours the hulls, and the destroyer takes
deep hold of all : nor does the heroes' strength avail nor
the floods they pour in. Then good Aeneas rent away the
raiment from his shoulders and called the gods to aid,
stretching forth his hands : 'Jupiter omnipotent, if thou
hatest not Troy yet wholly to her last man, if thine ancient
pity looks at all on human woes, now, O Lord, grant our
fleet to escape the flame, and rescue from doom the slender
Teucrian estate. Or do thou plunge to death this remnant,
if I deserve it, with levelled thunderbolt, and here with thine
own hand smite us down.' Scarce had he uttered this, when
a black tempest rages in streaming showers ; earth trembles

to the thunder on plain and steep; the water-flood rushes
in torrents from the whole heaven amid black darkness and
volleying blasts of the South. The ships are filled from overhead, the half-burnt timbers are soaking; till all the heat is
quenched, and all the hulls, but four that are lost, are rescued
from destruction.

But lord Aeneas, dismayed by the bitter mischance,
revolved at heart this way and that his shifting weight of care,
whether, forgetting fate, he should rest in Sicilian fields, or
reach forth to the borders of Italy. Then old Nautes,
whom Tritonian Pallas taught like none other, and made
famous in eminence of art — she granted him to reply
what the gods' heavy anger menaced or what the order of
fate claimed—he then in accents of comfort thus speaks to
Aeneas:

'Goddess-born, follow we fate's ebb and flow, whatsoever it shall be; fortune must be borne to be overcome.
Acestes is of thine own divine Dardanian race; take him,
for he is willing, to join thee in common counsel; deliver
to him those who are over, now these ships are lost, and
those who are quite weary of thy fortunes and the great
quest. Choose out the old men stricken in years, and the
matrons sick of the sea, and all that is weak and fearful of
peril in thy company. Let this land give a city to the
weary; they shall be allowed to call their town Acesta by
name.'

Then, indeed, kindled by these words of his aged
friend, his spirit is distracted among all his cares. And
now black Night rose chariot-borne, and held the sky;
when the likeness of his father Anchises seemed to descend
from heaven and suddenly utter thus:

'O son, more dear to me than life once of old while
life was yet mine; O son, hard wrought by the destinies of
Ilium! I come hither by Jove's command, who drove the

I

fire from thy fleets, and at last had pity out of high heaven.
Obey thou the fair counsel aged Nautes now gives.   Carry
through to Italy thy chosen men and bravest souls; in
Latium must thou war down a people hard and rough in
living.   Yet ere then draw thou nigh the nether chambers
of Dis, and in the deep tract of hell come, O son, to meet
me.   For I am not held in cruel Tartarus among wailing
ghosts, but inhabit Elysium and the sweet societies of the
good.   Hither with much blood of dark cattle shall the
holy Sibyl lead thee.   Then shalt thou learn of all thy
line, and what city is given thee.   And now farewell; dank
Night wheels her mid-career, and even now I feel the stern
breath of the panting horses of the East.'   He ended, and
retreated like a vapour into thin air.   'Ah, whither
hurriest thou?' cries Aeneas; 'whither so fast away?
From whom fliest thou? or who withholds thee from our
embrace?'   So speaking, he kindles the sleeping embers of
the fire, and with holy meal and laden censer does sacrifice
to the tutelar of Pergama and hoar Vesta's secret shrine.

Straightway he summons his crews and Acestes first of
all, and instructs them of Jove's command and his beloved
father's precepts, and what is now his fixed mind and
purpose.   They linger not in counsel, nor does Acestes
decline his bidden duty: they enrol the matrons in their
town, and plant a people there, souls that will have none
of glory.   The rest repair the thwarts and replace the
ships' timbers that the flames had gnawed upon, and fit up
oars and rigging, little in number, but alive and valiant for
war.   Meanwhile Aeneas traces the town with the plough
and allots the homesteads; this he bids be Ilium, and
these lands Troy.   Trojan Acestes, rejoicing in his kingdom, appoints a court and gathers his senators to give
them statutes.   Next, where the crest of Eryx is neighbour
to the stars, a dwelling is founded to Venus the Idalian;

and a priest and breadth of holy wood is attached to
Anchises' grave.

And now for nine days all the people hath feasted, and
offering been paid at the altars; quiet breezes have
smoothed the ocean floor, and the gathering south wind
blows, calling them again to sea. A mighty weeping arises
along the winding shore; a night and a day they linger in
mutual embraces. The very mothers now, the very men
to whom once the sight of the sea seemed cruel and the
name intolerable, would go on and endure the journey's
travail to the end. These Aeneas comforts with kindly
words, and commends with tears to his kinsman Acestes'
care. Then he bids slay three steers to Eryx and a she-
lamb to the Tempests, and loose the hawser as is due.
Himself, his head bound with stripped leaves of olive, he
stands apart on the prow holding the cup, and casts the
entrails into the salt flood and pours liquid wine. A wind
rising astern follows them forth on their way. Emulously
the crews strike the water, and sweep through the seas.

But Venus meanwhile, wrought upon with distress,
accosts Neptune, and thus pours forth her heart's complaint :
' Juno's bitter wrath and heart insatiable compel me, O
Neptune, to sink to the uttermost of entreaty: neither
length of days nor any goodness softens her, nor doth
Jove's command and fate itself break her to desistence.
It is not enough that her accursed hatred hath devoured
the Phrygian city from among the people, and exhausted
on it the stores of vengeance ; still she pursues this
remnant, the bones and ashes of murdered Troy. I pray
she know why her passion is so fierce. Thyself art my
witness what a sudden stir she raised of late on the Libyan
waters, flinging all the seas to heaven in vain reliance on
Aeolus' blasts; this she dared in thy realm . . . Lo too,
driving the Trojan matrons into guilt, she hath foully

burned their ships, and forced them, their fleet lost, to
leave the crews to an unknown land. Let the remnant, I
beseech thee, give their sails to thy safe keeping across the
seas; let them reach Laurentine Tiber; if I ask what is
permitted, if fate grants them a city there.'

Then the son of Saturn, compeller of the ocean deep,
uttered thus: 'It is wholly right, O Cytherean, that thy
trust should be in my realm, whence thou drawest birth;
and I have deserved it: often have I allayed the rage and
full fury of sky and sea. Nor less on land, I call Xanthus
and Simoïs to witness, hath been my care of thine Aeneas.
When Achilles pursued the Trojan armies and hurled them
breathless on their walls, and sent many thousands to
death,—when the choked rivers groaned and Xanthus could
not find passage or roll out to sea,—then I snatched Aeneas
away in sheltering mist as he met the brave son of Peleus
outmatched in strength and gods, eager as I was to overthrow the walls of perjured Troy that mine own hands had
built. Now too my mind rests the same; dismiss thy fear.
In safety, as thou desirest, shall he reach the haven of
Avernus. One will there be alone whom on the flood
thou shalt lose and require; one life shall be given for
many. . . .'

With these words the goddess' bosom is soothed to
Joy. Then their lord yokes his wild horses with gold and
fastens the foaming bits, and letting all the reins run slack
in his hand, flies lightly in his sea-coloured chariot over
the ocean surface. The waves sink to rest, and the
swoln water-ways smooth out under the thundering axle;
the storm-clouds scatter from the vast sky. Diverse shapes
attend him, monstrous whales, and Glaucus' aged choir,
and Palaemon, son of Ino, the swift Tritons, and Phorcus
with all his army. Thetis and Melite keep the left, and
maiden Panopea, Nesaea and Spio, Thalia and Cymodoce.

At this lord Aeneas' soul is thrilled with soft counterchange of delight. He bids all the masts be upreared
with speed, and the sails stretched on the yards. Together
all set their sheets, and all at once slacken their canvas to
left and again to right; together they brace and unbrace
the yard-arms aloft; prosperous gales waft the fleet along.
First, in front of all, Palinurus steered the close column;
the rest under orders ply their course by his. And now
dewy Night had just reached heaven's mid-cone; the
sailors, stretched on their hard benches under the oars,
relaxed their limbs in quiet rest: when Sleep, sliding
lightly down from the starry sky, parted the shadowy air
and cleft the dark, seeking thee, O Palinurus, carrying
dreams of bale to thee who dreamt not of harm, and lit on
the high stern, a god in Phorbas' likeness, dropping this
speech from his lips: 'Palinurus son of Iasus, the very
seas bear our fleet along; the breezes breathe steadily; for
an hour rest is given. Lay down thine head, and steal
thy worn eyes from their toil. I myself for a little will
take thy duty in thy stead.' To whom Palinurus, scarcely
lifting his eyes, returns : 'Wouldst thou have me ignorant
what the calm face of the brine means, and the waves at
rest? Shall I have faith in this perilous thing? How
shall I trust Aeneas to deceitful breezes, and the placid
treachery of sky that hath so often deceived me?' Such
words he uttered, and, clinging fast to the tiller, slackened
hold no whit, and looked up steadily on the stars. Lo!
the god shakes over either temple a bough dripping with
Lethean dew and made slumberous with the might of
Styx, and makes his swimming eyes relax their struggles.
Scarcely had sleep begun to slacken his limbs unaware,
when bending down, he flung him sheer into the clear
water, tearing rudder and half the stern away with him,
and many a time crying vainly on his comrades: himself

he rose on flying wings into the thin air. None the less does
the fleet run safe on its sea path, and glides on unalarmed
in lord Neptune's assurance. Yes, and now they were
sailing in to the cliffs of the Sirens, dangerous once of old
and white with the bones of many a man ; and the hoarse
rocks echoed afar in the ceaseless surf ; when her lord felt
the ship rocking astray for loss of her helmsman, and
himself steered her on over the darkling water, sighing
often the while, and heavy at heart for his friend's mischance. 'Ah too trustful in sky's and sea's serenity, thou
shalt lie, O Palinurus, naked on an alien sand !'

BOOK SIXTH

THE VISION OF THE UNDER WORLD

So speaks he weeping, and gives his fleet the rein, and at
last glides in to Euboïc Cumae's coast. They turn the
prows seaward; the ships grounded fast on their anchors'
teeth, and the curving ships line the beach. The warrior
band leaps forth eagerly on the Hesperian shore; some
seek the seeds of flame hidden in veins of flint, some scour
the woods, the thick coverts of wild beasts, and find and
shew the streams. But good Aeneas seeks the fortress
where Apollo sits high enthroned, and the lone mystery of
the awful Sibyl's cavern depth, over whose mind and soul
the prophetic Delian breathes high inspiration and reveals
futurity.

Now they draw nigh the groves of Trivia and the roof
of gold. Daedalus, as the story runs, when in flight from
Minos' realm he dared to spread his fleet wings to the sky,
glided on his unwonted way towards the icy northern star,
and at length lit gently on the Chalcidian fastness. Here,
on the first land he retrod, he dedicated his winged oarage
to thee, O Phoebus, in the vast temple he built. On the
doors is Androgeus' death; thereby the children of Cecrops,
bidden, ah me! to pay for yearly ransom seven souls of their
sons; the urn stands there, and the lots are drawn. Right

opposite the land of Gnosus rises from the sea ; on it is the
cruel love of the bull, the disguised stealth of Pasiphaë, and
the mingled breed and double issue of the Minotaur, record
of a shameful passion ; on it the famous dwelling's laborious
inextricable maze ; but Daedalus, pitying the great love of
the princess, himself unlocked the tangled treachery of the
palace, guiding with the clue her lover's blind footsteps.
Thou too hadst no slight part in the work he wrought, O
Icarus, did grief allow. Twice had he essayed to portray
thy fate in gold ; twice the father's hands dropped down.
Nay, their eyes would scan all the story in order, were not
Achates already returned from his errand, and with him the
priestess of Phoebus and Trivia, Deïphobe daughter of
Glaucus, who thus accosts the king : 'Other than this are
the sights the time demands : now were it well to sacrifice
seven unbroken bullocks of the herd, as many fitly chosen
sheep of two years old.' Thus speaks she to Aeneas ; nor
do they delay to do her sacred bidding ; and the priestess
calls the Teucrians into the lofty shrine.

A vast cavern is scooped in the side of the Euboïc cliff,
whither lead an hundred wide passages by an hundred gates,
whence peal forth as manifold the responses of the Sibyl.
They had reached the threshold, when the maiden cries :
It is time to enquire thy fate : the god, lo ! the god ! And
even as she spoke thus in the gateway, suddenly countenance nor colour nor ranged tresses stayed the same ; her
wild heart heaves madly in her panting bosom ; and she
expands to sight, and her voice is more than mortal, now
the god breathes on her in nearer deity. 'Lingerest thou
to vow and pray,' she cries, 'Aeneas of Troy ? lingerest
thou ? for not till then will the vast portals of the spell-
bound house swing open.' So spoke she, and sank to
silence. A cold shiver ran through the Teucrians' iron
frames, and the king pours heart-deep supplication :

'Phoebus, who hast ever pitied the sore travail of Troy, who didst guide the Dardanian shaft from Paris' hand full on the son of Aeacus, in thy leading have I pierced all these seas that skirt mighty lands, the Massylian nations far withdrawn, and the fields the Syrtes fringe ;/thus far let the fortune of Troy follow us. You too may now unforbidden spare the nation of Pergama, gods and goddesses to whomsoever Ilium and the great glory of Dardania did wrong. And thou, O prophetess most holy, foreknower of the future, grant (for no unearned realm does my destiny claim) a resting-place in Latium to the Teucrians, to their wandering gods and the storm-tossed deities of Troy. Then will I ordain to Phoebus and Trivia a temple of solid marble, and festal days in Phoebus' name. Thee likewise a mighty sanctuary awaits in our realm. For here will I place thine oracles and the secrets of destiny uttered to my people, and consecrate chosen men, O gracious one. Only commit not thou thy verses to leaves, lest they fly disordered, the sport of rushing winds ; thyself utter them, I beseech thee.' His lips made an end of utterance.

But the prophetess, not yet tame to Phoebus' hand, rages fiercely in the cavern, so she may shake the mighty godhead from her breast ; so much the more does he tire her maddened mouth and subdue her wild breast and shape her to his pressure. And now the hundred mighty portals of the house open of their own accord, and bring through the air the answer of the soothsayer :

'O past at length with the great perils of the sea ! though heavier yet by land await thee, the Dardanians shall come to the realm of Lavinium ; relieve thy heart of this care ; but not so shall they have joy of their coming. Wars, grim wars I discern, and Tiber afoam with streams of blood. A Simoïs shall not fail thee, a Xanthus, a Dorian camp ; another Achilles is already found for Latium, he too

goddess-born; nor shall Juno's presence ever leave the
Teucrians; while thou in thy need, to what nations or what
towns of Italy shalt thou not sue ! Again is an alien bride
the source of all that Teucrian woe, again a foreign mar-
riage-chamber. . . . Yield not thou to distresses, but all
the bolder go forth to meet them, as thy fortune shall allow
thee way. The path of rescue, little as thou deemest it,
shall first open from a Grecian town.'

In such words the Sibyl of Cumae chants from the
shrine her perplexing terrors, echoing through the cavern
truth wrapped in obscurity: so does Apollo clash the reins
and ply the goad in her maddened breast So soon as the
spasm ceased and the raving lips sank to silence, Aeneas
the hero begins : ' No shape of toil, O maiden, rises strange
or sudden on my sight; all this ere now have I guessed
and inly rehearsed in spirit One thing I pray; since here
is the gate named of the infernal king, and the darkling
marsh of Acheron's overflow, be it given me to go to my
beloved father, to see him face to face; teach thou the
way, and open the consecrated portals. Him on these
shoulders I rescued from encircling flames and a thousand
pursuing weapons, and brought him safe from amid the
enemy; he accompanied my way over all the seas, and bore
with me all the threats of ocean and sky, in weakness, beyond his age's strength and due. Nay, he it was who
besought and enjoined me to seek thy grace and draw nigh
thy courts. Have pity, I beseech thee, on son and father,
O gracious one ! for thou art all-powerful, nor in vain hath
Hecate given thee rule in the groves of Avernus. If
Orpheus could call up his wife's ghost in the strength of
his Thracian lyre and the music of the strings,—if Pollux
redeemed his brother by exchange of death, and passes and
repasses so often,—why make mention of great Theseus,
why of Alcides? I too am of Jove's sovereign race.'

In such words he pleaded and clasped the altars ; when
the soothsayer thus began to speak :

'O sprung of gods' blood, child of Anchises of Troy,
easy is the descent into hell; all night and day the gate of
dark Dis stands open ; but to recall thy steps and issue to
upper air, this is the task and burden. Some few of gods'
lineage have availed, such as Jupiter's gracious favour or
virtue's ardour hath upborne to heaven. Midway all is
muffled in forest, and the black coils of Cocytus circle it
round. Yet if thy soul is so passionate and so desirous
twice to float across the Stygian lake, twice to see dark
Tartarus, and thy pleasure is to plunge into the mad task,
learn what must first be accomplished. Hidden in a shady
tree is a bough with leafage and pliant shoot all of gold,
consecrate to nether Juno, wrapped in the depth of woodland and shut in by dim dusky vales. But to him only
who first hath plucked the golden-tressed fruitage from the
tree is it given to enter the hidden places of the earth.
This hath beautiful Proserpine ordained to be borne to
her for her proper gift. The first torn away, a second fills
the place in gold, and the spray burgeons with even such
ore again. So let thine eyes trace it home, and thine hand
pluck it duly when found ; for lightly and unreluctant will it
follow if thine is fate's summons; else will no strength of thine
avail to conquer it nor hard steel to cut it away. Yet again,
a friend of thine lies a lifeless corpse, alas ! thou knowest it
not, and defiles all the fleet with death, while thou seekest
our counsel and lingerest in our courts. First lay him in
his resting-place and hide him in the tomb ; lead thither
black cattle ; be this first thine expiation ; so at last shalt
thou behold the Stygian groves and the realm untrodden of
the living.' She spoke, and her lips shut to silence.

Aeneas goes forth, and leaves the cavern with fixed eyes
and sad countenance, his soul revolving inly the unseen

issues. By his side goes faithful Achates, and plants his footsteps in equal perplexity. Long they ran on in mutual change of talk; of what lifeless comrade spoke the sooth-sayer, of what body for burial? And even as they came, they see on the dry beach Misenus cut off by untimely death, Misenus the Aeolid, excelled of none other in stirring men with brazen breath and kindling battle with his trumpet-note. He had been attendant on mighty Hector; in Hector's train he waged battle, renowned alike for bugle and spear: after victorious Achilles robbed him of life the valiant hero had joined Dardanian Aeneas' company, and followed no meaner leader. But now, while he makes his hollow shell echo over the seas, ah fool! and calls the gods to rival his blast, jealous Triton, if belief is due, had caught him among the rocks and sunk him in the foaming waves. So all surrounded him with loud murmur and cries, good Aeneas the foremost. Then weeping they quickly hasten on the Sibyl's orders, and work hard to pile trees for the altar of burial, and heap it up into the sky. They move into the ancient forest, the deep coverts of game; pitch-pines fall flat, ilex rings to the stroke of axes, and ashen beams and oak are split in clefts with wedges; they roll in huge mountain-ashes from the hills. Aeneas likewise is first in the work, and cheers on his crew and arms himself with their weapons. And alone with his sad heart he ponders it all, gazing on the endless forest, and utters this prayer: 'If but now that bough of gold would shew itself to us on the tree in this depth of woodland! since all the soothsayer's tale of thee, Misenus, was, alas! too truly spoken.' Scarcely had he said thus, when twin doves haply came flying down the sky, and lit on the green sod right under his eyes. Then the kingly hero knows them for his mother's birds, and joyfully prays: 'Ah, be my guides, if way there be, and direct your aëry passage into the groves

where the rich bough overshadows the fertile ground ! and
thou, O goddess mother, fail not our wavering fortune.' So
spoke he and stayed his steps, marking what they signify,
whither they urge their way. Feeding and flying they
advance at such distance as following eyes could keep them
in view ; then, when they came to Avernus' pestilent gorge,
they tower swiftly, and sliding down through the liquid air,
choose their seat and light side by side on a tree, through
whose boughs shone out the contrasting flicker of gold.
As in chill mid-winter the woodland is wont to blossom
with the strange leafage of the mistletoe, sown on an alien
tree and wreathing the smooth stems with burgeoning
saffron ; so on the shadowy ilex seemed that leafy gold, so
the foil tinkled in the light breeze. Immediately Aeneas
seizes it and eagerly breaks off its resistance, and carries it
beneath the Sibyl's roof.

And therewithal the Teucrians on the beach wept
Misenus, and bore the last rites to the thankless ashes.
First they build up a vast pyre of resinous billets and sawn
oak, whose sides they entwine with dark leaves and plant
funereal cypresses in front, and adorn it above with his
shining armour. Some prepare warm water in cauldrons
bubbling over the flames, and wash and anoint the chill
body, and make their moan ; then, their weeping done, lay
his limbs on the pillow, and spread over it crimson raiment,
the accustomed pall. Some uplift the heavy bier, a melancholy service, and with averted faces in their ancestral
fashion hold and thrust in the torch. Gifts of frankincense,
food, and bowls of olive oil, are poured and piled upon the
fire. After the embers sank in and the flame died away,
they soaked with wine the remnant of thirsty ashes, and
Corynaeus gathered the bones and shut them in an urn of
brass ; and he too thrice encircled his comrades with fresh
water, and cleansed them with light spray sprinkled from a

bough of fruitful olive, and spoke the last words of all. But
good Aeneas heaps a mighty mounded tomb over him, with
his own armour and his oar and trumpet, beneath a skyey
mountain that now is called Misenus after him, and keeps
his name immortal from age to age.

This done, he hastens to fulfil the Sibyl's ordinance.
A deep cave yawned dreary and vast, shingle-strewn,
sheltered by the black lake and the gloom of the forests;
over it no flying things could wing their way unharmed,
such a vapour streamed from the dark gorge and rose into
the overarching sky. Here the priestess first arrays four
black-bodied bullocks and pours wine upon their forehead;
and plucking the topmost hairs from between the horns, lays
them on the sacred fire for first-offering, calling aloud on
Hecate, mistress of heaven and hell. Others lay knives beneath, and catch the warm blood in cups. Aeneas himself
smites with the sword a black-fleeced she-lamb to the mother
of the Eumenides and her mighty sister, and a barren heifer,
Proserpine, to thee. Then he uprears darkling altars to the
Stygian king, and lays whole carcases of bulls upon the
flames, pouring fat oil over the blazing entrails. And lo!
about the first rays of sunrise the ground moaned under-
foot, and the woodland ridges began to stir, and dogs
seemed to howl through the dusk as the goddess came.
'Apart, ah keep apart, O ye unsanctified!' cries the soothsayer; 'retire from all the grove; and thou, stride on and
unsheath thy steel; now is need of courage, O Aeneas,
now of strong resolve.' So much she spoke, and plunged
madly into the cavern's opening; he with unflinching steps
keeps pace with his advancing guide.

Gods who are sovereign over souls! silent ghosts, and
Chaos and Phlegethon, the wide dumb realm of night! as
I have heard, so let me tell, and according to your will
unfold things sunken deep under earth in gloom.

They went darkling through the dusk beneath the solitary night, through the empty dwellings and bodiless realm of Dis; even as one walks in the forest beneath the jealous light of a doubtful moon, when Jupiter shrouds the sky in shadow and black night blots out the world. Right in front of the doorway and in the entry of the jaws of hell Grief and avenging Cares have made their bed; there dwell wan Sicknesses and gloomy Eld, and Fear, and ill-counselling Hunger, and loathly Want, shapes terrible to see; and Death and Travail, and thereby Sleep, Death's kinsman, and the Soul's guilty Joys, and death-dealing War full in the gateway, and the Furies in their iron cells, and mad Discord with bloodstained fillets enwreathing her serpent locks.

Midway an elm, shadowy and high, spreads her boughs and secular arms, where, one saith, idle Dreams dwell clustering, and cling under every leaf. And monstrous creatures besides, many and diverse, keep covert at the gates, Centaurs and twy-shaped Scyllas, and the hundred-fold Briareus, and the beast of Lerna hissing horribly, and the Chimaera armed with flame, Gorgons and Harpies, and the body of the triform shade. Here Aeneas snatches at his sword in a sudden flutter of terror, and turns the naked edge on them as they come; and did not his wise fellow-passenger remind him that these lives flit thin and unessential in the hollow mask of body, he would rush on and vainly lash through phantoms with his steel.

Hence a road leads to Tartarus and Acheron's wave. Here the dreary pool swirls thick in muddy eddies and disgorges into Cocytus with its load of sand. Charon, the dread ferryman, guards these flowing streams, ragged and awful, his chin covered with untrimmed masses of hoary hair, and his glassy eyes aflame; his soiled raiment hangs knotted from his shoulders. Himself he plies the pole and trims the sails of his vessel, the steel-blue galley with freight

of dead ; stricken now in years, but a god's old age is lusty
and green. Hither all crowded, and rushed streaming to
the bank, matrons and men and high-hearted heroes dead
and done with life, boys and unwedded girls, and children
laid young on the bier before their parents' eyes, multitudinous as leaves fall dropping in the forests at autumn's earliest
frost, or birds swarm landward from the deep gulf, when
the chill of the year routs them overseas and drives them
to sunny lands. They stood pleading for the first passage
across, and stretched forth passionate hands to the farther
shore. But the grim sailor admits now one and now another,
while some he pushes back far apart on the strand. Moved
with marvel at the confused throng : 'Say, O maiden,' cries
Aeneas, 'what means this flocking to the river? of what are
the souls so fain? or what difference makes these retire from
the banks, those go with sweeping oars over the leaden
waterways?'

To him the long-lived priestess thus briefly returned :
'Seed of Anchises, most sure progeny of gods, thou seest
the deep pools of Cocytus and the Stygian marsh, by whose
divinity the gods fear to swear falsely. All this crowd thou
discernest is helpless and unsepultured ; Charon is the ferryman ; they who ride on the wave found a tomb. Nor is it
given to cross the awful banks and hoarse streams ere the
dust hath found a resting-place. An hundred years they
wander here flitting about the shore ; then at last they gain
entrance, and revisit the pools so sorely desired.'

Anchises' son stood still, and ponderingly stayed his
footsteps, pitying at heart their cruel lot. There he discerns, mournful and unhonoured dead, Leucaspis and
Orontes, captains of the Lycian squadron, whom, as they
sailed together from Troy over gusty seas, the south wind
overwhelmed and wrapped the waters round ship and
men.

Lo, there went by Palinurus the steersman, who of late,
while he watched the stars on their Libyan passage, had
slipped from the stern and fallen amid the waves. To
him, when he first knew the melancholy form in that depth
of shade, he thus opens speech : ' What god, O Palinurus,
reft thee from us and sank thee amid the seas ? forth and
tell. For in this single answer Apollo deceived me, never
found false before, when he prophesied thee safety on ocean
and arrival on the Ausonian coasts. See, is this his pro-
mise-keeping ?'

And he : ' Neither did Phoebus on his oracular seat
delude thee, O prince, Anchises' son, nor did any god
drown me in the sea. For while I clung to my appointed
charge and governed our course, I pulled the tiller with me
in my fall, and the shock as I slipped wrenched it away.
By the rough seas I swear, fear for myself never wrung me
so sore as for thy ship, lest, the rudder lost and the pilot
struck away, those gathering waves might master it. Three
wintry nights in the water the blustering south drove me
over the endless sea ; scarcely on the fourth dawn I descried
Italy as I rose on the climbing wave. Little by little I
swam shoreward ; already I clung safe ; but while, encum-
bered with my dripping raiment, I caught with crooked
fingers at the jagged needles of mountain rock, the barbarous people attacked me in arms and ignorantly deemed me
a prize. Now the wave holds me, and the winds toss me
on the shore. By heaven's pleasant light and breezes I
beseech thee, by thy father, by Iülus thy rising hope, rescue
me from these distresses, O unconquered one ! Either do
thou, for thou canst, cast earth over me and again seek the
haven of Velia ; or do thou, if in any wise that may be, if
in any wise the goddess who bore thee shews a way,—for
not without divine will do I deem thou wilt float across
these vast rivers and the Stygian pool,—lend me a pitying

K

hand, and bear me over the waves in thy company, that at least in death I may find a quiet resting-place.'

Thus he ended, and the soothsayer thus began : ' Whence, O Palinurus, this fierce longing of thine ? Shalt thou without burial behold the Stygian waters and the awful river of the Furies ? Cease to hope prayers may bend the decrees of heaven. But take my words to thy memory, for comfort in thy woeful case : far and wide shall the bordering cities be driven by celestial portents to appease thy dust ; they shall rear a tomb, and pay the tomb a yearly offering, and for evermore shall the place keep Palinurus' name.' The words soothed away his distress, and for a while drove grief away from his sorrowing heart ; he is glad in the land of his name.

So they complete their journey's beginning, and draw nigh the river. Just then the waterman descried them from the Stygian wave advancing through the silent woodland and turning their feet towards the bank, and opens on them in these words of challenge : ' Whoso thou art who marchest in arms towards our river, forth and say, there as thou art, why thou comest, and stay thine advance. This is the land of Shadows, of Sleep, and slumberous Night ; no living body may the Stygian hull convey. Nor truly had I joy of taking Alcides on the lake for passenger, nor Theseus and Pirithoüs, born of gods though they were and unconquered in might. He laid fettering hand on the warder of Tartarus, and dragged him cowering from the throne of my lord the King ; they essayed to ravish our mistress from the bridal chamber of Dis.' Thereto the Amphrysian soothsayer made brief reply : ' No such plot is here ; be not moved ; nor do our weapons offer violence ; the huge gatekeeper may bark on for ever in his cavern and affright the bloodless ghosts ; Proserpine may keep her honour within her uncle's gates. Aeneas of Troy, renowned

in goodness as in arms, goes down to meet his father in
the deep shades of Erebus.   If the sight of such affection
stirs thee in nowise, yet this bough' (she discovers the
bough hidden in her raiment) 'thou must know.'   Then
his heaving breast allays its anger, and he says no more;
but marvelling at the awful gift, the fated rod so long
unseen, he steers in his dusky vessel and draws to shore.
Next he routs out the souls that sate on the long benches,
and clears the thwarts, while he takes mighty Aeneas on
board.   The galley groaned under the weight in all her
seams, and the marsh-water leaked fast in.   At length
prophetess and prince are landed unscathed on the ugly
ooze and livid sedge.

This realm rings with the triple-throated baying of vast
Cerberus, couched huge in the cavern opposite; to whom
the prophetess, seeing the serpents already bristling up on
his neck, throws a cake made slumberous with honey and
drugged grain.   He, with threefold jaws gaping in ravenous
hunger, catches it when thrown, and sinks to earth with
monstrous body outstretched, and sprawling huge over all
his den.   The warder overwhelmed, Aeneas makes entrance,
and quickly issues from the bank of the irremeable wave.

Immediately wailing voices are loud in their ears, the
souls of babies crying on the doorway sill, whom, torn from
the breast and portionless in life's sweetness, a dark day
cut off and drowned in bitter death.   Hard by them are
those condemned to death on false accusation.   Neither
indeed are these dwellings assigned without lot and judgment; Minos presides and shakes the urn; he summons
a council of the silent people, and inquires of their lives
and charges.   Next in order have these mourners their
place whose own innocent hands dealt them death, who
flung away their souls in hatred of the day.   How fain
were they now in upper air to endure their poverty and

sore travail! It may not be; the unlovely pool locks
them in her gloomy wave, and Styx pours her ninefold
barrier between. And not far from here are shewn stretching on every side the Wailing Fields; so they call them by
name. Here they whom pitiless love hath wasted in cruel
decay hide among untrodden ways, shrouded in embosoming myrtle thickets; not death itself ends their distresses.
In this region he discerns Phaedra and Procris and woeful
Eriphyle, shewing on her the wounds of her merciless son,
and Evadne and Pasiphaë; Laodamia goes in their company, and she who was once Caeneus and a man, now
woman, and again returned by fate into her shape of old.
Among whom Dido the Phoenician, fresh from her death-
wound, wandered in the vast forest; by her the Trojan
hero stood, and knew the dim form through the darkness,
even as the moon at the month's beginning to him who sees
or thinks he sees her rising through the vapours; he let
tears fall, and spoke to her lovingly and sweet :

'Alas, Dido! so the news was true that reached me;
thou didst perish, and the sword sealed thy doom! Ah
me, was I cause of thy death? By the stars I swear, by
the heavenly powers and all that is sacred beneath the
earth, unwillingly, O queen, I left thy shore. But the gods,
at whose orders now I pass through this shadowy place,
this land of mouldering overgrowth and deep night, the
gods' commands drove me forth; nor could I deem my
departure would bring thee pain so great as this. Stay thy
footstep, and withdraw not from our gaze. From whom
fliest thou? the last speech of thee fate ordains me is this.'

In such words and with starting tears Aeneas soothed
the burning and fierce-eyed soul. She turned away with
looks fixed fast on the ground, stirred no more in countenance by the speech he essays than if she stood in iron flint
or Marpesian stone. At length she started, and fled wrath-

fully into the shadowy woodland, where Sychaeus, her
ancient husband, responds to her distresses and equals her
affection. Yet Aeneas, dismayed by her cruel doom, follows her far on her way with pitying tears.

Thence he pursues his appointed path. And now they
trod those utmost fields where the renowned in war have
their haunt apart. Here Tydeus meets him; here Parthen-
opaeus, glorious in arms, and the pallid phantom of Adras-
tus; here the Dardanians long wept on earth and fallen in
the war; sighing he discerns all their long array, Glaucus
and Medon and Thersilochus, the three children of Antenor,
and Polyphoetes, Ceres' priest, and Idaeus yet charioted,
yet grasping his arms. The souls throng round him to
right and left; nor is one look enough; lingering delighted,
they pace by his side and enquire wherefore he is come.
But the princes of the Grecians and Agamemnon's armies,
when they see him glittering in arms through the gloom,
hurry terror-stricken away; some turn backward, as when
of old they fled to the ships; some raise their voice faintly,
and gasp out a broken ineffectual cry.

And here he saw Deïphobus son of Priam, with face
cruelly torn, face and both hands, and ears lopped from his
mangled temples, and nostrils maimed by a shameful wound.
Barely he knew the cowering form that hid its dreadful
punishment; then he springs to accost it in familiar speech:

'Deïphobus mighty in arms, seed of Teucer's royal
blood, whose wantonness of vengeance was so cruel? who
was allowed to use thee thus? Rumour reached me that
on that last night, outwearied with endless slaughter, thou
hadst sunk on the heap of mingled carnage. Then mine
own hand reared an empty tomb on the Rhoetean shore,
mine own voice thrice called aloud upon thy ghost. Thy
name and armour keep the spot; thee, O my friend, I
could not see nor lay in the native earth I left.'

Whereto the son of Priam : ' In nothing, O my friend, wert thou wanting; thou hast paid the full to Deïphobus and the dead man's shade. But me my fate and the Laconian woman's murderous guilt thus dragged down to doom ; these are the records of her leaving. For how we spent that last night in delusive gladness thou knowest, and must needs remember too well. When the fated horse leapt down on the steep towers of Troy, bearing armed infantry for the burden of its womb, she, in feigned procession, led round our Phrygian women with Bacchic cries ; herself she upreared a mighty flame amid them, and called the Grecians out of the fortress height. Then was I fast in mine ill-fated bridal chamber, deep asleep and outworn with my charge, and lay overwhelmed in slumber sweet and profound and most like to easeful death. Meanwhile that crown of wives removes all the arms from my dwelling, and slips out the faithful sword from beneath my head : she calls Menelaus into the house and flings wide the gateway : be sure she hoped her lover would magnify the gift, and so she might quench the fame of her ill deeds of old. Why do I linger ? They burst into the chamber, they and the Aeolid, counsellor of crime, in their company. Gods, recompense the Greeks even thus, if with righteous lips I call for vengeance ! But come, tell in turn what hap hath brought thee hither yet alive. Comest thou driven on ocean wanderings, or by promptings from heaven ? or what fortune keeps thee from rest, that thou shouldst draw nigh these sad sunless dwellings, this disordered land ?'

In this change of talk Dawn had already crossed heaven's mid axle on her rose-charioted way; and haply had they thus drawn out all the allotted time ; but the Sibyl made brief warning speech to her companion : ' Night falls, Aeneas; we waste the hours in weeping. Here is the place where the road disparts ; by this that runs to the right

under great Dis' city is our path to Elysium; but the leftward wreaks vengeance on the wicked and sends them to
unrelenting hell.'   But Deïphobus: 'Be not angered,
mighty priestess; I will depart, I will refill my place and
return into darkness. Go, glory of our people, go, enjoy
a fairer fate than mine.' Thus much he spoke, and on the
word turned away his footsteps.

Aeneas looks swiftly back, and sees beneath the cliff on
the left hand a wide city, girt with a triple wall and encircled
by a racing river of boiling flame, Tartarean Phlegethon,
that echoes over its rolling rocks.   In front is the gate,
huge and pillared with solid adamant, that no warring force
of men nor the very habitants of heaven may avail to overthrow; it stands up a tower of iron, and Tisiphone sitting
girt in bloodstained pall keeps sleepless watch at the entry
by night and day.   Hence moans are heard and fierce
lashes resound, with the clank of iron and dragging chains.
Aeneas stopped and hung dismayed at the tumult.   'What
shapes of crime are here? declare, O maiden; or what the
punishment that pursues them, and all this upsurging wail?'
Then the soothsayer thus began to speak: 'Illustrious
chief of Troy, no pure foot may tread these guilty courts;
but to me Hecate herself, when she gave me rule over the
groves of Avernus, taught how the gods punish, and guided
me through all her realm.   Gnosian Rhadamanthus here
holds unrelaxing sway, chastises secret crime revealed, and
exacts confession, wheresoever in the upper world one
vainly exultant in stolen guilt hath till the dusk of death
kept clear from the evil he wrought.   Straightway avenging
Tisiphone, girt with her scourge, tramples down the shivering sinners, menaces them with the grim snakes in her left
hand, and summons forth her sisters in merciless train.
Then at last the sacred gates are flung open and grate on
the jarring hinge.   Markest thou what sentry is seated in

the doorway? what shape guards the threshold? More
grim within sits the monstrous Hydra with her fifty black
yawning throats: and Tartarus' self gapes sheer and strikes
into the gloom through twice the space that one looks
upward to Olympus and the skyey heaven. Here Earth's
ancient children, the Titans' brood, hurled down by the
thunderbolt, lie wallowing in the abyss. Here likewise I
saw the twin Aloïds, enormous of frame, who essayed with
violent hands to pluck down high heaven and thrust Jove
from his upper realm. Likewise I saw Salmoneus in the
cruel payment he gives for mocking Jove's flame and
Olympus' thunders. Borne by four horses and brandishing
a torch, he rode in triumph midway through the populous
city of Grecian Elis, and claimed for himself the worship
of deity; madman! who would mimic the storm-cloud
and the inimitable bolt with brass that rang under his
trampling horse-hoofs. But the Lord omnipotent hurled
his shaft through thickening clouds (no firebrand his nor
smoky glare of torches) and dashed him headlong in the
fury of the whirlwind. Therewithal Tityos might be seen,
fosterling of Earth the mother of all, whose body stretches
over nine full acres, and a monstrous vulture with crooked
beak eats away the imperishable liver and the entrails that
breed in suffering, and plunges deep into the breast that
gives it food and dwelling; nor is any rest given to the
fibres that ever grow anew. Why tell of the Lapithae, of
Ixion and Pirithoüs? over whom a stone hangs just slipping and just as though it fell; or the high banqueting
couches gleam golden-pillared, and the feast is spread in
royal luxury before their faces; couched hard by, the eldest
of the Furies wards the tables from their touch and rises
with torch upreared and thunderous lips. Here are they
who hated their brethren while life endured, or struck a
parent or entangled a client in wrong, or who brooded

alone over found treasure and shared it not with their
fellows, this the greatest multitude of all; and they who
were slain for adultery, and who followed unrighteous arms,
and feared not to betray their masters' plighted hand.
Imprisoned they await their doom. Seek not to be told
that doom, that fashion of fortune wherein they are sunk.
Some roll a vast stone, or hang outstretched on the spokes
of wheels; hapless Theseus sits and shall sit for ever, and
Phlegyas in his misery gives counsel to all and witnesses
aloud through the gloom, *Learn by this warning to do justly
and not to slight the gods.* This man sold his country for
gold, and laid her under a tyrant's sway; he set up and
pulled down laws at a price; this other forced his daughter's
bridal chamber and a forbidden marriage; all dared some
monstrous wickedness, and had success in what they dared.
Not had I an hundred tongues, an hundred mouths, and a
voice of iron, could I sum up all the shapes of crime or
name over all their punishments.'

Thus spoke Phoebus' long-lived priestess; then 'But
come now,' she cries; 'haste on the way and perfect the
service begun; let us go faster; I descry the ramparts cast
in Cyclopean furnaces, and in front the arched gateway
where they bid us lay the gifts foreordained.' She ended,
and advancing side by side along the shadowy ways, they
pass over and draw nigh the gates. Aeneas makes entrance,
and sprinkling his body with fresh water, plants the bough
full in the gateway.

Now at length, this fully done, and the service of the
goddess perfected, they came to the happy place, the green
pleasances and blissful seats of the Fortunate Woodlands.
Here an ampler air clothes the meadows in lustrous sheen,
and they know their own sun and a starlight of their own.
Some exercise their limbs in tournament on the greensward,
contend in games, and wrestle on the yellow sand. Some

dance with beating footfall and lips that sing ; with them is
the Thracian priest in sweeping robe, and makes music to
their measures with the notes' sevenfold interval, the notes
struck now with his fingers, now with his ivory rod.   Here
is Teucer's ancient brood, a generation excellent in beauty,
high-hearted heroes born in happier years, Ilus and Assaracus, and Dardanus, founder of Troy.   Afar he marvels at
the armour and chariots empty of their lords : their spears
stand fixed in the ground, and their unyoked horses pasture
at large over the plain : their life's delight in chariot and
armour, their care in pasturing their sleek horses, follows
them in like wise low under earth.   Others, lo ! he beholds
feasting on the sward to right and left, and singing in
chorus the glad Paean-cry, within a scented laurel-grove
whence Eridanus river surges upward full-volumed through
the wood.   Here is the band of them who bore wounds in
fighting for their country, and they who were pure in priest-
hood while life endured, and the good poets whose speech
abased not Apollo ; and they who made life beautiful by the
arts of their invention, and who won by service a memory
among men, the brows of all girt with the snow-white fillet.
To their encircling throng the Sibyl spoke thus, and to
Musaeus before them all ; for he is midmost of all the
multitude, and stands out head and shoulders among their
upward gaze :
    ' Tell, O blissful souls, and thou, poet most gracious,
what region, what place hath Anchises for his own ?   For
his sake are we come, and have sailed across the wide rivers
of Erebus.'
    And to her the hero thus made brief reply : ' None hath
a fixed dwelling ; we live in the shady woodlands ; soft-
swelling banks and meadows fresh with streams are our
habitation.   But you, if this be your heart's desire, scale
this ridge, and I will even now set you on an easy path-

way,' He spoke, and paced on before them, and from
above shews the shining plains; thereafter they leave the
mountain heights.

But lord Anchises, deep in the green valley, was
musing in earnest survey over the imprisoned souls destined
to the daylight above, and haply reviewing his beloved
children and all the tale of his people, them and their fates
and fortunes, their works and ways. And he, when he
saw Aeneas advancing to meet him over the greensward,
stretched forth both hands eagerly, while tears rolled over
his cheeks, and his lips parted in a cry: 'Art thou come
at last, and hath thy love, O child of my desire, conquered
the difficult road? Is it granted, O my son, to gaze on
thy face and hear and answer in familiar tones? Thus
indeed I forecast in spirit, counting the days between; nor
hath my care misled me. What lands, what space of seas
hast thou traversed to reach me, through what surge of
perils, O my son! How I dreaded the realm of Libya
might work thee harm!'

And he: 'Thy melancholy phantom, thine, O my
father, came before me often and often, and drove me to
steer to these portals. My fleet is anchored on the Tyrrhenian brine. Give thine hand to clasp, O my father, give
it, and withdraw not from our embrace.'

So spoke he, his face wet with abundant weeping.
Thrice there did he essay to fling his arms about his neck;
thrice the phantom vainly grasped fled out of his hands
even as light wind, and most like to fluttering sleep.

Meanwhile Aeneas sees deep withdrawn in the covert
of the vale a woodland and rustling forest thickets, and the
river of Lethe that floats past their peaceful dwellings.
Around it flitted nations and peoples innumerable; even
as in the meadows when in clear summer weather bees
settle on the variegated flowers and stream round the snow-

white lilies, all the plain is murmurous with their humming.
Aeneas starts at the sudden view, and asks the reason he
knows not; what are those spreading streams, or who are
they whose vast train fills the banks?   Then lord Anchises :
' Souls, for whom second bodies are destined and due, drink
at the wave of the Lethean stream the heedless water of
long forgetfulness.   These of a truth have I long desired
to tell and shew thee face to face, and number all the
generation of thy children, that so thou mayest the more
rejoice with me in finding Italy.'—'O father, must we think
that any souls travel hence into upper air, and return again
to bodily fetters ?   why this their strange sad longing for
the light ? '   ' I will tell,' rejoins Anchises, ' nor will I hold
thee in suspense, my son.'   And he unfolds all things in
order one by one.

' First of all, heaven and earth and the liquid fields, the
shining orb of the moon and the Titanian star, doth a spirit
sustain inly, and a soul shed abroad in them sways all their
members and mingles in the mighty frame.   Thence is the
generation of man and beast, the life of winged things, and
the monstrous forms that ocean breeds under his glittering
floor.   Those seeds have fiery force and divine birth, so far
as they are not clogged by taint of the body and dulled by
earthy frames and limbs ready to die.   Hence is it they
fear and desire, sorrow and rejoice ; nor can they pierce
the air while barred in the blind darkness of their prison-
house.   Nay, and when the last ray of life is gone, not yet,
alas ! does all their woe, nor do all the plagues of the body
wholly leave them free ; and needs must be that many a
long ingrained evil should take root marvellously deep.
Therefore they are schooled in punishment, and pay all the
forfeit of a lifelong ill ; some are hung stretched to the
viewless winds ; some have the taint of guilt washed out
beneath the dreary deep, or burned away in fire.   We

suffer, each a several ghost ; thereafter we are sent to the broad spaces of Elysium, some few of us to possess the happy fields ; till length of days completing time's circle takes out the ingrained soilure and leaves untainted the ethereal sense and pure spiritual flame. All these before thee, when the wheel of a thousand years hath come fully round, a God summons in vast train to the river of Lethe, that so they may regain in forgetfulness the slopes of upper. earth, and begin to desire to return again into the body.'

Anchises ceased, and leads his son and the Sibyl likewise amid the assembled murmurous throng, and mounts a hillock whence he might scan all the long ranks and learn their countenances as they came.

'Now come, the glory hereafter to follow our Dardanian progeny, the posterity to abide in our Italian people, illustrious souls and inheritors of our name to be, these will I rehearse, and instruct thee of thy destinies. He yonder, seest thou ? the warrior leaning on his pointless spear, holds the nearest place allotted in our groves, and shall rise first into the air of heaven from the mingling blood of Italy, Silvius of Alban name, the child of thine age, whom late in thy length of days thy wife Lavinia shall nurture in the woodland, king and father of kings ; from him in Alba the Long shall our house have dominion. He next him is Procas, glory of the Trojan race ; and Capys and Numitor ; and he who shall renew thy name, Silvius Aeneas, eminent alike in goodness or in arms, if ever he shall receive his kingdom in Alba. Men of men ! see what strength they display, and wear the civic oak shading their brows. They shall establish Nomentum and Gabii and Fidena city, they the Collatine hill-fortress, Pometii and the Fort of Inuus, Bola and Cora : these shall be names that are now nameless lands. Nay, Romulus likewise, seed of Mavors, shall join

his grandsire's company, from his mother Ilia's nurture and
Assaracus' blood. Seest thou how the twin plumes straighten
on his crest, and his father's own emblazonment already
marks him for upper air? Behold, O son! by his augury
shall Rome the renowned fill earth with her empire and
heaven with her pride, and gird about seven fortresses with
her single wall, prosperous mother of men; even as our
lady of Berecyntus rides in her chariot turret-crowned
through the Phrygian cities, glad in the gods she hath
borne, clasping an hundred of her children's children, all
habitants of heaven, all dwellers on the upper heights.
Hither now bend thy twin-eyed gaze; behold this people,
the Romans that are thine. Here is Caesar and all Iülus'
posterity that shall arise under the mighty cope of heaven.
Here is he, he of whose promise once and again thou
hearest, Caesar Augustus, a god's son, who shall again
establish the ages of gold in Latium over the fields that
once were Saturn's realm, and carry his empire afar to
Garamant and Indian, to the land that lies beyond our
stars, beyond the sun's yearlong ways, where Atlas the sky-
bearer wheels on his shoulder the glittering star-spangled
pole. Before his coming even now the kingdoms of the
Caspian shudder at oracular answers, and the Maeotic land
and the mouths of sevenfold Nile flutter in alarm. Nor
indeed did Alcides traverse such spaces of earth, though he
pierced the brazen-footed deer, or though he stilled the
Erymanthian woodlands and made Lerna tremble at his
bow: nor he who sways his team with reins of vine, Liber
the conqueror, when he drives his tigers from Nysa's lofty
crest. And do we yet hesitate to give valour scope in deeds,
or shrink in fear from setting foot on Ausonian land? Ah,
and who is he apart, marked out with sprays of olive, offering sacrifice? I know the locks and hoary chin of the
king of Rome who shall establish the infant city in his

laws, sent from little Cures' sterile land to the majesty of empire. To him Tullus shall next succeed, who shall break the peace of his country and stir to arms men rusted from war and armies now disused to triumphs; and hard on him over-vaunting Ancus follows, even now too elate in popular breath. Wilt thou see also the Tarquin kings, and the haughty soul of Brutus the Avenger, and the fasces regained? He shall first receive a consul's power and the merciless axes, and when his children would stir fresh war, the father, for fair freedom's sake, shall summon them to doom. Unhappy! yet howsoever posterity shall take the deed, love of country and limitless passion for honour shall prevail. Nay, behold apart the Decii and the Drusi, Torquatus with his cruel axe, and Camillus returning with the standards. Yonder souls likewise, whom thou discernest gleaming in equal arms, at one now, while shut in Night, ah me! what mutual war, what battle-lines and bloodshed shall they arouse, so they attain the light of the living! father-in-law descending from the Alpine barriers and the fortress of the Dweller Alone, son-in-law facing him with the embattled East. Nay, O my children, harden not your hearts to such warfare, neither turn upon her own heart the mastering might of your country; and thou, be thou first to forgive, who drawest thy descent from heaven; cast down the weapons from thy hand, O blood of mine. . . . He shall drive his conquering chariot to the Capitoline height triumphant over Corinth, glorious in Achaean slaughter. He shall uproot Argos and Agamemnonian Mycenae, and the Aeacid's own heir, the seed of Achilles mighty in arms, avenging his ancestors in Troy and Minerva's polluted temple. Who might leave thee, lordly Cato, or thee, Cossus, to silence? who the Gracchan family, or these two sons of the Scipios, a double thunderbolt of war, Libya's bale? and Fabricius potent in poverty, or

thee, Serranus, sowing in the furrow? Whither whirl you
me all breathless, O Fabii? thou art he, the most mighty,
the one man whose lingering retrieves our State. Others
shall beat out the breathing bronze to softer lines, I believe
it well ; shall draw living lineaments from the marble ; the
cause shall be more eloquent on their lips ; their pencil
shall portray the pathways of heaven, and tell the stars in
their arising : be thy charge, O Roman, to rule the nations
in thine empire ; this shall be thine art, to lay down the
law of peace, to be merciful to the conquered and beat the
haughty down.'

Thus lord Anchises, and as they marvel, he so pursues :
' Look how Marcellus the conqueror marches glorious in
the splendid spoils, towering high above them all ! He
shall stay the Roman State, reeling beneath the invading
shock, shall ride down Carthaginian and insurgent Gaul,
and a third time hang up the captured armour before lord
Quirinus.'

And at this Aeneas, for he saw going by his side one
excellent in beauty and glittering in arms, but his brow had
little cheer, and his eyes looked down :

' Who, O my father, is he who thus attends him on his
way ? son, or other of his children's princely race ? How
his comrades murmur around him ! how goodly of presence
he is ! but dark Night flutters round his head with melancholy shade.'

Then lord Anchises with welling tears began : ' O my
son, ask not of the great sorrow of thy people. Him shall
fate but shew to earth, and suffer not to stay further. Too
mighty, lords of heaven, did you deem the brood of Rome,
had this your gift been abiding. What moaning of men
shall arise from the Field of Mavors by the imperial city !
what a funeral train shalt thou see, O Tiber, as thou flowest
by the new-made grave ! Neither shall the boyhood of any

of Ilian race raise his Latin forefathers' hope so high ; nor
shall the land of Romulus ever boast of any fosterling like
this. Alas his goodness, alas his antique honour, and
right hand invincible in war ! none had faced him unscathed
in armed shock, whether he met the foe on foot, or ran his
spurs into the flanks of his foaming horse Ah me, the
pity of thee, O boy ! if in any wise thou breakest the grim
bar of fate, thou shalt be Marcellus. Give me lilies in full
hands ; let me strew bright blossoms, and these gifts at
least let me lavish on my descendant's soul, and do the
unavailing service.'

Thus they wander up and down over the whole region
of broad vaporous plains, and scan all the scene. And
when Anchises had led his son over it, each point by each,
and kindled his spirit with passion for the glories on their
way, he tells him thereafter of the war he next must wage,
and instructs him of the Laurentine peoples and the city of
Latinus, and in what wise each task may be turned aside
or borne.

There are twin portals of Sleep, whereof the one is
fabled of horn, and by it real shadows are given easy outlet ;
the other shining white of polished ivory, but false visions
issue upward from the ghostly world. With these words
then Anchises follows forth his son and the Sibyl together
there, and dismisses them by the ivory gate. He pursues
his way to the ships and revisits his comrades ; then bears
on to Caieta's haven straight along the shore. The anchor
is cast from the prow ; the sterns are grounded on the
beach.

BOOK SEVENTH

THE LANDING IN LATIUM, AND THE ROLL OF THE ARMIES OF ITALY

THOU also, Caieta, nurse of Aeneas, gavest our shores an everlasting renown in death; and still thine honour haunts thy resting-place, and a name in broad Hesperia, if that be glory, marks thy dust. But when the last rites are duly paid, and the mound smoothed over the grave, good Aeneas, now the high seas are hushed, bears on under sail and leaves his haven. Breezes blow into the night, and the white moonshine speeds them on; the sea glitters in her quivering radiance. Soon they skirt the shores of Circe's land, where the rich daughter of the Sun makes her untrodden groves echo with ceaseless song; and her stately house glows nightlong with burning odorous cedarwood, as she runs over her delicate web with the ringing comb. Hence are heard afar angry cries of lions chafing at their fetters and roaring in the deep night; bears and bristly swine rage in their pens, and vast shapes of wolves howl; whom with her potent herbs the deadly divine Circe had disfashioned, face and body, into wild beasts from the likeness of men. But lest the good Trojans might suffer so dread a change, might enter her haven or draw nigh the ominous shores, Neptune filled

their sails with favourable winds, and gave them escape,
and bore them past the seething shallows.

And now the sea reddened with shafts of light, and
high in heaven the yellow dawn shone rose-charioted;
when the winds fell, and every breath sank suddenly, and
the oar-blades toil through the heavy ocean-floor. And on
this Aeneas descries from sea a mighty forest. Midway in
it the pleasant Tiber stream breaks to sea in swirling
eddies, laden with yellow sand. Around and above fowl
many in sort, that haunt his banks and river-channel,
solaced heaven with song and flew about the forest. He
orders his crew to bend their course and turn their prows
to land, and glides joyfully into the shady river.

Forth now, Erato! and I will unfold who were the
kings, what the tides of circumstance, how it was with
ancient Latium when first that foreign army drew their
fleet ashore on Ausonia's coast; I will recall the prelud-
ing of battle. Thou, divine one, inspire thou thy poet.
I will tell of grim wars, tell of embattled lines, of kings
whom honour drove on death, of the Tyrrhenian forces,
and all Hesperia enrolled in arms. A greater history opens
before me, a greater work I essay.

Latinus the King, now growing old, ruled in a long
peace over quiet tilth and town. He, men say, was sprung
of Faunus and the nymph Marica of Laurentum. Faunus'
father was Picus; and he boasts himself, Saturn, thy son;
thou art the first source of their blood. Son of his, by
divine ordinance, and male descent was none, cut off in
the early spring of youth. One alone kept the household
and its august home, a daughter now ripe for a husband
and of full years for marriage. Many wooed her from
wide Latium and all Ausonia. Fairest and foremost of all

is Turnus, of long and lordly ancestry; but boding signs
from heaven, many and terrible, bar the way. Within the
palace, in the lofty inner courts, was a laurel of sacred
foliage, guarded in awe through many years, which lord
Latinus, it was said, himself found and dedicated to Phoebus
when first he would build his citadel; and from it gave
his settlers their name, Laurentines. High atop of it,
wonderful to tell, bees borne with loud humming across
the liquid air girt it thickly about, and with interlinked
feet hung in a sudden swarm from the leafy bough.
Straightway the prophet cries : ' I see a foreigner draw nigh,
an army from the same quarter seek the same quarter, and
reign high in our fortress.'   Furthermore, while maiden
Lavinia stands beside her father feeding the altars with holy
fuel, she was seen, oh, horror ! to catch fire in her long
tresses, and burn with flickering flame in all her array, her
queenly hair lit up, lit up her jewelled circlet; till, enwreathed in smoke and lurid light, she scattered fire over
all the palace.   That sight was rumoured wonderful and
terrible.   Herself, they prophesied, she should be glorious
in fame and fortune; but a great war was foreshadowed
for her people.   But the King, troubled by the omen,
visits the oracle of his father Faunus the soothsayer, and
the groves deep under Albunea, where, queen of the woods,
she echoes from her holy well, and breathes forth a dim and
deadly vapour.   Hence do the tribes of Italy and all the
Oenotrian land seek answers in perplexity; hither the
priest bears his gifts, and when he hath lain down and
sought slumber under the silent night on the spread fleeces
of slaughtered sheep, sees many flitting phantoms of wonderful wise, hears manifold voices, and attains converse of
the gods, and hath speech with Acheron and the deep
tract of hell.   Here then, likewise seeking an answer, lord
Latinus paid fit sacrifice of an hundred woolly ewes, and

lay couched on the strewn fleeces they had worn. Out of
the lofty grove a sudden voice was uttered : 'Seek not,
O my child, to unite thy daughter in Latin espousals, nor
trust her to the bridal chambers ready to thine hand ;
foreigners shall come to be thy sons, whose blood shall
raise our name to heaven, and the children of whose race
shall see, where the circling sun looks on either ocean, all
the rolling world swayed beneath their feet.' This his
father Faunus' answer and counsel given in the silent night
Latinus restrains not in his lips ; but wide-flitting Rumour
had already borne it round among the Ausonian cities,
when the children of Laomedon moored their fleet to the
grassy slope of the river bank.

Aeneas, with the foremost of his captains and fair
Iülus, lay them down under the boughs of a high tree and
array the feast. They spread wheaten cakes along the
sward under their meats—so Jove on high prompted—and
crown the platter of corn with wilding fruits. Here haply
when the rest was spent, and scantness of food set them to
eat their thin bread, and with hand and venturous teeth do
violence to the round cakes fraught with fate and spare not
the flattened squares : *Ha ! Are we eating our tables too ?*
cries Iülus jesting, and stops. At once that accent heard
set their toils a limit ; and at once as he spoke his father
caught it from his lips and hushed him, in amazement at the
omen. Straightway 'Hail, O land !' he cries, 'my destined
inheritance ! and hail, O household gods, faithful to your
Troy ! here is home ; this is our native country. For my
father Anchises, now I remember it, bequeathed me this
secret of fate : "When hunger shall drive thee, O son, to
consume thy tables where the feast fails, on the unknown
shores whither thou shalt sail ; then, though outwearied,
hope for home, and there at last let thine hand remember
to set thy house's foundations and bulwarks." This was

the hunger, this the last that awaited us, to set the promised
end to our desolations . . . Up then, and, glad with the first
sunbeam, let us explore and search all abroad from our
harbour, what is the country, who its habitants, where is
the town of the nation. Now pour your cups to Jove, and
call in prayer on Anchises our father, setting the wine again
upon the board.' So speaks he, and binding his brows
with a leafy bough, he makes supplication to the Genius of
the ground, and Earth first of deities, and the Nymphs,
and the Rivers yet unknown; then calls on Night and
Night's rising signs, and next on Jove of Ida, and our lady
of Phrygia, and on his twain parents, in heaven and in the
under world. At this the Lord omnipotent thrice thundered sharp from high heaven, and with his own hand
shook out for a sign in the sky a cloud ablaze with luminous shafts of gold. A sudden rumour spreads among the
Trojan array, that the day is come to found their destined
city. Emulously they renew the feast, and, glad at the high
omen, array the flagons and engarland the wine.

Soon as the morrow bathed the lands in its dawning
light, they part to search out the town, and the borders
and shores of the nation : these are the pools and spring of
Numicus ; this is the Tiber river; here dwell the brave
Latins. Then the seed of Anchises commands an hundred
envoys chosen of every degree to go to the stately royal
city, all with the wreathed boughs of Pallas, to bear him
gifts and desire grace for the Teucrians. Without delay
they hasten on their message, and advance with swift
step. Himself he traces the city walls with a shallow
trench, and builds on it; and in fashion of a camp girdles
this first settlement on the shore with mound and battlements. And now his men had traversed their way ; they
espied the towers and steep roofs of the Latins, and drew
near the wall. Before the city boys and men in their early

bloom exercise on horseback, and break in their teams on
the dusty ground, or draw ringing bows, or hurl tough
javelins from the shoulder, and contend in running and
boxing : when a messenger riding forward brings news to
the ears of the aged King that mighty men are come thither
in unknown raiment. He gives orders to call them within
his house, and takes his seat in the midst on his ancestral
throne. His house, stately and vast, crowned the city,
upreared on an hundred columns, once the palace of
Laurentian Picus, amid awful groves of ancestral sanctity.
Here their kings receive the inaugural sceptre, and have
the fasces first raised before them ; this temple was their
senate-house ; this their sacred banqueting-hall ; here, after
sacrifice of rams, the elders were wont to sit down at long
tables. Further, there stood arow in the entry images of the
forefathers of old in ancient cedar, Italus, and lord Sabinus,
planter of the vine, still holding in show the curved prun-
ing-hook, and gray Saturn, and the likeness of Janus the
double-facing, and the rest of their primal kings, and they
who had borne wounds of war in fighting for their country.
Armour besides hangs thickly on the sacred doors, captured
chariots and curved axes, helmet-crests and massy gateway-
bars, lances and shields, and beaks torn from warships.
He too sat there, with the divining-rod of Quirinus, girt
in the short augural gown, and carrying on his left arm the
sacred shield, Picus the tamer of horses ; he whom Circe,
desperate with amorous desire, smote with her golden rod
and turned by her poisons into a bird with patches of
colour on his wings. Of such wise was the temple of the
gods wherein Latinus, sitting on his father's seat, summoned
the Teucrians to his house and presence ; and when they
entered in, he thus opened with placid mien :

'Tell, O Dardanians, for we are not ignorant of your
city and race, nor unheard of do you bend your course

overseas, what seek you? what the cause or whereof the
need that hath borne you over all these blue waterways to
the Ausonian shore? Whether wandering in your course,
or tempest-driven (such perils manifold on the high seas do
sailors suffer), you have entered the river banks and lie in
harbour; shun not our welcome, and be not ignorant that
the Latins are Saturn's people, whom no laws fetter to
justice, upright of their own free will and the custom of the
god of old. And now I remember, though the story is
dimmed with years, thus Auruncan elders told, how Dardanus, born in this our country, made his way to the towns
of Phrygian Ida and to the Thracian Samos that is now
called Samothrace. Here was the home he left, Tyrrhenian
Corythus; now the palace of heaven, glittering with golden
stars, enthrones and adds him to the ranged altars of
the gods.'

He ended; and Ilioneus pursued his speech with these
words:

'King, Faunus' illustrious progeny, neither hath black
tempest driven us with stress of waves to shelter in your
lands, nor hath star or shore misled us on the way we went.
Of set purpose and willing mind do we draw nigh this thy
city, outcasts from a realm once the greatest that the sun
looked on as he came from Olympus' utmost border. From
Jove hath our race beginning; in Jove the men of Dardania
rejoice as ancestor; our King himself of Jove's supreme
race, Aeneas of Troy, hath sent us to thy courts. How
terrible the tempest that burst from fierce Mycenae over
the plains of Ida, driven by what fate Europe and Asia
met in the shock of two worlds, even he hath heard who is
sundered in the utmost land where the ocean surge recoils,
and he whom stretching midmost of the four zones the
zone of the intolerable sun holds in severance. Borne by
that flood over many desolate seas, we crave a scant dwell-

ing for our country's gods, an unmolested landing-place,
and the air and water that are free to all. We shall not
disgrace the kingdom ; nor will the rumour of your renown
be lightly gone or the grace of all you have done fade away;
nor will Ausonia be sorry to have taken Troy to her breast.
By the fortunes of Aeneas I swear, by that right hand
mighty, whether tried in friendship or in warlike arms, many
and many a people and nation—scorn us not because we
advance with hands proffering chaplets and words of supplication—hath sought us for itself and desired our alliance ;
but yours is the land that heaven's high ordinance drove us
forth to find. Hence sprung Dardanus: hither Apollo recalls
us, and pushes us on with imperious orders to Tyrrhenian
Tiber and the holy pools of Numicus' spring. Further, he
presents to thee these small guerdons of our past estate,
relics saved from burning Troy. From this gold did lord
Anchises pour libation at the altars ; this was Priam's array
when he delivered statutes to the nations assembled in
order ; the sceptre, the sacred mitre, the raiment wrought
by the women of Ilium. . . .'

At these words of Ilioneus Latinus holds his countenance in a steady gaze, and stays motionless on the floor,
casting his intent eyes around. Nor does the embroidered
purple so move the King, nor the sceptre of Priam, as
his daughter's marriage and the bridal chamber absorb
him, and the oracle of ancient Faunus stirs deep in his
heart. This is he, the wanderer from a foreign home, fore-
shewn of fate for his son, and called to a realm of equal
dominion, whose race should be excellent in valour and
their might overbear all the world. At last he speaks with
good cheer :

'The gods prosper our undertaking and their own
augury ! What thou desirest, Trojan, shall be given ; nor
do I spurn your gifts. While Latinus reigns you shall not

lack foison of rich land nor Troy's own riches. Only let
Aeneas himself come hither, if desire of us be so strong, if
he be in haste to join our friendship and be called our ally.
Let him not shrink in terror from a friendly face. A term
of the peace for me shall be to touch your monarch's hand.
Do you now convey in answer my message to your King.
I have a daughter whom the oracles of my father's shrine
and many a celestial token alike forbid me to unite to one
of our own nation ; sons shall come, they prophesy, from
foreign coasts, such is the destiny of Latium, whose blood
shall exalt our name to heaven. He it is on whom fate
calls ; this I think, this I choose, if there be any truth in
my soul's foreshadowing.'

Thus he speaks, and chooses horses for all the company. Three hundred stood sleek in their high stalls ; for
all the Teucrians in order he straightway commands them
to be led forth, fleet-footed, covered with embroidered
purple : golden chains hang drooping over their chests,
golden their housings, and they champ on bits of ruddy
gold : for the absent Aeneas a chariot and pair of chariot
horses of celestial breed, with nostrils breathing flame ; of
the race of those which subtle Circe bred by sleight on her
father, the bastard issue of a stolen union. With these
gifts and words the Aeneadae ride back from Latinus
carrying peace.

And lo ! the fierce wife of Jove was returning from
Inachian Argos, and held her way along the air, when out
of the distant sky, far as from Sicilian Pachynus, she espied
the rejoicing of Aeneas and the Dardanian fleet. She sees
them already house-building, already trusting in the land,
their ships left empty. She stops, shot with sharp pain ;
then shaking her head, she pours forth these words :

'Ah, hated brood, and doom of the Phrygians that
thwarts our doom ! Could they perish on the Sigean

plains? Could they be ensnared when taken? Did the
fires of Troy consume her people? Through the midst of
armies and through the midst of flames they have found
their way. But, I think, my deity lies at last outwearied,
or my hatred sleeps and is satisfied? Nay, it is I who
have been fierce to follow them over the waves when
hurled from their country, and on all the seas have crossed
their flight. Against the Teucrians the forces of sky and
sea are spent. What hath availed me Syrtes or Scylla,
what desolate Charybdis? they find shelter in their desired
Tiber-bed, careless of ocean and of me. Mars availed to
destroy the giant race of the Lapithae; the very father of
the gods gave over ancient Calydon to Diana's wrath:
for forfeit of what crime in the Lapithae, what in Calydon?
But I, Jove's imperial consort, who have borne, ah me!
to leave naught undared, who have shifted to every device,
I am vanquished by Aeneas. If my deity is not great
enough, I will not assuredly falter to seek succour where
it may be; if the powers of heaven are inflexible, I will
stir up Acheron. It may not be to debar him of a Latin
realm; well; and Lavinia is destined his bride unalterably.
But it may be yet to defer, to make all this action linger;
but it may be yet to waste away the nation of either king;
at such forfeit of their people may son-in-law and father-in-
law enter into union. Blood of Troy and Rutulia shall be
thy dower, O maiden, and Bellona is the bridesmaid who
awaits thee. Nor did Cisseus' daughter alone conceive a
firebrand and travail of bridal flames. Nay, even such a
birth hath Venus of her own, a second Paris, another bale-
fire for Troy towers reborn.'

These words uttered, she descends to earth in all her
terrors, and calls dolorous Allecto from the home of the
Fatal Sisters in nether gloom, whose delight is in woeful
wars, in wrath and treachery and evil feuds: hateful to

lord Pluto himself, hateful and horrible to her hell-born sisters; into so many faces does she turn, so savage the guise of each, so thick and black bristles she with vipers. And her Juno spurs on with words, saying thus :

'Grant me, virgin born of Night, this thy proper task and service, that the rumour of our renown may not crumble away, nor the Aeneadae have power to win Latinus by marriage or beset the borders of Italy. Thou canst set brothers once united in armed conflict, and overturn families with hatreds; thou canst launch into houses thy whips and deadly brands; thine are a thousand names, a thousand devices of injury. Stir up thy teeming breast, sunder the peace they have joined, and sow seeds of quarrel; let all at once desire and demand and seize on arms.'

Thereon Allecto, steeped in Gorgonian venom, first seeks Latium and the high house of the Laurentine monarch, and silently sits down before Amata's doors, whom a woman's distress and anger heated to frenzy over the Teucrians' coming and the marriage of Turnus. At her the goddess flings a snake out of her dusky tresses, and slips it into her bosom to her very inmost heart, that she may embroil all her house under its maddening magic. Sliding between her raiment and smooth breasts, it coils without touch, and instils its viperous breath unseen; the great serpent turns into the twisted gold about her neck, turns into the long ribbon of her chaplet, inweaves her hair, and winds slippery over her body. And while the gliding infection of the clammy poison begins to penetrate her sense and run in fire through her frame, nor as yet hath all her breast caught fire, softly she spoke and in mothers' wonted wise, with many a tear over her daughter and the Phrygian bridal :

'Is it to exiles, to Teucrians, that Lavinia is proffered in marriage, O father? and hast thou no compassion on

thy daughter and on thyself? no compassion on her
mother, whom with the first northern wind the treacherous
rover will abandon, steering to sea with his maiden prize?
Is it not thus the Phrygian herdsman wound his way to
Lacedaemon, and carried Leda's Helen to the Trojan
towns? Where is thy plighted faith? Where thine ancient
care for thy people, and the hand Turnus thy kinsman hath
so often clasped? If one of alien race from the Latins is
sought for our son, if this stands fixed, and thy father
Faunus' commands are heavy upon thee, all the land whose
freedom severs it from our sway is to my mind alien, and
of this is the divine word. And Turnus, if one retrace the
earliest source of his line, is born of Inachus and Acrisius,
and of the midmost of Mycenae.'

When in this vain essay of words she sees Latinus fixed
against her, and the serpent's maddening poison is sunk
deep in her vitals and runs through and through her, then
indeed, stung by infinite horrors, hapless and frenzied, she
rages wildly through the endless city. As whilome a top
flying under the twisted whipcord, which boys busy at their
play drive circling wide round an empty hall, runs before
the lash and spins in wide gyrations; the witless ungrown
band hang wondering over it and admire the whirling boxwood; the strokes lend it life: with pace no slacker is she
borne midway through towns and valiant nations. Nay,
she flies into the woodland under feigned Bacchic influence,
assumes a greater guilt, arouses a greater frenzy, and hides
her daughter in the mountain coverts to rob the Teucrians
of their bridal and stay the marriage torches. 'Hail,
Bacchus!' she shrieks and clamours; 'thou only art worthy
of the maiden; for to thee she takes up the lissom wands,
thee she circles in the dance, to thee she trains and con-
secrates her tresses.' Rumour flies abroad; and the
matrons, their breasts kindled by the furies, run all at once

with a single ardour to seek out strange dwellings. They have left their homes empty, they throw neck and hair free to the winds; while others fill the air with ringing cries, girt about with fawnskins, and carrying spears of vine. Amid them the infuriate queen holds her blazing pine-torch on high, and chants the wedding of Turnus and her daughter; and rolling her bloodshot gaze, cries sudden and harsh: 'Hear, O mothers of Latium, wheresoever you be; if unhappy Amata hath yet any favour in your affection, if care for a mother's right pierces you, untie the chaplets from your hair, begin the orgies with me.' Thus, amid woods and wild beasts' solitary places, does Allecto goad the queen with the encircling Bacchic madness.

When their frenzy seemed heightened and her first task complete, the purpose and all the house of Latinus turned upside down, the dolorous goddess flies on thence, soaring on dusky wing, to the walls of the gallant Rutulian, the city which Danaë, they say, borne down on the boister-ous south wind, built and planted with Acrision's people. The place was called Ardea once of old; and still Ardea remains a mighty name; but its fortune is no more. Here in his high house Turnus now took rest in the black mid-night. Allecto puts off her grim feature and the body of a Fury; she transforms her face to an aged woman's, and furrows her brow with ugly wrinkles; she puts on white tresses chaplet-bound, and entwines them with an olive spray; she becomes aged Calybe, priestess of Juno's temple, and presents herself before his eyes, uttering thus:

'Turnus, wilt thou brook all these toils poured out in vain, and the conveyance of thy crown to Dardanian settlers? The King denies thee thy bride and the dower thy blood had earned; and a foreigner is sought for heir to the kingdom. Forth now, dupe, and face thankless perils; forth, cut down the Tyrrhenian lines; give the

Latins peace in thy protection. This Saturn's omnipotent daughter in very presence commanded me to pronounce to thee, as thou wert lying in the still night. Wherefore arise, and make ready with good cheer to arm thy people and march through thy gates to battle; consume those Phrygian captains that lie with their painted hulls in the beautiful river. All the force of heaven orders thee on. Let King Latinus himself know of it, unless he consents to give thee thy bridal, and abide by his words, when he shall at last make proof of Turnus' arms.'

But he, deriding her inspiration, with the words of his mouth thus answers her again :

'The fleets ride on the Tiber wave; that news hath not, as thou deemest, escaped mine ears. Frame not such terrors before me. Neither is Queen Juno forgetful of us. . . . But thee, O mother, overworn old age, exhausted and untrue, frets with vain distress, and amid embattled kings mocks thy presage with false dismay. Thy charge it is to keep the divine image and temple; war and peace shall be in the hands of men and warriors.'

At such words Allecto's wrath blazed out. But amid his utterance a quick shudder overruns his limbs; his eyes are fixed in horror; so thickly hiss the snakes of the Fury, so vast her form expands. Then rolling her fiery eyes, she thrust him back as he would stammer out more, raised two serpents in her hair, and, sounding her whip, resumed with furious tone :

'Behold me the overworn ! me whom old age, exhausted and untrue, mocks with false dismay amid embattled kings ! Look on this ! I am come from the home of the Dread Sisters : war and death are in my hand. . . .'

So speaking, she hurled her torch at him, and pierced his breast with the lurid smoking brand. He breaks from sleep in overpowering fear, his limbs and body bathed in sweat that breaks out all over him; he shrieks madly for arms, searches for arms on his bed and in his palace. The passion of the sword rages high, the accursed fury of war, and wrath over all : even as when flaming sticks are heaped roaring loud under the sides of a seething cauldron, and the boiling water leaps up; the river of water within smokes furiously and swells high in overflowing foam, and now the wave contains itself no longer; the dark steam flies aloft. So, for the stain of the broken peace, he orders his chief warriors to march on King Latinus, and bids prepare for battle, to defend Italy and drive the foe from their borders ; himself will suffice for Trojans and Latins together. When he uttered these words and called the gods to hear his vows, the Rutulians stir one another up to arms. One is moved by the splendour of his youthful beauty, one by his royal ancestry, another by the noble deeds of his hand.

While Turnus fills the Rutulian minds with valour, Allecto on Stygian wing hastens towards the Trojans. With fresh wiles she marked the spot where beautiful Iülus was trapping and coursing game on the bank; here the infernal maiden suddenly crosses his hounds with the maddening touch of a familiar scent, and drives them hotly on the stag-hunt. This was the source and spring of ill, and kindled the country-folk to war. The stag, beautiful and high-antlered, was stolen from his mother's udder and bred by Tyrrheus' boys and their father Tyrrheus, master of the royal herds, and ranger of the plain. Their sister Silvia tamed him to her rule, and lavished her care on his adornment, twining his antlers with delicate garlands, and combed his wild coat and washed him in the clear spring. Tame to her hand, and familiar to his master's table, he would wander the woods, and, however late the night, return home to the door he knew. Far astray, he floated idly down the stream, and allayed his heat on the green bank, when Iülus'

mad hounds started him in their hunting; and Ascanius
himself, kindled with desire of the chief honour, aimed a
shaft from his bended bow. A present deity suffered not
his hand to stray, and the loud whistling reed came driven
through his belly and flanks. But the wounded beast fled
within the familiar roof and crept moaning to the courtyard,
dabbled with blood, and filling all the house with moans as
of one beseeching. Sister Silvia, smiting her arms with
open hands, begins to call for aid, and gathers the hardy
rustics with her cries. They, for a fell destroyer is hidden
in the silent woodland, are there before her expectation,
one armed with a stake hardened in the fire, one with a
heavy knotted trunk; what each one searches and finds,
wrath turns into a weapon. Tyrrheus cheers on his array,
panting hard, with his axe caught up in his hand, as he was
haply splitting an oaken log in four clefts with cross-driven
wedges.

But the grim goddess, seizing from her watch-tower the
moment of mischief, seeks the steep farm-roof and sounds
the pastoral war-note from the ridge, straining the infernal
cry on her twisted horn; it spread shuddering over all the
woodland, and echoed through the deep forests: the lake
of Trivia heard it afar; Nar river heard it with white sul-
phurous water, and the springs of Velinus; and fluttered
mothers clasped their children to their breast. Then, hurrying to the voice of the terrible trumpet-note, on all sides
the wild rustics snatch their arms and stream in: therewithal the men of Troy pour out from their camp's open
gates to succour Ascanius. The lines are ranged; not now
in rustic strife do they fight with hard trunks or burned
stakes; the two-edged steel sways the fight, the broad corn-
fields bristle dark with drawn swords, and brass flashes
smitten by the sunlight, and casts a gleam high into the
cloudy air: as when the wind begins to blow and the flood

to whiten, gradually the sea lifts his waves higher and yet
higher, then rises from the bottom right into the air.   Here
in the front rank young Almo, once Tyrrheus' eldest son,
is struck down by a whistling arrow; for the wound, staying
in his throat, cut off in blood the moist voice's passage and
the thin life.   Around many a one lies dead, aged Galaesus
among them, slain as he throws himself between them for a
peacemaker, once incomparable in justice and wealth of
Ausonian fields; for him five flocks bleated, a five-fold herd
returned from pasture, and an hundred ploughs upturned
the soil.

But while thus in even battle they fight on the broad
plain, the goddess, her promise fulfilled, when she hath
dyed the war in blood, and mingled death in the first
encounter, quits Hesperia, and, glancing through the sky,
addresses Juno in exultant tone:

'Lo, discord is ripened at thy desire into baleful war:
tell them now to mix in amity and join alliance.   Insomuch
as I have imbued the Trojans in Ausonian blood, this
likewise will I add, if I have assurance of thy will.   With
my rumours I will sweep the bordering towns into war,
and kindle their spirit with furious desire for battle, that
from all quarters help may come; I will sow the land with
arms.'

Then Juno answering: 'Terror and harm is wrought
abundantly.   The springs of war are aflow: they fight with
arms in their grasp, the arms that chance first supplied, that
fresh blood stains.   Let this be the union, this the bridal
that Venus' illustrious progeny and Latinus the King shall
celebrate.   Our Lord who reigns on Olympus' summit
would not have thee stray too freely in heaven's upper air.
Withdraw thy presence.   Whatsoever future remains in the
struggle, that I myself will sway.'

Such accents uttered the daughter of Saturn; and the

other raises her rustling snaky wings and darts away from
the high upper air to Cocytus her home. There is a place
midmost of Italy, deep in the hills, notable and famed of
rumour in many a country, the Vale of Amsanctus; on
either hand a wooded ridge, dark with thick foliage, hems
it in, and midway a torrent in swirling eddies shivers and
echoes over the rocks. Here is shewn a ghastly pool, a
breathing-hole of the grim lord of hell, and a vast chasm
breaking into Acheron yawns with pestilential throat. In it
the Fury sank, and relieved earth and heaven of her hateful
influence.

But therewithal the queenly daughter of Saturn puts the
last touch to war. The shepherds pour in full tale from
the battlefield into the town, bearing back their slain, the
boy Almo and Galaesus' disfigured face, and cry on the gods
and call on Latinus. Turnus is there, and amid the heat
and outcry at the slaughter redoubles his terrors, crying that
Teucrians are bidden to the kingdom, that a Phrygian race
is mingling its taint with theirs, and he is thrust out of their
gates. They too, the matrons of whose kin, struck by
Bacchus, trample in choirs down the pathless woods—nor
is Amata's name a little thing—they too gather together
from all sides and weary themselves with the battle-cry.
Omens and oracles of gods go down before them, and all
under malign influence clamour for awful war. Emulously
they surround Latinus' royal house. He withstands, even
as a rock in ocean unremoved, as a rock in ocean when the
great crash comes down, firm in its own mass among many
waves slapping all about: in vain the crags and boulders
hiss round it in foam, and the seaweed on its side is flung
up and sucked away. But when he may in nowise overbear their blind counsel, and all goes at fierce Juno's beck,
with many an appeal to gods and void sky, ' Alas! ' he
cries, ' we are broken of fate and driven helpless in the

storm. With your very blood will you pay the price of
this, O wretched men! Thee, O Turnus, thy crime, thee
thine awful punishment shall await; too late wilt thou
address to heaven thy prayers and supplication. For my
rest was won, and my haven full at hand; I am robbed but
of a happy death.' And without further speech he shut
himself in the palace, and dropped the reins of state.

There was a use in Hesperian Latium, which the Alban
towns kept in holy observance, now Rome keeps, the mistress of the world, when they stir the War-God to enter
battle; whether their hands prepare to carry war and
weeping among Getae or Hyrcanians or Arabs, or to reach
to India and pursue the Dawn, and reclaim their standards
from the Parthian. There are twain gates of War, so runs
their name, consecrate in grim Mars' sanctity and terror.
An hundred bolts of brass and masses of everlasting iron
shut them fast, and Janus the guardian never sets foot from
their threshold. There, when the sentence of the Fathers
stands fixed for battle, the Consul, arrayed in the robe of
Quirinus and the Gabine cincture, with his own hand un-
bars the grating doors, with his own lips calls battles forth;
then all the rest follow on, and the brazen trumpets blare
harsh with consenting breath. With this use then likewise
they bade Latinus proclaim war on the Aeneadae, and unclose
the baleful gates. He withheld his hand, and shrank away
averse from the abhorred service, and hid himself blindly
in the dark. Then the Saturnian queen of heaven glided
from the sky, with her own hand thrust open the lingering
gates, and swung sharply back on their hinges the iron-
bound doors of war. Ausonia is ablaze, till then unstirred
and immoveable. Some make ready to march afoot over
the plains; some, mounted on tall horses, ride amain in
clouds of dust. All seek out arms; and now they rub
their shields smooth and make their spearheads glitter with

fat lard, and grind their axes on the whetstone : rejoicingly
they advance under their standards and hear the trumpet
note. Five great cities set up the anvil and sharpen the
sword, strong Atina and proud Tibur, Ardea and Crustu-
meri, and turreted Antemnae. They hollow out head-gear
to guard them, and plait wickerwork round shield-bosses;
others forge breastplates of brass or smooth greaves of flexible
silver. To this is come the honour of share and pruning-
hook, to this all the love of the plough : they re-temper
their fathers' swords in the furnace. And now the trumpets blare; the watchword for war passes along. One
snatches a helmet hurriedly from his house, another backs
his neighing horses into the yoke ; and arrays himself in
shield and mail-coat triple-linked with gold, and girds on
his trusty sword.

Open now the gates of Helicon, goddesses, and stir the
song of the kings that rose for war, the array that followed
each and filled the plains, the men that even then blossomed,
the arms that blazed in Italy the bountiful land : for you
remember, divine ones, and you can recall ; to us but a
breath of rumour, scant and slight, is wafted down.

First from the Tyrrhene coast savage Mezentius, scorner
of the gods, opens the war and arrays his columns. By
him is Lausus, his son, unexcelled in bodily beauty by any
save Laurentine Turnus, Lausus tamer of horses and destroyer of wild beasts; he leads a thousand men who
followed him in vain from Agylla town ; worthy to be
happier in ancestral rule, and to have other than Mezentius
for father.

After them beautiful Aventinus, born of beautiful Hercules, displays on the sward his palm-crowned chariot and
victorious horses, and carries on his shield his father's
device, the hundred snakes of the Hydra's serpent-wreath.
Him, in the wood of the hill Aventine, Rhea the priestess

bore by stealth into the borders of light, a woman mingled with a god, after the Tirynthian Conqueror had slain Geryon and set foot on the fields of Laurentum, and bathed his Iberian oxen in the Tuscan river. These carry for war javelins and grim stabbing weapons, and fight with the round shaft and sharp point of the Sabellian pike. Himself he went on foot swathed in a vast lion skin, shaggy with bristling terrors, whose white teeth encircled his head ; in such wild dress, the garb of Hercules clasped over his shoulders, he entered the royal house.

Next twin brothers leave Tibur town, and the people called by their brother Tiburtus' name, Catillus and valiant Coras, the Argives, and advance in the forefront of battle among the throng of spears : as when two cloud-born Centaurs descend from a lofty mountain peak, leaving Homole or snowy Othrys in rapid race ; the mighty forest yields before them as they go, and the crashing thickets give them way.

Nor was the founder of Praeneste city absent, the king who, as every age hath believed, was born of Vulcan among the pasturing herds, and found beside the hearth, Caeculus. On him a rustic battalion attends in loose order, they who dwell in steep Praeneste and the fields of Juno of Gabii, on the cool Anio and the Hernican rocks dewy with streams; they whom rich Anagnia, and whom thou, lord Amasenus, pasturest. Not all of them have armour, nor shields and clattering chariots. The most part shower bullets of dull lead ; some wield in their hand two darts, and have for head-covering caps of tawny wolfskin ; their left foot is bare wherewith to plant their steps ; the other is covered with a boot of raw hide.

But Messapus, tamer of horses, the seed of Neptune, whom none might ever strike down with steel or fire, calls quickly to arms his long unstirred peoples and bands dis-

used to war, and again handles the sword. These are of
the Fescennine ranks and of Aequi Falisci, these of Soracte's
fortresses and the fields of Flavina, and Ciminus' lake and
hill, and the groves of Capena. They marched in even
time, singing their King; as whilome snowy swans among
the thin clouds, when they return from pasturage, and utter
resonant notes through their long necks ; far off echoes the
river and the smitten Asian fen. . . . Nor would one think
these vast streaming masses were ranks clad in brass; rather
that, high in air, a cloud of hoarse birds from the deep gulf
was pressing to the shore.

Lo, Clausus of the ancient Sabine blood, leading a
great host, a great host himself; from whom now the
Claudian tribe and family is spread abroad since Rome
was shared with the Sabines. Alongside is the broad battalion of Amiternum, and the Old Latins, and all the force
of Eretum and the Mutuscan oliveyards ; they who dwell in
Nomentum town, and the Rosean country by Velinus, who
keep the crags of rough Tetrica and Mount Severus, Cas-
peria and Foruli, and the river of Himella; they who drink
of Tiber and Fabaris, they whom cold Nursia hath sent,
and the squadrons of Horta and the tribes of Latinium ;
and they whom Allia, the ill-ominous name, severs with its
current ; as many as the waves that roll on the Libyan sea-
floor when fierce Orion sets in the wintry surge ; as thick
as the ears that ripen in the morning sunlight on the plain
of the Hermus or the yellowing Lycian tilth. Their shields
clatter, and earth is amazed under the trampling of their
feet.

Here Agamemnonian Halaesus, foe of the Trojan name,
yokes his chariot horses, and draws a thousand warlike
peoples to Turnus ; those who turn with spades the Massic
soil that is glad with wine ; whom the elders of Aurunca
sent from their high hills, and the Sidicine low country

hard by ; and those who leave Cales, and the dweller by the shallows of Volturnus river, and side by side the rough Saticulan and the Oscan bands. Polished maces are their weapons, and these it is their wont to fit with a tough thong ; a target covers their left side, and for close fighting they have crooked swords.

Nor shalt thou, Oebalus, depart untold of in our verses, who wast borne, men say, by the nymph Sebethis to Telon, when he grew old in rule over Capreae the Teleboïc realm : but not so content with his ancestral fields, his son even then held down in wide sway the Sarrastian peoples and the meadows watered by Sarnus, and the dwellers in Rufrae and Batulum, and the fields of Celemnae, and they on whom from her apple orchards Abella city looks down. Their wont was to hurl lances in Teutonic fashion ; their head covering was stripped bark of the cork tree, their shield-plates glittering brass, glittering brass their sword.

Thee too, Ufens, mountainous Nersae sent forth to battle, of noble fame and prosperous arms, whose race on the stiff Aequiculan clods is rough beyond all other, and bred to continual hunting in the woodland ; they till the soil in arms, and it is ever their delight to drive in fresh spoils and live on plunder.

Furthermore there came, sent by King Archippus, the priest of the Marruvian people, dressed with prosperous olive leaves over his helmet, Umbro excellent in valour, who was wont with charm and touch to sprinkle slumberous dew on the viper's brood and water-snakes of noisome breath. Yet he availed not to heal the stroke of the Dar-danian spear-point, nor was the wound of him helped by his sleepy charms and herbs culled on the Massic hills. Thee the woodland of Angitia, thee Fucinus' glassy wave, thee the clear pools wept. . . .

Likewise the seed of Hippolytus marched to war, Virbius

most excellent in beauty, sent by his mother Aricia. The
groves of Egeria nursed him round the spongy shore where
Diana's altar stands rich and gracious. For they say in
story that Hippolytus, after he fell by his stepmother's
treachery, torn asunder by his frightened horses to fulfil a
father's revenge, came again to the daylight and heaven's
upper air, recalled by Diana's love and the drugs of the
Healer. Then the Lord omnipotent, indignant that any
mortal should rise from the nether shades to the light of
life, launched his thunder and hurled down to the Stygian
water the Phoebus-born, the discoverer of such craft and
cure. But Trivia the bountiful hides Hippolytus in a secret
habitation, and sends him away to the nymph Egeria and
the woodland's keeping, where, solitary in Italian forests, he
should spend an inglorious life, and have Virbius for his
altered name. Whence also hoofed horses are kept away
from Trivia's temple and consecrated groves, because,
affrighted at the portents of the sea, they overset the chariot
and flung him out upon the shore. Notwithstanding did
his son train his ruddy steeds on the level plain, and sped
charioted to war.

Himself too among the foremost, splendid in beauty
of body, Turnus moves armed and towers a whole head over
all. His lofty helmet, triple-tressed with horse-hair, holds
high a Chimaera breathing from her throat Aetnean fires,
raging the more and exasperate with baleful flames, as the
battle and bloodshed grow fiercer. But on his polished
shield was emblazoned in gold Io with uplifted horns,
already a heifer and overgrown with hair, a lofty design,
and Argus the maiden's warder, and lord Inachus pouring
his stream from his embossed urn. Behind comes a cloud
of infantry, and shielded columns thicken over all the plains;
the Argive men and Auruncan forces, the Rutulians and
old Sicanians, the Sacranian ranks and Labicians with

painted shields; they who till thy dells, O Tiber, and Numicus' sacred shore, and whose ploughshare goes up and down on the Rutulian hills and the Circaean headland, over whose fields Jupiter of Anxur watches, and Feronia glad in her greenwood: and where the marsh of Satura lies black, and cold Ufens winds his way along the valley-bottoms and sinks into the sea.

Therewithal came Camilla the Volscian, leading a train of cavalry, squadrons splendid with brass: a warrior maiden who had never used her woman's hands to Minerva's distaff or wool-baskets, but hardened to endure the battle shock and outstrip the winds with racing feet. She might have flown across the topmost blades of unmown corn and left the tender ears unhurt as she ran; or sped her way over mid sea upborne by the swelling flood, nor dipt her swift feet in the water. All the people pour from house and field, and mothers crowd to wonder and gaze at her as she goes, in rapturous astonishment at the royal lustre of purple that drapes her smooth shoulders, at the clasp of gold that intertwines her tresses, at the Lycian quiver she carries, and the pastoral myrtle shaft topped with steel.

BOOK EIGHTH

THE EMBASSAGE TO EVANDER

WHEN Turnus ran up the flag of war on the towers of
Laurentum, and the trumpets blared with harsh music,
when he spurred his fiery steeds and clashed his armour,
straightway men's hearts are in tumult; all Latium
at once flutters in banded uprisal, and her warriors rage
furiously. Their chiefs, Messapus, and Ufens, and Mezentius, scorner of the gods, begin to enrol forces on all sides,
and dispeople the wide fields of husbandmen. Venulus
too is sent to the town of mighty Diomede to seek succour,
to instruct him that Teucrians set foot in Latium; that
Aeneas in his fleet invades them with the vanquished gods
of his home, and proclaims himself the King summoned of
fate; that many tribes join the Dardanian, and his name
swells high in Latium. What he will rear on these foundations, what issue of battle he desires, if Fortune attend him,
lies clearer to his own sight than to King Turnus or King
Latinus.

Thus was it in Latium. And the hero of Laomedon's
blood, seeing it all, tosses on a heavy surge of care, and
throws his mind rapidly this way and that, and turns it on
all hands in swift change of thought: even as when the
quivering light of water brimming in brass, struck back

from the sunlight or the moon's glittering reflection, flickers abroad over all the room, and now mounts aloft and strikes the high panelled roof. Night fell, and over all lands weary creatures were fast in deep slumber, the race of fowl and of cattle; when lord Aeneas, sick at heart of the dismal warfare, stretched him on the river bank under the cope of the cold sky, and let sleep, though late, overspread his limbs. To him the very god of the ground, the pleasant Tiber stream, seemed to raise his aged form among the poplar boughs; thin lawn veiled him with its gray covering, and shadowy reeds hid his hair. Thereon he addressed him thus, and with these words allayed his distresses:

'O born of the family of the gods, thou who bearest back our Trojan city from hostile hands, and keepest Troy towers in eternal life; O long looked for on Laurentine ground and Latin fields! here is thine assured home, thine home's assured gods. Draw not thou back, nor be alarmed by menace of war. All the anger and wrath of the gods is passed away . . . And even now for thine · assurance, that thou think not this the idle fashioning of sleep, a great sow shall be found lying under the oaks on the shore, with her new-born litter of thirty head: white she couches on the ground, and the brood about her teats is white. By this token in thirty revolving years shall Ascanius found a city, Alba of bright name. My prophecy is sure. Now hearken, and I will briefly instruct thee how thou mayest unravel and overcome thy present task. An Arcadian people sprung of Pallas, following in their king Evander's company beneath his banners, have chosen a place in these coasts, and set a city on the hills, called Pallanteum after Pallas their forefather. These wage perpetual war with the Latin race; these do thou take to thy camp's alliance, and join with them in league. Myself I will lead thee by my banks and straight along my stream, that thou mayest oar thy way upward against the river. Up and arise, goddess-born, and even with the setting stars address thy prayers to Juno as is meet, and vanquish her wrath and menaces with humble vows. To me thou shalt pay a conqueror's sacrifice. I am he whom thou seest washing the banks with full flood and severing the rich tilth, glassy Tiber, best beloved by heaven of rivers. Here is my stately home; my fountain-head is among high cities.'

Thus spoke the River, and sank in the depth of the pool: night and sleep left Aeneas. He arises, and, looking towards the radiant sky of the sunrising, holds up water from the river in fitly-hollowed palms, and pours to heaven these accents :

Nymphs, Laurentine Nymphs, from whom is the generation of rivers, and thou, O father Tiber, with thine holy flood, receive Aeneas and deign to save him out of danger. What pool soever holds thy source, who pitiest our discomforts, from whatsoever soil thou dost spring excellent in beauty, ever shall my worship, ever my gifts frequent thee, the hornèd river lord of Hesperian waters. Ah, be thou only by me, and graciously confirm thy will.' So speaks he, and chooses two galleys from his fleet, and mans them with rowers, and withal equips a crew with arms.

And lo! suddenly, ominous and wonderful to tell, the milk-white sow, of one colour with her white brood, is espied through the forest couched on the green brink; whom to thee, yes to thee, queenly Juno, good Aeneas offers in sacrifice, and sets with her offspring before thine altar. All that night long Tiber assuaged his swelling stream, and silently stayed his refluent wave, smoothing the surface of his waters to the fashion of still pool and quiet mere, to spare

labour to the oar. So they set out and speed on their way
with prosperous cries; the painted fir slides along the water-
way; the waves and unwonted woods marvel at their far-
gleaming shields, and the gay hulls afloat on the river.
They outwear a night and a day in rowing, ascend the long
reaches, and pass under the chequered shadows of the
trees, and cut through the green woodland in the calm
water. The fiery sun had climbed midway in the circle of
the sky when they see afar fortress walls and scattered
house roofs, where now the might of Rome hath risen high
as heaven ; then Evander held a slender state. Quickly
they turn their prows to land and draw near the town.

It chanced on that day the Arcadian king paid his
accustomed sacrifice to the great son of Amphitryon and
all the gods in a grove before the city. With him his son
Pallas, with him all the chief of his people and his poor
senate were offering incense, and the blood steamed warm
at their altars. When they saw the high ships, saw them
glide up between the shady woodlands and rest on their
silent oars, the sudden sight appals them, and all at once
they rise and stop the banquet. Pallas courageously forbids them to break off the rites; snatching up a spear, he
flies forward, and from a hillock cries afar: ' O men, what
cause hath driven you to explore these unknown ways ?
or whither do you steer ? What is your kin, whence your
habitation ? Is it peace or arms you carry hither ?' Then
from the lofty stern lord Aeneas thus speaks, stretching
forth in his hand an olive bough of peace-bearing :

' Thou seest men born of Troy and arms hostile to the
Latins, who have driven us to flight in insolent warfare. We
seek Evander ; carry this message, and tell him that chosen
men of the Dardanian captains are come pleading for an
armed alliance.'

Pallas stood amazed at the august name. ' Descend,'

he cries, 'whoso thou art, and speak with my father face to face, and enter our home and hospitality.' And giving him the grasp of welcome, he caught and clung to his hand. Advancing, they enter the grove and leave the river.   Then Aeneas in courteous words addresses the King:

'Best of the Grecian race, thou whom fortune hath willed that I supplicate, holding before me boughs dressed in fillets, no fear stayed me because thou wert a Grecian chief and an Arcadian, or allied by descent to the twin sons of Atreus.   Nay, mine own prowess and the sanctity of divine oracles, our ancestral kinship, and the fame of thee that is spread abroad over the earth, have allied me to thee and led me willingly on the path of fate.   Dardanus, who sailed to the Teucrian land, the first father and founder of the Ilian city, was born, as Greeks relate, of Electra the Atlantid ; Electra's sire is ancient Atlas, whose shoulder sustains the heavenly spheres.   Your father is Mercury, whom white Maia conceived and bore on the cold summit of Cyllene ; but Maia, if we give any credence to report, is daughter of Atlas, that same Atlas who bears up the starry heavens ; so both our families branch from a single blood. In this confidence I sent no embassy, I framed no crafty overtures ; myself I have presented mine own person, and come a suppliant to thy courts.   The same Daunian race pursues us and thee in merciless warfare ; we once expelled, they trust nothing will withhold them from laying all Hesperia wholly beneath their yoke, and holding the seas that wash it above and below.   Accept and return our friendship.   We can give brave hearts in war, high souls and men approved in deeds.'

Aeneas ended.   The other ere now scanned in a long gaze the face and eyes and all the form of the speaker ; then thus briefly returns :

'How gladly, bravest of the Teucrians, do I hail and

own thee! how I recall thy father's words and the very
tone and glance of great Anchises! For I remember how
Priam son of Laomedon, when he sought Salamis on his
way to the realm of his sister Hesione, went on to visit the
cold borders of Arcadia. Then early youth clad my cheeks
with bloom. I admired the Teucrian captains, admired
their lord, the son of Laomedon; but Anchises moved high
above them all. My heart burned with youthful passion
to accost him and clasp hand in hand; I made my way to
him, and led him eagerly to Pheneus' high town. Departing
he gave me an adorned quiver and Lycian arrows, a scarf
inwoven with gold, and a pair of golden bits that now my
Pallas possesses. Therefore my hand is already joined in
the alliance you seek, and soon as to-morrow's dawn rises
again over earth, I will send you away rejoicing in mine
aid, and supply you from my store. Meanwhile, since you
are come hither in friendship, solemnise with us these
yearly rites which we may not defer, and even now learn
to be familiar at your comrades' board.'

This said, he commands the feast and the wine-cups to
be replaced whence they were taken, and with his own
hand ranges them on the grassy seat, and welcomes Aeneas
to the place of honour, with a lion's shaggy fell for cushion
and a hospitable chair of maple. Then chosen men with
the priest of the altar in emulous haste bring roasted flesh
of bulls, and pile baskets with the gift of ground corn, and
serve the wine. Aeneas and the men of Troy with him
feed on the long chines of oxen and the entrails of the
sacrifice.

After hunger is driven away and the desire of food
stayed, King Evander speaks: 'No idle superstition that
knows not the gods of old hath ordered these our solemn
rites, this customary feast, this altar of august sanctity;
saved from bitter perils, O Trojan guest, do we worship, and

most due are the rites we inaugurate. Look now first on
this overhanging cliff of stone, where shattered masses lie
strewn, and the mountain dwelling stands desolate, and
rocks are rent away in vast ruin. Here was a cavern, awful
and deep-withdrawn, impenetrable to the sunbeams, where
the monstrous half-human shape of Cacus had his hold : the
ground was ever wet with fresh slaughter, and pallid faces
of men, ghastly with gore, hung nailed on the haughty
doors. This monster was the son of Vulcan, and spouted
his black fires from his mouth as he moved in giant bulk.
To us also in our desire time bore a god's aid and arrival.
For princely Alcides the avenger came glorious in the spoils
of triple Geryon slain ; this way the Conqueror drove the
huge bulls, and his oxen filled the river valley. But savage
Cacus, infatuate to leave nothing undared or unhandled in
craft or crime, drives four bulls of choice shape away from
their pasturage, and as many heifers of excellent beauty.
And these, that there should be no straightforward footprints, he dragged by the tail into his cavern, the track of
their compelled path reversed, and hid them behind the
screen of rock. No marks were there to lead a seeker to
the cavern. Meanwhile the son of Amphitryon, his herds
filled with food, was now breaking up his pasturage and
making ready to go. The oxen low as they depart ; all the
woodland is filled with their complaint as they clamorously quit the hills. One heifer returned the cry, and, lowing from the depth of the dreary cave, baffled the hope of
Cacus from her imprisonment. ` At this the grief and choler
of Alcides blazed forth dark and infuriate. Seizing in his
hand his club of heavy knotted oak, he seeks with swift
pace the aëry mountain steep. Then, as never before, did
we see Cacus afraid and his countenance troubled ; he goes
flying swifter than the wind and seeks his cavern ; fear
wings his feet. As he shut himself in, and, bursting the

N

chains, dropped the vast rock slung in iron by his father's craft, and blocked the doorway with its pressure, lo! the Tirynthian came in furious wrath, and, scanning all the entry, turned his face this way and that and ground his teeth. Thrice, hot with rage, he circles all Mount Aventine; thrice he assails the rocky portals in vain; thrice he sinks down outwearied in the valley. There stood a sharp rock of flint with sides cut sheer away, rising over the cavern's ridge a vast height to see, fit haunt for foul birds to build on. This—for, sloping from the ridge, it leaned on the left towards the river—he loosened, urging it from the right till he tore it loose from its deep foundations; then suddenly shook it free; with the shock the vast sky thunders, the banks leap apart, and the amazed river recoils. But the den, Cacus' huge palace, lay open and revealed, and the depths of gloomy cavern were made manifest; even as though some force tearing earth apart should unlock the infernal house, and disclose the pallid realms abhorred of heaven, and deep down the monstrous gulf be descried where the ghosts flutter in the streaming daylight. On him then, surprised in unexpected light, shut in the rock's recesses and howling in strange fashion, Alcides from above hurls missiles and calls all his arms to aid, and presses hard on him with boughs and enormous millstones. And he, for none other escape from peril is left, vomits from his throat vast jets of smoke, wonderful to tell, and enwreathes his dwelling in blind gloom, blotting view from the eyes, while in the cave's depth night thickens with smoke-bursts in a darkness shot with fire. Alcides broke forth in anger, and with a bound hurled himself sheer amid the flames, where the smoke rolls billowing and voluminous, and the cloud surges black through the enormous den. Here, as Cacus in the darkness spouts forth his idle fires, he grasps and twines tight round him, till his eyes start out and his throat

is drained of blood under the strangling pressure. Straightway the doors are torn open and the dark house laid plain ;
the stolen oxen and forsworn plunder are shewn forth to
heaven, and the misshapen carcase dragged forward by the
feet. Men cannot satisfy their soul with gazing on the
terrible eyes, the monstrous face and shaggy bristling chest,
and the throat with its quenched fires. Thenceforth this
sacrifice is solemnised, and a younger race have gladly kept
the day ; Potitius the inaugurator, and the Pinarian family,
guardians of the rites of Hercules, have set in the grove
this altar, which shall ever be called of us Most Mighty, and
shall be our mightiest evermore. Wherefore arise, O men,
and enwreathe your hair with leafy sprays, and stretch forth
the cups in your hands ; call on our common god and pour
the glad wine.' He ended ; when the twy-coloured poplar
of Hercules hid his shaded hair with pendulous plaited leaf,
and the sacred goblet filled his hand. Speedily all pour
glad libation on the board, and supplicate the gods.

　　Meanwhile the evening star draws nigher down the
slope of heaven, and now the priests went forth, Potitius at
their head, girt with skins after their fashion, and bore
torches aflame. They renew the banquet, and bring the
grateful gift of a second repast, and heap the altars with
loaded platters. Then the Salii stand round the lit altar-fires
to sing, their brows bound with poplar boughs, one chorus
of young men, one of elders, and extol in song the praises
and deeds of Hercules ; how first he strangled in his gripe
the twin terrors, the snakes of his stepmother ; how he
likewise shattered in war famous cities, Troy and Oechalia ;
how under Eurystheus the King he bore the toil of a
thousand labours by Juno's malign decrees. Thine hand,
unconquered, slays the cloud-born double-bodied race,
Hylaeus and Pholus, the Cretan monster, and the huge lion
in the hollow Nemean rock. Before thee the Stygian pools

shook for fear, before thee the warder of hell, couched on
half-gnawn bones in his blood-stained cavern; to thee not
any form was terrible, not Typhoeus' self towering in arms;
thou wast not bereft of counsel when the snake of Lerna
encompassed thee with thronging heads. Hail, true seed
of Jove, deified glory! graciously visit us and these thy
rites with favourable feet. Such are their songs of praise;
they crown all with the cavern of Cacus and its fire-breathing
lord. All the woodland echoes with their clamour, and
the hills resound.

Thence all at once, the sacred rites accomplished,
retrace their way to the city. The age-worn King walked
holding Aeneas and his son by his side for companions on
his way, and lightened the road with changing talk. Aeneas
admires and turns his eyes lightly round about, pleased with
the country; and gladly on spot after spot inquires and
hears of the memorials of earlier men. Then King Evander,
founder of the fortress of Rome:

'In these woodlands dwelt Fauns and Nymphs sprung
of the soil, and a tribe of men born of stocks and hard oak;
who had neither law nor grace of life, nor did they know to
yoke bulls or lay up stores or save their gains, but were
nurtured by the forest boughs and the hard living of the
huntsman. Long ago Saturn came from heaven on high in
flight before Jove's arms, an exile from his lost realm. He
gathered together the unruly race scattered on the mountain
heights, and gave them statutes, and chose Latium to be
their name, since in these borders he had found a safe
hiding-place. Beneath his reign were the ages named of
gold; thus, in peace and quietness, did he rule the nations;
till gradually there crept in a sunken and stained time, the
rage of war, and the lust of possession. Then came the
Ausonian clan and the tribes of Sicania, and many a time
the land of Saturn put away her name. Then were kings,

and fierce Thybris with his giant bulk, from whose name we
of Italy afterwards called the Tiber river, when it lost the
true name of old, Albula. Me, cast out from my country
and following the utmost limits of the sea, Fortune the
omnipotent and irreversible doom settled in this region ;
and my mother the Nymph Carmentis' awful warnings and
Apollo's divine counsel drove me hither.'

Scarce was this said ; next advancing he points out the
altar and the Carmental Gate, which the Romans call
anciently by that name in honour of the Nymph Carmentis,
seer and soothsayer, who sang of old the coming greatness
of the Aeneadae and the glory of Pallanteum. Next he
points out the wide grove where valiant Romulus set his
sanctuary, and the Lupercal in the cool hollow of the rock,
dedicate to Lycean Pan after the manner of Parrhasia.
Therewithal he shows the holy wood of Argiletum, and
calls the spot to witness as he tells the slaying of his guest
Argus. Hence he leads him to the Tarpeian house, and
the Capitol golden now, of old rough with forest thickets.
Even then men trembled before the wood and rock. 'This
grove,' he cries, 'this hill with its leafy crown, is a god's
dwelling, though whose we know not ; the Arcadians
believe Jove himself hath been visible, when often he shook
the darkening aegis in his hand and gathered the storm-
clouds. Thou seest these two towns likewise with walls
overthrown, relics and memorials of men of old. This
fortress lord Janus built, this Saturn ; the name of this was
once Janiculum, of that Saturnia.'

With such mutual words they drew nigh the house
of poor Evander, and saw scattered herds lowing on the
Roman Forum and down the gay Carinae. When they
reached his dwelling, 'This threshold,' he cries, 'Alcides
the Conqueror stooped to cross ; in this palace he rested.
Dare thou, my guest, to despise riches ; mould thyself to

like dignity of godhead, and come not exacting to our poverty.' He spoke, and led tall Aeneas under the low roof of his narrow dwelling, and laid him on a couch of stuffed leaves and the skin of a Libyan she-bear. Night falls and clasps the earth in her dusky wings.

But Venus, stirred in spirit by no vain mother's alarms, and moved by the threats and stern uprisal of the Laurentines, addresses herself to Vulcan, and in her golden bridal chamber begins thus, breathing divine passion in her speech:

'While Argolic kings wasted in war the doomed towers of Troy, the fortress fated to fall in hostile fires, no succour did I require for her wretched people, no weapons of thine art and aid: nor would I task, dear my lord, thee or thy toils for naught, though I owed many and many a debt to the children of Priam, and had often wept the sore labour of Aeneas. Now by Jove's commands he hath set foot in the Rutulian borders; I now therefore come with entreaty, and ask armour of the god I worship. For the son she bore, the tears of Nereus' daughter, of Tithonus' consort, could melt thine heart. Look what nations are gathering, what cities bar their gates and sharpen the sword against me for the desolation of my children.'

The goddess ended, and, as he hesitates, clasps him round in the soft embrace of her snowy arms. He suddenly caught the wonted flame, and the heat known of old pierced him to the heart and overran his melting frame: even as when, bursting from the thunder peal, a sparkling cleft of fire shoots through the storm-clouds with dazzling light. His consort knew, rejoiced in her wiles, and felt her beauty. Then her lord speaks, enchained by Love the immortal:

'Why these far-fetched pleas? Whither, O goddess, is thy trust in me gone? Had like distress been thine,

even then we might unblamed have armed thy Trojans,
nor did doom nor the Lord omnipotent forbid Troy to
stand, and Priam to survive yet ten other years. And
now, if thou purposest war, and this is thy counsel, whatever charge I can undertake in my craft, in aught that may
be made of iron or molten electrum, whatever fire and air
can do, cease thou to entreat as doubtful of thy strength.'
These words spoken, he clasped his wife in the desired
embrace, and, sinking in her lap, wooed quiet slumber to
overspread his limbs.

Thereon, so soon as sleep, now in mid-career of waning
night, had given rest and gone ; soon as a woman, whose
task is to sustain life with her distaff and the slender labours
of the loom, kindles the ashes of her slumbering fire, her
toil encroaching on the night, and sets a long task of fire-
lit spinning to her maidens, that so she may keep her
husband's bed unsullied and nourish her little children,—
even so the Lord of Fire, nor slacker in his hours than she,
rises from his soft couch to the work of his smithy. An
island rises by the side of Sicily and Aeolian Lipare, steep
with smoking cliffs, whereunder the vaulted and thunderous
Aetnean caverns are hollowed out for Cyclopean forges, the
strong strokes on the anvils echo in groans, ore of steel
hisses in the vaults, and the fire pants in the furnaces : the
house of Vulcan, and Vulcania the land's name. Hither
now the Lord of Fire descends from heaven's height. In
the vast cavern the Cyclopes were forging iron, Brontes
and Steropes and Pyracmon with bared limbs. Shaped in
their hands was a thunderbolt, in part already polished,
such as the Father of Heaven hurls down on earth in multi-
tudes, part yet unfinished. Three coils of frozen rain, three
of watery mist they had enwrought in it, three of ruddy fire
and winged south wind ; now they were mingling in their
work the awful splendours, the sound and terror, and the

angry pursuing flames. Elsewhere they hurried on a chariot
for Mars with flying wheels, wherewith he stirs up men
and cities; and burnished the golden serpent-scales of the
awful aegis, the armour of wrathful Pallas, and the entwined
snakes on the breast of the goddess, the Gorgon head with
severed neck and rolling eyes. 'Away with all!' he cries:
'stop your tasks unfinished, Cyclopes of Aetna, and attend
to this; a warrior's armour must be made. Now must
strength, now quickness of hand be tried, now all our art
lend her guidance. Fling off delay.' He spoke no more;
but they all bent rapidly to the work, allotting their labours
equally. Brass and ore of gold flow in streams, and
wounding steel is molten in the vast furnace. They shape
a mighty shield, to receive singly all the weapons of the
Latins, and weld it sevenfold, circle on circle. Some fill and
empty the windy bellows of their blast, some dip the hissing
brass in the trough. They raise their arms mightily in re-
sponsive time, and turn the mass of metal about in the
grasp of their tongs.

While the lord of Lemnos is busied thus in the borders
of Aeolia, Evander is roused from his low dwelling by the
gracious daylight and the matin songs of birds from the
eaves. The old man arises, and draws on his body raiment,
and ties the Tyrrhene shoe latchets about his feet; then
buckles to his side and shoulder his Tegeaean sword, and
swathes himself in a panther skin that droops upon his left.
Therewithal two watch-dogs go before him from the high
threshold, and accompany their master's steps. The hero
sought his guest Aeneas in the privacy of his dwelling,
mindful of their talk and his promised bounty. Nor did
Aeneas fail to be astir with the dawn. With the one went
his son Pallas, with the other Achates. They meet and
clasp hands, and, sitting down within the house, at length
enjoy unchecked converse. The King begins thus: . . .

'Princely chief of the Teucrians, in whose lifetime I will
never allow the state or realm of Troy vanquished, our
strength is scant to succour in war for so great a name. On
this side the Tuscan river shuts us in ; on that the Rutulian
drives us hard, and thunders in arms about our walls. But
I purpose to unite to thee mighty peoples and the camp of
a wealthy realm; an unforeseen chance offers this for thy
salvation. Fate summons thy approach. Not far from
here stands fast Agylla city, an ancient pile of stone, where
of old the Lydian race, eminent in war, settled on the
Etruscan ridges. For many years it flourished, till King
Mezentius ruled it with insolent sway and armed terror.
Why should I relate the horrible murders, the savage deeds
of the monarch ? May the gods keep them in store for himself and his line ! Nay, he would even link dead bodies to
living, fitting hand to hand and face to face (the torture !),
and in the oozy foulness and corruption of the dreadful
embrace so slay them by a lingering death. But at last his
citizens, outwearied by his mad excesses, surround him and
his house in arms, cut down his comrades, and hurl fire on
his roof. Amid the massacre he escaped to the refuge of
Rutulian land and the armed defence of Turnus' friendship.
So all Etruria hath risen in righteous fury, and in immedi-
ate battle claim their king for punishment. Over these
thousands will I make thee chief, O Aeneas ; for their noisy
ships crowd all the shore, and they bid the standards
advance, while the aged diviner stays them with prophecies :
" O chosen men of Maeonia, flower and strength of them,
of old time, whom righteous anger urges on the enemy, and
Mezentius inflames with deserved wrath, to no Italian is it
permitted to hold this great nation in control : choose
foreigners to lead you." At that, terrified by the divine
warning, the Etruscan lines have encamped on the plain ;
Tarchon himself hath sent ambassadors to me with the crown

and sceptre of the kingdom, and offers the royal attire will I but enter their camp and take the Tyrrhene realm. But old age, frozen to dulness, and exhausted with length of life, denies me the load of empire, and my prowess is past its day. I would urge it on my son, did not the mixture of blood by his Sabellian mother make this half his native land. Thou, to whose years and race alike the fates extend their favour, on whom fortune calls, enter thou in, a leader supreme in bravery over Teucrians and Italians. Mine own Pallas likewise, our hope and comfort, I will send with thee ; let him grow used to endure warfare and the stern work of battle under thy teaching, to regard thine actions, and from his earliest years look up to thee. To him will I give two hundred Arcadian cavalry, the choice of our warlike strength, and Pallas as many more to thee in his own name.'

Scarce had he ended ; Aeneas, son of Anchises, and trusty Achates gazed with steadfast face, and, sad at heart, were revolving inly many a labour, had not the Cytherean sent a sign from the clear sky. For suddenly a flash and peal comes quivering from heaven, and all seemed in a moment to totter, and the Tyrrhene trumpet-blast to roar along the sky. They look up ; again and yet again the heavy crash re-echoes. They see in the serene space of sky armour gleam red through a cloud in the clear air, and ring clashing out. The others stood in amaze ; but the Trojan hero knew the sound for the promise of his goddess mother; then he speaks : 'Ask not, O friend, ask not in any wise what fortune this presage announces ; it is I who am summoned of heaven. This sign the goddess who bore me foretold she would send if war assailed, and would bring through the air to my succour armour from Vulcan's hands. . . . Ah, what slaughter awaits the wretched Laurentines ! what a price, O Turnus, wilt thou pay me ! how many shields and helmets and brave bodies of men shalt thou,

Lord Tiber, roll under thy waves !   Let them call for armed
array and break the league !'

These words uttered, he rises from the high seat, and
first wakes with fresh fire the slumbering altars of Hercules,
and gladly draws nigh his tutelar god of yesternight and the
small deities of the household.   Alike Evander, and alike
the men of Troy, offer up, as is right, choice sheep of two
years old.   Thereafter he goes to the ships and revisits his
crew, of whose company he chooses the foremost in valour
to attend him to war ; the rest glide down the water and
float idly with the descending stream, to come with news to
Ascanius of his father's state.   They give horses to the
Teucrians who seek the fields of Tyrrhenia ; a chosen one
is brought for Aeneas, housed in a tawny lion skin that
glitters with claws of gold.   Rumour flies suddenly, spreading over the little town, that they ride in haste to the courts
of the Tyrrhene king.   Mothers redouble their prayers in
terror, as fear treads closer on peril and the likeness of the
War God looms larger in sight.   Then Evander, clasping
the hand of his departing son, clings to him weeping incon-
solably, and speaks thus :

'Oh, if Jupiter would restore me the years that are
past, as I was when, close under Praeneste, I cut down their
foremost ranks and burned the piled shields of the conquered !   Then this right hand sent King Erulus down to
hell, though to him at his birth his mother Feronia (awful
to tell) had given three lives and triple arms to wield ; thrice
must he be laid low in death ; yet then this hand took all
his lives and as often stripped him of his arms.   Never
should I now, O son, be severed from thy dear embrace ;
never had the insolent sword of Mezentius on my borders
dealt so many cruel deaths, widowed the city of so many
citizens.   But you, O heavenly powers, and thou, Jupiter,
Lord and Governor of Heaven, have compassion, I pray, on

the Arcadian king, and hear a father's prayers. If your
deity and decrees keep my Pallas safe for me, if I live that
I may see him and meet him yet, I pray for life; any toil
soever I have patience to endure.   But if, O Fortune, thou
threatenest some dread calamity, now, ah now, may I break
off a cruel life, while anxiety still wavers and expectation is
in doubt, while thou, dear boy, my one last delight, art yet
clasped in my embrace; let no bitterer message wound
mine ear.'   These words the father poured forth at the final
parting; his servants bore him swooning within.

    And now the cavalry had issued from the open gates,
Aeneas and trusty Achates among the foremost, then other
of the Trojan princes, Pallas conspicuous amid the column
in scarf and inlaid armour; like the Morning Star, when,
newly washed in the ocean wave, he shews his holy face in
heaven, and melts the darkness away. Fearful mothers
stand on the walls and follow with their eyes the cloud of
dust and the squadrons gleaming in brass. They, where
the goal of their way lies nearest, bear through the brushwood in armed array. Forming in column, they advance
noisily, and the horse hoof shakes the crumbling plain with
four-footed trampling. There is a high grove by the cold
river of Caere, widely revered in ancestral awe; sheltering
hills shut it in all about and girdle the woodland with their
dark firs. Rumour is that the old Pelasgians, who once long
ago held the Latin borders, consecrated the grove and its
festal day to Silvanus, god of the tilth and flock. Not far
from it Tarchon and his Tyrrhenians were encamped in a
protected place; and now from the hill-top the tents of all
their army might be seen outspread on the fields. Lord
Aeneas and his chosen warriors draw hither and refresh their
weary horses and limbs.

    But Venus the white goddess drew nigh, bearing her
gifts through the clouds of heaven; and when she saw her

son withdrawn far apart in the valley's recess by the cold
river, cast herself in his way, and addressed him thus :
' Behold perfected the presents of my husband's promised
craftsmanship : so shalt thou not shun, O my child, soon to
challenge the haughty Laurentines or fiery Turnus to battle.'
The Cytherean spoke, and sought her son's embrace, and
laid the armour glittering under an oak over against him.
He, rejoicing in the magnificence of the goddess' gift, cannot have his fill of turning his eyes over it piece by piece,
and admires and handles between his arms the helmet,
dread with plumes and spouting flame, as when a blue cloud
takes fire in the sunbeams and gleams afar; then the
smooth greaves of electrum and refined gold, the spear, and
the shield's ineffable design.   There the Lord of Fire
had fashioned the story of Italy and the triumphs of the
Romans, not witless of prophecy or ignorant of the age to
be ; there all the race of Ascanius' future seed, and their
wars fought one by one.   Likewise had he fashioned the
she-wolf couched after the birth in the green cave of Mars ;
round her teats the twin boys hung playing, and fearlessly
mouthed their foster-mother; she, with round neck bent
back, stroked them by turns and shaped their bodies with
her tongue.   Thereto not far from this he had set Rome
and the lawless rape of the Sabines in the concourse of the
theatre when the great Circensian games were celebrated,
and a fresh war suddenly arising between the people of
Romulus and aged Tatius and austere Cures.   Next these
same kings laid down their mutual strife and stood armed
before Jove's altar with cup in hand, and joined treaty over
a slain sow.   Not far from there four-horse chariots
driven apart had torn Mettus asunder (but thou, O Alban,
shouldst have kept by thy words !), and Tullus tore the
flesh of the liar through the forest, his splashed blood
dripping from the briars.   Therewithal Porsena commanded

to admit the exiled Tarquin, and held the city in the grasp
of a strong blockade; the Aeneadae rushed on the sword
for liberty.　Him thou couldst espy like one who chafes
and like one who threatens, because Cocles dared to tear
down the bridge, and Cloelia broke her bonds and swam
the river.　Highest of all Manlius, warder of the Tarpeian
fortress, stood with the temple behind him and held the
high Capitoline; and the thatch of Romulus' palace stood
rough and fresh.　And here the silver goose, fluttering in
the gilded colonnades, cried that the Gauls were there on
the threshold.　The Gauls were there among the brushwood,
hard on the fortress, secure in the darkness and the dower
of shadowy night.　Their clustering locks are of gold, and
of gold their attire; their striped cloaks glitter, and their
milk-white necks are entwined with gold.　Two Alpine
pikes sparkle in the hand of each, and long shields guard
their bodies.　Here he had embossed the dancing Salii
and the naked Luperci, the crests wreathed in wool, and
the sacred shields that fell from heaven; in cushioned cars
the virtuous matrons led on their rites through the city.
Far hence he adds the habitations of hell also, the high
gates of Dis and the dooms of guilt; and thee, O Catiline,
clinging on the beetling rock, and shuddering at the faces
of the Furies; and far apart the good, and Cato delivering
them statutes.　Amidst it all flows wide the likeness of the
swelling sea, wrought in gold, though the foam surged gray
upon blue water; and round about dolphins, in shining
silver, swept the seas with their tails in circle as they cleft
the tide.　In the centre were visible the brazen war-
fleets of Actium; thou mightest see all Leucate swarm in
embattled array, and the waves gleam with gold.　Here
Caesar Augustus, leading Italy to battle with Fathers and
People, with gods of household and of state, stands on the
lofty stern; prosperous flames jet round his brow, and his

ancestral star dawns overhead. Elsewhere Agrippa, with
favouring winds and gods, proudly leads on his column ;
on his brows glitters the prow-girt naval crown, the haughty
emblazonment of the war.   Here Antonius with barbarian
aid and motley arms, from the conquered nations of the
Dawn and the shore of the southern sea, carries with him
Egypt and the Eastern forces of utmost Bactra, and the
shameful Egyptian woman goes as his consort.   All at
once rush on, and the whole ocean is torn into foam by
straining oars and triple-pointed prows.   They steer to sea ;
one might think that the Cyclades were uptorn and floated
on the main, or that lofty mountains clashed with mountains, so mightily do their crews urge on the turreted ships.
Flaming tow and the winged steel of darts shower thickly
from their hands ; the fields of ocean redden with fresh
slaughter.   Midmost the Queen calls on her squadron with
the timbrel of her country, nor yet casts back a glance on
the twin snakes behind her.   Howling Anubis, and gods
monstrous and multitudinous, level their arms against Neptune and Venus and against Minerva ; Mars rages amid the
havoc, graven in iron, and the Fatal Sisters hang aloft, and
Discord strides rejoicing with garment rent, and Bellona
attends her with blood-stained scourge.   Looking thereon,
Actian Apollo above drew his bow ; with the terror of it
all Egypt and India, every Arab and Sabaean, turned back
in flight.   The Queen herself seemed to call the winds and
spread her sails, and even now let her sheets run slack.
Her the Lord of Fire had fashioned amid the carnage,
wan with the shadow of death, borne along by the waves
and the north-west wind ; and over against her the vast
bulk of mourning Nile, opening out his folds and calling
with all his raiment the conquered people into his blue lap
and the coverture of his streams.   But Caesar rode into the
city of Rome in triple triumph, and dedicated his vowed

offering to the gods to stand for ever, three hundred stately shrines all about the city. The streets were loud with gladness and games and shouting. In all the temples was a band of matrons, in all were altars, and before the altars slain steers strewed the ground. Himself he sits on the snowy threshold of Phoebus the bright, reviews the gifts of the nations and ranges them on the haughty doors. The conquered tribes move in long line, diverse as in tongue, so in fashion of dress and armour. Here Mulciber had designed the Nomad race and the ungirt Africans, here the Leleges and Carians and archer Gelonians. Euphrates went by now with smoother waves, and the Morini utmost of men, and the hornèd Rhine, the untamed Dahae, and Araxes chafing under his bridge.

These things he admires on the shield of Vulcan, his mother's gift, and rejoicing in the portraiture of unknown history, lifts on his shoulder the destined glories of his children.

BOOK NINTH

THE SIEGE OF THE TROJAN CAMP

AND while thus things pass far in the distance, Juno
daughter of Saturn sent Iris down the sky to gallant
Turnus, then haply seated in his forefather Pilumnus' holy
forest dell. To him the child of Thaumas spoke thus with
roseate lips :

'Turnus, what no god had dared promise to thy prayer,
behold, is brought unasked by the circling day. Aeneas
hath quitted town and comrades and fleet to seek Evander's
throne and Palatine dwelling-place. Nor is it enough ; he
hath pierced to Corythus' utmost cities, and is mustering in
arms a troop of Lydian rustics. Why hesitate ? now, now
is the time to call for chariot and horses. Break through
all hindrance and seize the bewildered camp.'

She spoke, and rose into the sky on poised wings, and
flashed under the clouds in a long flying bow. He knew
her, and lifting either hand to heaven, with this cry pursued her flight : 'Iris, grace of the sky, who hath driven
thee down the clouds to me and borne thee to earth ?
Whence is this sudden sheen of weather ? I see the sky
parting asunder, and the wandering stars in the firmament.
I follow the high omen, whoso thou art that callest me to
arms.' And with these words he drew nigh the wave, and

o

caught up water from its brimming eddy, making many prayers to the gods and burdening the air with vows.

And now all the army was advancing on the open plain, rich in horses, rich in raiment of broidered gold. Messapus rules the foremost ranks, the sons of Tyrrheus the rear. Turnus commands the centre: even as Ganges rising high in silence when his seven streams are still, or the rich flood of Nile when he ebbs from the plains, and is now sunk into his channel. On this the Teucrians descry a sudden cloud of dark dust gathering, and the blackness rising on the plain. Caïcus raises a cry from the mound in front: 'What mass of misty gloom, O citizens, is rolling hitherward? to arms in haste! serve out weapons, climb the walls. The enemy approaches, ho!' With mighty clamour the Teucrians pour in through all the gates and fill the works. For so at his departure Aeneas the great captain had enjoined; were aught to chance meanwhile, they should not venture to range their line or trust the plain, but keep their camp and the safety of the entrenched walls. So, though shame and wrath beckon them on to battle, they yet bar the gates and do his bidding, and await the foe armed and in shelter of the towers. Turnus, who had flown forward in advance of his tardy column, comes up suddenly to the town with a train of twenty chosen cavalry, borne on a Thracian horse dappled with white, and covered by a golden helmet with scarlet plume. 'Who will be with me, my men, to be first on the foe? See!' he cries; and sends a javelin spinning into the air to open battle, and advances towering on the plain. His comrades take up the cry, and follow with dreadful din, wondering at the Teucrians' coward hearts, that they issue not on even field nor face them in arms, but keep in shelter of the camp. Hither and thither he rides furiously, tracing the walls, and seeking entrance where way is none. And as a wolf prowl-

ing about some crowded sheepfold, when, beaten sore of
winds and rains, he howls at the pens by midnight ; safe
beneath their mothers the lambs keep bleating on ; he,
savage and insatiate, rages in anger against the flock he
cannot reach, tired by the long-gathering madness for food,
and the throat unslaked with blood : even so the Rutulian,
as he gazes on the walled camp, kindles in anger, and indignation is hot in his iron frame. By what means may
he essay entrance ? by what passage hurl the imprisoned
Trojans from the rampart and fling them on the plain ?
Close under the flanking camp lay the fleet, fenced about
with mounds and the waters of the river ; it he attacks, and
calls for fire to his exultant comrades, and eagerly catches
a blazing pine-torch in his hand. Then indeed they press
on, quickened by Turnus' presence, and all the band arm
them with black faggots. The hearth-fires are plundered ;
the smoky brand trails a resinous glare, and the Fire-god
sends clouds of glowing ashes upward.

What god, O Muses, guarded the Trojans from the
rage of the fire ? who repelled the fierce flame from their
ships ? Tell it ; ancient is the assurance thereof, but the
fame everlasting. What time Aeneas began to shape his
fleet on Phrygian Ida, and prepared to seek the high seas,
the Berecyntian, they say, the very Mother of gods, spoke
to high Jove in these words : 'Grant, O son, to my
prayer, what her dearness claims who bore thee and laid
Olympus under thy feet. My pine forest beloved of me
these many years, my grove was on the mountain's crown,
whither men bore my holy things, dim with dusky pine and
pillared maples. These, when he required a fleet, I gave
gladly to the Dardanian ; now fear wrings me with sharp
distress. Relieve my terrors, and grant a mother's prayers
such power that they may yield to no stress of voyaging or
of stormy gust : be birth on our hills their avail.'

Thus her son in answer, who wheels the starry worlds :
'O mother, whither callest thou fate? or what dost thou
seek for these of thine?   May hulls have the right of
immortality that were fashioned by mortal hand? and may
Aeneas traverse perils secure in insecurity?   To what god
is power so great given?   Nay, but when, their duty done,
they shall lie at last in their Ausonian haven, from all that
have outgone the waves and borne their Dardanian captain
to the fields of Laurentum, will I take their mortal body,
and bid them be goddesses of the mighty deep, even as
Doto the Nereïd and Galatea, when they cut the sea that
falls away from their breasts in foam.'   He ended; and by
his brother's Stygian streams, by the banks of the pitchy
black-boiling chasm he nodded confirmation, and shook all
Olympus with his nod.

So the promised day was come, and the destinies had
fulfilled their due time, when Turnus' injury stirred the
Mother to ward the brands from her holy ships.   First
then a strange light flashed on all eyes, and a great glory
from the Dawn seemed to dart over the sky, with the choirs
of Ida; then an awful voice fell through air, filling the
Trojan and Rutulian ranks : 'Disquiet not yourselves, O
Teucrians, to guard ships of mine; neither arm your hands :
sooner shall Turnus burn the seas than these holy pines.
You, go free ; go, goddesses of the sea ; the Mother bids it.'
And immediately each ship breaks the bond that held it,
as with dipping prows they plunge like dolphins deep into
the water : from it again (O wonderful and strange !) they
rise with maidens' faces in like number, and bear out
to sea.

The Rutulians stood dumb : Messapus himself is terror-
stricken among his disordered cavalry ; even the stream of
Tiber pauses with hoarse murmur, and recoils from sea.
But bold Turnus fails not a whit in confidence ; nay, he

raises their courage with words, nay, he chides them : ' On
the Trojans are these portents aimed ; Jupiter himself hath
bereft them of their wonted succour ; nor do they abide
Rutulian sword and fire. So are the seas pathless for the
Teucrians, nor is there any hope in flight ; they have lost
half their world. And we hold the land : in all their
thousands the nations of Italy are under arms. In no wise
am I dismayed by those divine oracles of doom the Phrygians insolently advance. Fate and Venus are satisfied, in
that the Trojans have touched our fruitful Ausonian fields.
I too have my fate in reply to theirs, to put utterly to the
sword the guilty nation who have robbed me of my bride ;
not the sons of Atreus alone are touched by that pain, nor
may Mycenae only rise in arms. But to have perished
once is enough I To have sinned once should have been
enough, in all but utter hatred of the whole of womankind.
Trust in the sundering rampart, and the hindrance of their
trenches, so little between them and death, gives these their
courage : yet have they not seen Troy town, the work of
Neptune's hand, sink into fire ? But you, my chosen, who
of you makes ready to breach their palisade at the sword's
point, and join my attack on their fluttered camp ? I have
no need of Vulcanian arms, of a thousand ships, to meet
the Teucrians. All Etruria may join on with them in
alliance : nor let them fear the darkness, and the cowardly
theft of their Palladium, and the guards cut down on the
fortress height. Nor will we hide ourselves unseen in a
horse's belly ; in daylight and unconcealed are we resolved
to girdle their walls with flame. Not with Grecians will I
make them think they have to do, nor a Pelasgic force
kept off till the tenth year by Hector. Now, since the
better part of day is spent, for what remains refresh your
bodies, glad that we have done so well, and expect the
order of battle.'

Meanwhile charge is given to Messapus to blockade the
gates with pickets of sentries, and encircle the works with
watchfires. Twice seven are chosen to guard the walls
with Rutulian soldiery; but each leads an hundred men,
crimson-plumed and sparkling in gold. They spread
themselves about and keep alternate watch, and, lying
along the grass, drink deep and set brazen bowls atilt.
The fires glow, and the sentinels spend the night awake in
games. . . .

Down on this the Trojans look forth from the rampart,
as they hold the height in arms; withal in fearful haste
they try the gates and lay gangways from bastion to bastion,
and bring up missiles. Mnestheus and valiant Serestus
speed the work, whom lord Aeneas appointed, should mis-
fortune call, to be rulers of the people and governors of
the state. All their battalions, sharing the lot of peril,
keep watch along the walls, and take alternate charge of
all that requires defence.

On guard at the gate was Nisus son of Hyrtacus, most
valiant in arms, whom Ida the huntress had sent in Aeneas'
company with fleet javelin and light arrows; and by his
side Euryalus, fairest of all the Aeneadae and the wearers
of Trojan arms, showing on his unshaven boy's face the
first bloom of youth. These two were one in affection,
and charged in battle together; now likewise their common guard kept the gate. Nisus cries: 'Lend the gods
this fervour to the soul, Euryalus? or does fatal passion
become a proper god to each? Long ere now my soul is
restless to begin some great deed of arms, and quiet peace
delights it not. Thou seest how confident in fortune the
Rutulians stand. Their lights glimmer far apart; buried
in drunken sleep they have sunk to rest; silence stretches
all about. Learn then what doubt, what purpose, now rises
in my spirit. People and senate, they all cry that Aeneas

be summoned, and men be sent to carry him tidings. If
they promise what I ask in thy name—for to me the glory
of the deed is enough—methinks I can find beneath
yonder hillock a path to the walls of Pallanteum town.'

Euryalus stood fixed, struck through with high ambition, and therewith speaks thus to his fervid friend :
' Dost thou shun me then, Nisus, to share thy company in
highest deeds ? shall I send thee alone into so great perils ?
Not thus did my warrior father Opheltes rear and nurture
me amid the Argive terror and the agony of Troy, nor thus
have I borne myself by thy side while following noble
Aeneas to his utmost fate.   Here is a spirit, yes here, that
scorns the light of day, that deems lightly bought at a life's
price that honour to which thou dost aspire.'

To this Nisus : ' Assuredly I had no such fear of thee ;
no, nor could I ; so may great Jupiter, or whoso looks on
earth with equal eyes, restore me to thee triumphant.   But
if haply—as thou seest often and often in so forlorn a hope
—if haply chance or deity sweep me to adverse doom, I
would have thee survive ; thine age is worthier to live.
Be there one to commit me duly to earth, rescued or ran-
somed from the battlefield : or, if fortune deny that, to pay
me far away the rites of funeral and the grace of a tomb.
Neither would I bring such pain on thy poor mother, she
who singly of many matrons hath dared to follow her boy
to the end, and slights great Acestes' city.'

And he : ' In vain dost thou string idle reasons ; nor
does my purpose yield or change its place so soon.   Let
us make haste.'   He speaks, and rouses the watch ; they
come up, and relieve the guard ; quitting their post, he and
Nisus stride on to seek the prince.

The rest of living things over all lands were soothing
their cares in sleep, and their hearts forgot their pain ;
the foremost Trojan captains, a chosen band, held council

of state upon the kingdom; what should they do, or who
would now be their messenger to Aeneas? They stand,
leaning on their long spears and grasping their shields, in
mid level of the camp.   Then Nisus and Euryalus together pray with quick urgency to be given audience ; their
matter is weighty and will be worth the delay.   Iülus at
once heard their hurried plea, and bade Nisus speak.
Thereon the son of Hyrtacus: 'Hear, O people of Aeneas,
with favourable mind, nor regard our years in what we
offer.   Sunk in sleep and wine, the Rutulians are silent ;
we have stealthily spied the open ground that lies in the
path through the gate next the sea.   The line of fires is
broken, and their smoke rises darkly upwards.   If you
allow us to use the chance towards seeking Aeneas in Pallanteum town, you will soon descry us here at hand with
the spoils of the great slaughter we have dealt.   Nor shall
we miss the way we go; up the dim valleys we have seen
the skirts of the town, and learned all the river in continual hunting.'

    Thereon aged Aletes, sage in counsel : 'Gods of our
fathers, under whose deity Troy ever stands, not wholly yet
do you purpose to blot out the Trojan race, when you have
brought us young honour and hearts so sure as this.'   So
speaking, he caught both by shoulder and hand, with tears
showering down over face and feature.   'What guerdon shall
I deem may be given you, O men, what recompense for these
noble deeds?   First and fairest shall be your reward from
the gods and your own conduct ; and Aeneas the good
shall speedily repay the rest, and Ascanius' fresh youth
never forget so great a service.'—'Nay,' breaks in Ascanius,
'I whose sole safety is in my father's return, I adjure thee
and him, O Nisus, by our great household gods, by the
tutelar spirit of Assaracus and hoar Vesta's sanctuary—on
your knees I lay all my fortune and trust—recall my father ;

give him back to sight; all sorrow disappears in his
recovery. I will give a pair of cups my father took in
vanquished Arisba, wrought in silver and rough with
tracery, twin tripods, and two large talents of gold, and an
ancient bowl of Sidonian Dido's giving. If it be indeed
our lot to possess Italy and grasp a conquering sceptre, and
to assign the spoil; thou sawest the horse and armour of
Turnus as he went all in gold; that same horse, the shield
and the ruddy plume, will I reserve from partition, thy
reward, O Nisus, even from now. My father will give
besides twelve mothers of the choicest beauty, and men
captives, all in their due array; above these, the space of
meadow-land that is now King Latinus' own domain.
Thee, O noble boy, whom mine age follows at a nearer
interval, even now I welcome to all my heart, and embrace
as my companion in every fortune. No glory shall be
sought for my state without thee; whether peace or war be
in conduct, my chiefest trust for deed and word shall be
in thee.'

Answering whom Euryalus speaks thus: 'Let but the
day never come to prove me degenerate from this daring
valour; fortune may fall prosperous or adverse. But
above all thy gifts, one thing I ask of thee. My poor
mother of Priam's ancient race, whom neither the Ilian
land nor King Acestes' city kept from following me forth,
her I now leave in ignorance of this danger, such as it is,
and without a farewell, because—night and thine hand be
witness!—I cannot bear a parent's tears. But thou, I
pray, support her want and relieve her loneliness. Let me
take with me this hope in thee, I shall go more daringly
to every fortune.' Deeply stirred at heart, the Dardanians
shed tears, fair Iülus before them all, as the likeness of his
own father's love wrung his soul. Then he speaks thus:
. . . 'Assure thyself all that is due to thy mighty enterprise;

for she shall be a mother to me, and only in name fail to
be Crëusa ; nor slight is the honour reserved for the mother
of such a son. What chance soever follow this deed, I
swear by this head whereby my father was wont to swear,
what I promise to thee on thy prosperous return shall
abide the same for thy mother and kindred.' So speaks he
weeping, and ungirds from his shoulder the sword inlaid
with gold, fashioned with marvellous skill by Lycaon of
Gnosus and fitly set in a sheath of ivory. Mnestheus gives
Nisus the shaggy spoils of a lion's hide; faithful Aletes
exchanges his helmet. They advance onward in arms, and
as they go all the company of captains, young and old,
speed them to the gates with vows. Likewise fair Iülus,
with a man's thought and a spirit beyond his years, gave
many messages to be carried to his father. But the
breezes shred all asunder and give them unaccomplished
to the clouds.

They issue and cross the trenches, and through the
shadow of night seek the fatal camp, themselves first to be
the death of many a man. All about they see bodies
strewn along the grass in drunken sleep, chariots atilt on the
shore, the men lying among their traces and wheels, with
their armour by them, and their wine. The son of
Hyrtacus began thus : 'Euryalus, now for daring hands ;
all invites them ; here lies our way ; see thou that none
raise a hand from behind against us, and keep far-sighted
watch. Here will I deal desolation, and make a broad
path for thee to follow.' So speaks he and checks his voice ;
therewith he drives his sword at lordly Rhamnes, who
haply on carpets heaped high was drawing the full breath of
sleep ; a king himself, and King Turnus' best-beloved
augur, but not all his augury could avert his doom. Three
of his household beside him, lying carelessly among their
arms, and the armour-bearer and charioteer of Remus go

down before him, caught at the horses' feet. Their drooping necks he severs with the sword, then beheads their lord
likewise and leaves the trunk spouting blood ; the dark
warm gore soaks ground and cushions. Therewithal Lamyrus
and Lamus, and beautiful young Serranus, who that night
had played long and late, and lay with the conquering god
heavy on every limb ; happy, had he played out the night,
and carried his game to day ! Even thus an unfed lion
riots through full sheepfolds, for the madness of hunger
urges him, and champs and rends the fleecy flock that are
dumb with fear, and roars with blood-stained mouth.   Nor
less is the slaughter of Euryalus ; he too rages all aflame ; an
unnamed multitude go down before his path, and Fadus
and Herbesus and Rhoetus and Abaris, unaware ; Rhoetus
awake and seeing all, but he hid in fear behind a great
bowl ; right in whose breast, as he rose close by, he plunged
the sword all its length, and drew it back heavy with death.
He vomits forth the crimson life-blood, and throws up wine
mixed with blood in the death agony.   The other presses
hotly on his stealthy errand, and now bent his way towards
Messapus' comrades, where he saw the last flicker of the
fires go down, and the horses tethered in order cropping
the grass ; when Nisus briefly speaks thus, for he saw him
carried away by excess of murderous desire ; ' Let us stop ;
for unfriendly daylight draws nigh.   Vengeance is sated to
the full ; a path is cut through the enemy.'   Much they
leave behind, men's armour wrought in solid silver, and
bowls therewith, and beautiful carpets.   Euryalus tears
away the decorations of Rhamnes and his sword-belt
embossed with gold, a gift which Caedicus, wealthiest of
men of old, sends to Remulus of Tibur when plighting
friendship far away ; he on his death-bed gives them to his
grandson for his own ; after his death the Rutulians captured
them as spoil of war ; these he fits on the shoulders valiant

in vain, then puts on Messapus' light helmet with its graceful plumes.   They issue from the camp and make for
safety.

Meanwhile an advanced guard of cavalry were on their
way from the Latin city, while the rest of their marshalled
battalions linger on the plains, and bore a reply to King
Turnus; three hundred men all under shield, in Volscens'
leading. And now they approached the camp and drew
near the wall, when they descry the two turning away by the
pathway to the left; and in the glimmering darkness of
night the forgotten helmet betrayed Euryalus, glittering as
it met the light.   It seemed no thing of chance.   Volscens
cries aloud from his column : 'Stand, men ! why on the
march, or how are you in arms ? or whither hold you your
way ?' They offer nothing in reply, but quicken their
flight into the forest, and throw themselves on the night.
On this side and that the horsemen bar the familiar crossways, and encircle every outlet with sentinels.   The forest
spread wide in tangled thickets and dark ilex ; thick growth
of briars choked it all about, and the muffled pathway
glimmered in a broken track.   Hampered by the shadowy
boughs and his cumbrous spoil, Euryalus in his fright misses
the line of way.   Nisus gets clear ; and now unthinkingly
he had passed the enemy, and the place afterwards called
Albani from Alba's name; then the deep coverts were of
King Latinus' domain ; when he stopped, and looked back
in vain for his lost friend.   ' Euryalus, unhappy ! on what
ground have I left thee ? or where shall I follow, again
unwinding all the entanglement of the treacherous woodland
way ?' Therewith he marks and retraces his footsteps, and
wanders down the silent thickets.   He hears the horses,
hears the clatter and signal-notes of the pursuers.   Nor had
he long to wait, when shouts reach his ears, and he sees
Euryalus, whom even now, in the perplexity of ground and

darkness, the whole squadron have borne down in a sudden
rush, and seize in spite of all his vain struggles. What
shall he do? with what force, what arms dare his rescue?
or shall he rush on his doom amid their swords, and find
in their wounds a speedy and glorious death? Quickly he
draws back his arm with poised spear, and looking up to
the moon on high, utters this prayer: ' Do thou give present
aid to our enterprise, O Latonian goddess, glory of the
stars and guardian of the woodlands : by all the gifts my
father Hyrtacus ever bore for my sake to thine altars, by
all mine own hand hath added from my hunting, or hung
in thy dome, or fixed on thy holy roof, grant me to confound
these masses, and guide my javelin through the air.' He
ended, and with all the force of his body hurls the steel.
The flying spear whistles through the darkness of the night,
and comes full on the shield of Sulmo, and there snaps,
and the broken shaft passes on through his heart. Spouting
a warm tide from his breast he rolls over chill in death,
and his sides throb with long-drawn gasps. Hither and
thither they gaze round. Lo, he all the fiercer was poising
another weapon high by his ear; while they hesitate, the
spear went whizzing through both Tagus' temples, and
pierced and stuck fast in the warm brain. Volscens is mad
with rage, and nowhere espies the sender of the weapon,
nor where to direct his fury. ' Yet meanwhile thy warm
blood shalt pay me vengeance for both,' he cries; and
unsheathing his sword, he made at Euryalus. Then indeed
frantic with terror Nisus shrieks out; no longer could he
shroud himself in darkness or endure such agony. 'On
me, on me, I am here, I did it, on me turn your steel, O
Rutulians! Mine is all the guilt; he dared not, no, nor
could not; to this heaven I appeal and the stars that know;
he only loved his hapless friend too well.' Such words he
was uttering; but the sword driven hard home is gone

clean through his ribs and pierces the white breast.
Euryalus rolls over in death, and the blood runs over his
lovely limbs, and his neck sinks and settles on his shoulder;
even as when a lustrous flower cut away by the plough
droops in death, or weary-necked poppies bow down their
head if overweighted with a random shower. But Nisus
rushes amidst them, and alone among them all makes at
Volscens, keeps to Volscens alone : round him the foe
cluster, and on this side and that hurl him back : none the
less he presses on, and whirls his sword like lightning, till
he plunges it full in the face of the shrieking Rutulian, and
slays his enemy as he dies. Then, stabbed through and
through, he flung himself above his lifeless friend, and there
at last found the quiet sleep of death.

Happy pair ! if my verse is aught of avail, no length of
days shall ever blot you from the memory of time, while
the house of Aeneas shall dwell by the Capitoline's stedfast
stone, and the lord of Rome hold sovereignty.

The victorious Rutulians, with their spoils and the
plunder regained, bore dead Volscens weeping to the camp.
Nor in the camp was the wailing less, when Rhamnes was
found a bloodless corpse, and Serranus and Numa and all
their princes destroyed in a single slaughter. Crowds
throng towards the corpses and the men wounded to death,
the ground fresh with warm slaughter and the swoln run-
lets of frothing blood. They mutually recognise the spoils,
Messapus' shining helmet and the decorations that cost
such sweat to win back.

And now Dawn, leaving the saffron bed of Tithonus,
scattered over earth her fresh shafts of early light ; now the
sunlight streams in, now daylight unveils the world. Turnus,
himself fully armed, awakes his men to arms, and each
leader marshals to battle his brazen lines and whets their
ardour with varying rumours. Nay, pitiable sight ! they

fix on spear-points and uprear and follow with loud shouts
the heads of Euryalus and Nisus. . . . The Aeneadae
stubbornly face them, lining the left hand wall (for their
right is girdled by the river), hold the deep trenches and
stand gloomily on the high towers, stirred withal by the
faces they know, alas, too well, in their dark dripping gore.
Meanwhile Rumour on flutttering wings rushes with the
news through the alarmed town and glides to the ears of
Euryalus' mother.   But instantly the warmth leaves her
woeful body, the shuttle starts from her hand and the threads
unroll.   She darts forth in agony, and with woman's wailing and torn hair runs distractedly towards the walls and
the foremost columns, recking naught of men, naught of
peril or weapons ; thereon she fills the air with her complaint : ' Is it thus I behold thee, O Euryalus ?   Couldst
thou, the latest solace of mine age, leave me alone so
cruelly ? nor when sent into such danger was one last word
of thee allowed thine unhappy mother ?   Alas, thou liest
in a strange land, given for a prey to the dogs and fowls of
Latium ! nor was I, thy mother, there for chief mourner, to
lay thee out or close thine eyes or wash thy wounds, and
cover thee with the garment I hastened on for thee whole
nights and days, an anxious old woman taking comfort from
the loom.   Whither shall I follow ? or what land now holds
thy mangled corpse, thy body torn limb from limb ?   Is this
all of what thou wert that returns to me, O my son ? is it this
I have followed by land and sea ?   Strike me through of your
pity, on me cast all your weapons, Rutulians ; make me
the first sacrifice of your steel.   Or do thou, mighty lord of
heaven, be merciful, and with thine own weapon hurl this
hateful life to the nether deep, since in no wise else may I
break away from life's cruelty.'   At this weeping cry their
courage falters, and a sigh of sorrow passes all along ; their
strength is benumbed and broken for battle.   Her, while

her grief kindled, at Ilioneus' and weeping Iülus' bidding
Idaeus and Actor catch up and carry home in their arms.

But the terrible trumpet-note afar rang on the shrill
brass; a shout follows, and is echoed from the sky. The
Volscians hasten up in even line under their advancing roof
of shields, and set to fill up the trenches and tear down the
palisades. Some seek entrance by scaling the walls with
ladders, where the defenders' battle-line is thin, and light
shows through gaps in the ring of men. The Teucrians in
return shower weapons of every sort, and push them down
with stiff poles, practised by long warfare in their ramparts'
defence : and fiercely hurl heavy stones, so be they may
break the shielded line ; while they, crowded under their
shell, lightly bear all the downpour. But now they fail;
for where the vast mass presses close, the Teucrians roll a
huge block tumbling down that makes a wide gap in the
Rutulians and crashes through their armour-plating. Nor
do the bold Rutulians care longer to continue the blind
fight, but strive to clear the rampart with missiles. . . . Elsewhere in dreadful guise Mezentius brandishes his Etruscan
pine and hurls smoking brands ; but Messapus, tamer of
horses, seed of Neptune, tears away the palisading and calls
for ladders to the ramparts.

Thy sisterhood, O Calliope, I pray inspire me while I sing
the destruction spread then and there by Turnus' sword, the
deaths dealt from his hand, and whom each warrior sent
down to the under world ; and unroll with me the broad
borders of war.

A tower loomed vast with lofty gangways at a point of
vantage ; this all the Italians strove with main strength to
storm, and set all their might and device to overthrow it ;
the Trojans in return defended it with stones and hurled
showers of darts through the loopholes. Turnus, leading
the attack, threw a blazing torch that caught flaming on the

side wall; swoln by the wind, the flame seized the plank-
ing and clung devouring to the standards. Those within, in
hurry and confusion, desire retreat from their distress; in
vain; while they cluster together and fall back to the side
free from the destroyer, the tower sinks prone under the
sudden weight with a crash that thunders through all the
sky. Pierced by their own weapons, and impaled on hard
splinters of wood, they come half slain to the ground with
the vast mass behind them. Scarcely do Helenor alone
and Lycus struggle out; Helenor in his early prime, whom
a slave woman of Licymnos bore in secret to the Maeonian
king, and sent to Troy in forbidden weapons, lightly armed
with sheathless sword and white unemblazoned shield.
And he, when he saw himself among Turnus' encircling
thousands, ranks on this side and ranks on this of Latins,
as a wild beast which, girt with a crowded ring of
hunters, dashes at their weapons, hurls herself unblinded
on death, and comes with a bound upon the spears; even
so he rushes to his death amid the enemy, and presses on
where he sees their weapons thickest. But Lycus, far
fleeter of foot, holds by the walls in flight midway among
foes and arms, and strives to catch the coping in his grasp
and reach the hands of his comrades. And Turnus pursuing and aiming as he ran, thus upbraids him in triumph:
'Didst thou hope, madman, thou mightest escape our
hands?' and catches him as he clings, and tears him and
a great piece of the wall away: as when, with a hare or
snowy-bodied swan in his crooked talons, Jove's armour-
bearer soars aloft, or the wolf of Mars snatches from the
folds some lamb sought of his mother with incessant
bleating. On all sides a shout goes up. They advance
and fill the trenches with heaps of earth; some toss glowing
brands on the roofs. Ilioneus strikes down Lucetius with a
great fragment of mountain rock as, carrying fire, he draws

·   P

nigh the gate. Liger slays Emathion, Asylas Corinaeus, the one skilled with the javelin, the other with the stealthy arrow from afar. Caeneus slays Ortygius; Turnus victorious Caeneus; Turnus Itys and Clonius, Dioxippus, and Promolus, and Sagaris, and Idas where he stood in front of the turret top; Capys Privernus: him Themillas' spear had first grazed lightly; the madman threw down his shield to carry his hand to the wound; so the arrow winged her way, and pinning his hand to his left side, broke into the lungs with deadly wound. The son of Arcens stood splendid in arms, and scarf embroidered with needlework and bright with Iberian blue, the beautiful boy sent by his father Arcens from nurture in the grove of our Lady about the streams of Symaethus, where Palicus' altar is rich and gracious. Laying down his spear, Mezentius whirled thrice round his head the tightened cord of his whistling sling, pierced him full between the temples with the molten bullet, and stretched him all his length upon the sand.

Then, it is said, Ascanius first aimed his flying shaft in war, wont before to frighten beasts of the chase, and struck down a brave Numanian, Remulus by name, but lately allied in bridal to Turnus' younger sister. He advancing before his ranks clamoured things fit and unfit to tell, and strode along lofty and voluble, his heart lifted up with his fresh royalty.

'Take you not shame to be again held‧leaguered in your ramparts, O Phrygians twice taken, and to make walls your fence from death? Behold them who demand in war our wives for theirs! What god, what madness, hath driven you to Italy? Here are no sons of Atreus nor glozing Ulysses. A race of hardy breed, we carry our newborn children to the streams and harden them in the bitter icy water; as boys they spend wakeful nights over the chase, and tire out the woodland; but in manhood,

unwearied by toil and trained to poverty, they subdue the
soil with their mattocks, or shake towns in war. Every
age wears iron, and we goad the flanks of our oxen with
reversed spear; nor does creeping old age weaken our
strength of spirit or abate our force. White hairs bear
the weight of the helmet; and it is ever our delight to
drive in fresh spoil and live on our plunder. Yours is
embroidered raiment of saffron and shining sea-purple.
Indolence is your pleasure, your delight the luxurious
dance; you wear sleeved tunics and ribboned turbans. O
right Phrygian women, not even Phrygian men! traverse
the heights of Dindymus, where the double-mouthed flute
breathes familiar music. The drums call you, and the
Berecyntian boxwood of the mother of Ida; leave arms to
men, and lay down the sword.'

   As he flung forth such words of ill-ominous strain,
Ascanius brooked it not, and aimed an arrow on him from
the stretched horse sinew; and as he drew his arms
asunder, first stayed to supplicate Jove in lowly vows:
' Jupiter omnipotent, deign to favour this daring deed.
My hands shall bear yearly gifts to thee in thy temple, and
bring to stand before thine altars a steer with gilded forehead, snow-white, carrying his head high as his mother's,
already pushing with his horn and making the sand fly up
under his feet.' The Father heard and from a clear space
of sky thundered on the left; at once the fated bow rings,
the grim-whistling arrow flies from the tense string, and
goes through the head of Remulus, the steel piercing
through from temple to temple. 'Go, mock valour with
insolence of speech! Phrygians twice taken return this
answer to Rutulians.' Thus and no further Ascanius; the
Teucrians respond in cheers, and shout for joy in rising
height of courage. Then haply in the tract of heaven
tressed Apollo sate looking down from his cloud on the

Ausonian ranks and town, and thus addresses triumphant
Iülus: 'Good speed to thy young valour, O boy! this is
the way to heaven, child of gods and parent of gods to be!
Rightly shall all wars fated to come sink to peace beneath
the line of Assaracus; nor art thou bounded in a Troy.'
So speaking, he darts from heaven's height, and cleaving
the breezy air, seeks Ascanius. Then he changes the
fashion of his countenance, and becomes aged Butes,
armour-bearer of old to Dardanian Anchises, and the faithful porter of his threshold; thereafter his lord gave him
for Ascanius' attendant. In all points like the old man
Apollo came, voice and colour, white hair, and grimly
clashing arms, and speaks these words to eager Iülus:
    'Be it enough, son of Aeneas, that the Numanian hath
fallen unavenged beneath thine arrows; this first honour
great Apollo allows thee, nor envies the arms that match
his own. Further, O boy, let war alone.' Thus Apollo
began, and yet speaking retreated from mortal view,
vanishing into thin air away out of their eyes. The
Dardanian princes knew the god and the arms of deity,
and heard the clash of his quiver as he went. So they
restrain Ascanius' keenness for battle by the words of
Phoebus' will; themselves they again close in conflict, and
cast their lives into the perilous breach. Shouts run all
along the battlemented walls; ringing bows are drawn and
javelin thongs twisted: all the ground is strewn with
missiles. Shields and hollow helmets ring to blows; the
battle swells fierce; heavy as the shower lashes the ground
that sets in when the Kids are rainy in the West; thick
as hail pours down from storm-clouds on the shallows,
when the rough lord of the winds congeals his watery
deluge and breaks up the hollow vapours in the sky.
    Pandarus and Bitias, sprung of Alcanor of Ida, whom
woodland Iaera bore in the grove of Jupiter, grown now

tall as their ancestral pines and hills, fling open the gates
barred by their captain's order, and confident in arms,
wilfully invite the enemy within the walls. Themselves
within they stand to right and left in front of the towers,
sheathed in iron, the plumes flickering over their stately
heads: even as high in air around the gliding streams,
whether on Padus' banks or by pleasant Athesis, twin oaks
rise lifting their unshorn heads into the sky with high tops
asway. The Rutulians pour in when they see the entrance
open. Straightway Quercens and Aquicolus beautiful in
arms, and desperate Tmarus, and Haemon, seed of Mars,
either gave back in rout with all their columns, or in the
very gateway laid down their life. Then the spirits of the
combatants swell in rising wrath, and now the Trojans
gather swarming to the spot, and dare to close hand to
hand and to sally farther out.

News is brought to Turnus the captain, as he rages
afar among the routed foe, that the enemy surges forth
into fresh slaughter and flings wide his gates. He breaks
off unfinished, and, fired with immense anger, rushes towards
the haughty brethren at the Dardanian gate. And on
Antiphates first, for first he came, the bastard son of
mighty Sarpedon by a Theban mother, he hurls his javelin
and strikes him down; the Italian cornel flies through the
yielding air, and, piercing the gullet, runs deep into his
breast; a frothing tide pours from the dark yawning wound,
and the steel grows warm where it pierces the lung. Then
Meropes and Erymas, then Aphidnus goes down before his
hand; then Bitias, fiery-eyed and exultant, not with a
javelin; for not to a javelin had he given his life; but the
loud-whistling pike came hurled with a thunderbolt's force;
neither twofold bull's hide kept it back, nor the trusty
corslet's double scales of gold: his vast limbs sink in a
heap; earth utters a groan, and the great shield clashes

over him : even as once and again on the Euboïc shore
of Baiae falls a mass of stone, built up of great blocks
and so cast into the sea ; thus does it tumble prone,
crashes into the shoal water and sinks deep to rest ;
the seas are stirred, and the dark sand eddies up ; therewith the depth of Prochyta quivers at the sound, and the
couchant rocks of Inarime, piled above Typhoeus by Jove's
commands.

   On this Mars armipotent raised the spirit and strength
of the Latins, and goaded their hearts to rage, and sent
Flight and dark Fear among the Teucrians. From all
quarters they gather, since battle is freely offered ; and the
warrior god inspires. . . . Pandarus, at his brother's fall,
sees how fortune stands, what hap rules the day ; and
swinging the gate round on its hinge with all his force,
pushes it to with his broad shoulders, leaving many of his
own people shut outside the walls in the desperate conflict,
but shutting others in with him as they pour back in retreat.
Madman ! who saw not the Rutulian prince burst in amid
their columns, and fairly shut him into the town, like a
monstrous tiger among the silly flocks. At once strange
light flashed from his eyes, and his armour rang terribly ;
the blood-red plumes flicker on his head, and lightnings
shoot sparkling from his shield. In sudden dismay the
Aeneadae know the hated form and giant limbs. Then
tall Pandarus leaps forward, in burning rage at his brother's
death : ' This is not the palace of Amata's dower,' he cries,
' nor does Ardea enclose Turnus in her native walls. Thou
seest a hostile camp ; escape hence is hopeless.' To him
Turnus, smiling and cool : ' Begin with all thy valiance,
and close hand to hand ; here too shalt thou tell that a
Priam found his Achilles.' He ended ; the other, putting
out all his strength, hurls his rough spear, knotty and un-
peeled. The breezes caught it ; Juno, daughter of Saturn,

made the wound glance off as it came, and the spear sticks
fast in the gate. 'But this weapon that my strong hand
whirls, this thou shalt not escape; for not such is he who
sends weapon and wound.' So speaks he, and rises high on
his uplifted sword; the steel severs the forehead midway
right between the temples, and divides the beardless cheeks
with ghastly wound. He crashes down; earth shakes under
the vast weight; dying limbs and brain-spattered armour
tumble in a heap to the ground, and the head, evenly
severed, dangles this way and that from either shoulder.
The Trojans scatter and turn in hasty terror; and had the
conqueror forthwith taken thought to burst the bars and let
in his comrades at the gate, that had been the last day of
the war and of the nation. But rage and mad thirst of
slaughter drive him like fire on the foe. . . . First he
catches up Phalaris; then Gyges, and hamstrings him; he
plucks away their spears, and hurls them on the backs of
the flying crowd; Juno lends strength and courage. Halys
he sends to join them, and Phegeus, pierced right through
the shield; then, as they ignorantly raised their war-cry on
the walls, Alcander and Halius, Noëmon and Prytanis.
Lynceus advanced to meet him, calling up his comrades;
from the rampart the glittering sword sweeps to the left and
catches him; struck off by the one downright blow, head
and helmet lay far away. Next Amycus fell, the deadly
huntsman, incomparable in skill of hand to anoint his
arrows and arm their steel with venom; and Clytius the
Aeolid, and Cretheus beloved of the Muses, Cretheus of
the Muses' company, whose delight was ever in songs and
harps and stringing of verses; ever he sang of steeds and
armed men and battles.

At last, hearing of the slaughter of their men, the
Teucrian captains, Mnestheus and gallant Serestus, come
up, and see their comrades in disordered flight and the foe

let in. And Mnestheus : 'Whither next, whither press you
in flight ? what other walls, what farther city have you yet ?
Shall one man, and he girt in on all sides, fellow-citizens,
by your entrenchments, thus unchecked deal devastation
throughout our city, and send all our best warriors to the
under world ? Have you no pity, no shame, cowards, for
your unhappy country, for your ancient gods, for great
Aeneas ?'

Kindled by such words, they take heart and rally in
dense array. Little by little Turnus drew away from the
fight towards the river, and the side encircled by the stream :
the more bravely the Teucrians press on him with loud
shouts and thickening masses, even as a band that fall on
a wrathful lion with levelled weapons, but he, frightened
back, retires surly and grim-glaring ; and neither does wrath
nor courage let him turn his back, nor can he make head, for
all that he desires it, against the surrounding arms and men.
Even thus Turnus draws lingeringly backward, with un-
hastened steps, and soul boiling in anger. Nay, twice even
then did he charge amid the enemy, twice drove them in
flying rout along the walls. But all the force of the camp
gathers hastily up ; nor does Juno, daughter of Saturn, dare
to supply him strength to countervail ; for Jupiter sent Iris
down through the aery sky, bearing stern orders to his sister
that Turnus shall withdraw from the high Trojan town.
Therefore neither with shield nor hand can he keep his
ground, so overpoweringly from all sides comes upon him
the storm of weapons. About the hollows of his temples
the helmet rings with incessant clash, and the solid brass is
riven beneath the stones ; the horsehair crest is rent away ;
the shield-boss avails not under the blows ; Mnestheus
thunders on with his Trojans, and pours in a storm of
spears. All over him the sweat trickles and pours in swart
stream, and no breathing space is given ; sick gasps shake

his exhausted limbs.   Then at last, with a headlong bound,
he leapt fully armed into the river; the river's yellow
eddies opened for him as he came, and the buoyant water
brought him up, and, washing away the slaughter, returned
him triumphant to his comrades.

BOOK TENTH

THE BATTLE ON THE BEACH

MEANWHILE the heavenly house omnipotent unfolds her doors, and the father of gods and king of men calls a council in the starry dwelling; whence he looks sheer down on the whole earth, the Dardanian camp, and the peoples of Latium. They sit down within from doorway to doorway: their lord begins:

'Lords of heaven, wherefore is your decree turned back, and your minds thus jealously at strife? I forbade Italy to join battle with the Teucrians; why this quarrel in face of my injunction? What terror hath bidden one or another run after arms and tempt the sword? The due time of battle will arrive, call it not forth, when furious Carthage shall one day sunder the Alps to hurl ruin full on the towers of Rome. Then hatred may grapple with hatred, then hostilities be opened; now let them be, and cheerfully join in the treaty we ordain.'

Thus Jupiter in brief; but not briefly golden Venus returns in answer: . . .

'O Lord, O everlasting Governor of men and things—for what else may we yet supplicate?—beholdest thou how the Rutulians brave it, and Turnus, borne charioted through the ranks, proudly sweeps down the tide of battle? Dar

and bulwark no longer shelter the Trojans ; nay, within the
gates and even on the mounded walls they clash in battle
and make the trenches swim with blood.   Aeneas is away
and ignorant.   Wilt thou never then let our leaguer be
raised ?   Again a foe overhangs the walls of infant Troy ;
and another army, and a second son of Tydeus rises from
Aetolian Arpi against the Trojans.   Truly I think my
wounds are yet to come, and I thy child am keeping some
mortal weapons idle.   If the Trojans steered for Italy without thy leave and defiant of thy deity, let them expiate their
sin ; aid not such with thy succour.   But if so many oracles
guided them, given by god and ghost, why may aught now
reverse thine ordinance or write destiny anew ?   Why should
I recall the fleets burned on the coast of Eryx ?   why the
king of storms, and the raging winds roused from Aeolia, or
Iris driven down the clouds ?   Now hell too is stirred (this
share of the world was yet untried) and Allecto suddenly
let loose above to riot through the Italian towns.   In no
wise am I moved for empire ; that was our hope while
Fortune stood ; let those conquer whom thou wilt.   If thy
cruel wife leave no region free to Teucrians, by the smoking
ruins of desolated Troy, O father, I beseech thee, grant
Ascanius unhurt retreat from arms, grant me my child's
life.   Aeneas may well be tossed over unknown seas and
follow what path soever fortune open to him ; him let me
avail to shelter and withdraw from the turmoil of battle.
Amathus is mine, high Paphos and Cythera, and my house
of Idalia ; here, far from arms, let him spend an inglorious
life.   Bid Carthage in high lordship rule Ausonia ; there
will be nothing there to check the Tyrian cities.   What help
was it for the Trojans to escape war's doom and thread
their flight through Argive fires, to have exhausted all those
perils of sea and desolate lands, while they seek Latium
and the towers of a Troy rebuilt ?   Were it not better to have

clung to the last ashes of their country, and the ground
where once was Troy?   Give back, I pray, Xanthus and
Simoïs to a wretched people, and let the Teucrians again,
O Lord, circle through the fates of Ilium.'
     Then Queen Juno, swift and passionate :
     'Why forcest thou me to break long silence and pro-
claim my hidden pain?   Hath any man or god constrained
Aeneas to court war or make armed attack on King Latinus?
In oracular guidance he steered for Italy : be it so : he
whom raving Cassandra sent on his way !   Did we urge him
to quit the camp or entrust his life to the winds? to give
the issue of war and the charge of his ramparts to a child?
to stir the loyalty of Tyrrhenia or throw peaceful nations
into tumult?   What god, what potent cruelty of ours, hath
driven him on his hurt?   Where is Juno in this, or Iris
sped down the clouds?   It shocks thee that Italians should
enring an infant Troy with flame, and Turnus set foot on
his own ancestral soil—he, grandchild of Pilumnus, son of
Venilia the goddess : how, that the dark brands of Troy
assail the Latins? that Trojans subjugate and plunder fields
not their own? how, that they choose their brides and tear
plighted bosom from bosom? that their gestures plead for
peace, and their ships are lined with arms?   Thou canst
steal thine Aeneas from Grecian hands, and spread before
them a human semblance of mist and empty air; thou canst
turn his fleet into nymphs of like number : is it dreadful if
we retaliate with any aid to the Rutulians?   Aeneas is away
and ignorant; away and ignorant let him be.   Paphos is
thine and Idalium, thine high Cythera ; why meddlest thou
with fierce spirits and a city big with war?   Is it we who
would overthrow the tottering state of Phrygia? we? or he
who brought the Achaeans down on the hapless Trojans?
who made Europe and Asia bristle up in arms, and whose
theft shattered the alliance?   Was it in my guidance the

adulterous Dardanian broke into Sparta ? or did I send the shafts of passion that kindled war ? Then terror for thy children had graced thee ; too late now dost thou rise with unjust complaints, and reproaches leave thy lips in vain.'

Thus Juno pleaded ; and all the heavenly people murmured in diverse consent ; even as rising gusts murmur when caught in the forests, and eddy in blind moanings, betraying to sailors the gale's approach. Then the Lord omnipotent and primal power of the world begins ; as he speaks the high house of the gods and trembling floor of earth sink to silence ; silent is the deep sky, and the breezes are stilled ; ocean hushes his waters into calm.

'Take then to heart and lay deep these words of mine. Since it may not be that Ausonians and Teucrians join alliance, and your quarrel finds no term, to-day, what fortune each wins, what hope each follows, be he Trojan or Rutulian, I will hold in even poise ; whether it be Italy's fate or Trojan blundering and ill advice that holds the camp in leaguer. Nor do I acquit the Rutulians. Each as he hath begun shall work out his destiny. Jupiter is one and king over all ; the fates will find their way.' By his brother's infernal streams, by the banks of the pitchy black-boiling chasm he signed assent, and made all Olympus quiver at his nod. Here speaking ended : thereon Jupiter rises from his golden throne, and the heavenly people surround and escort him to the doorway.

Meanwhile the Rutulians press round all the gates, dealing grim slaughter and girdling the walls with flame. But the army of the Aeneadae are held leaguered within their trenches, with no hope of retreat. They stand helpless and disconsolate on their high towers, and their thin ring girdles the walls,—Asius, son of Imbrasus, and Thymoetes, son of Hicetaon, and the two Assaraci, and Castor, and old Thymbris together in the front rank : by them Clarus and

Themon, both full brothers to Sarpedon, out of high Lycia. Acmon of Lyrnesus, great as his father Clytius, or his brother Mnestheus, carries a stone, straining all his vast frame to the huge mountain fragment. Emulously they keep their guard, these with javelins, those with stones, and wield fire and fit arrows on the string. Amid them he, Venus' fittest care, lo! the Dardanian boy, his graceful head uncovered, shines even as a gem set in red gold on ornament of throat or head, or even as gleaming ivory cunningly inlaid in boxwood or Orician terebinth ; his tresses lie spread over his milk-white neck, bound by a flexible circlet of gold. Thee, too, Ismarus, proud nations saw aiming wounds and arming thy shafts with poison,— thee, of house illustrious in Maeonia, where the rich tilth is wrought by men's hands, and Pactolus waters it with gold. There too was Mnestheus, exalted in fame as he who erewhile had driven Turnus from the ramparts ; and Capys, from whom is drawn the name of the Campanian city.

They had closed in grim war's mutual conflict ; Aeneas, while night was. yet deep, clove the seas. For when, leaving Evander for the Etruscan camp, he hath audience of the king, and tells the king of his name and race, and what he asks or offers, instructs him of the arms Mezentius is winning to his side, and of Turnus' overbearing spirit, reminds him what is all the certainty of human things, and mingles all with entreaties ; delaying not, Tarchon joins forces and strikes alliance. Then, freed from the oracle, the Lydian people man their fleet, laid by divine ordinance in the foreign captain's hand. Aeneas' galley keeps in front, with the lions of Phrygia fastened on her prow, above them overhanging Ida, sight most welcome to the Trojan exiles. Here great Aeneas sits revolving the changing issues of war ; and Pallas, clinging on his left side, asks now

of the stars and their pathway through the dark night, now
of his fortunes by land and sea.

Open now the gates of Helicon, goddesses, and stir the
song of the band that come the while with Aeneas from the
Tuscan borders, and sail in armed ships overseas.

First in the brazen-plated Tiger Massicus cuts the flood;
beneath him are ranked a thousand men who have left
Clusium town and the city of Cosae; their weapons are
arrows, and light quivers on the shoulder, and their deadly
bow. With him goes grim Abas, all his train in shining
armour, and a gilded Apollo glittering astern. To him
Populonia had given six hundred of her children, tried in
war, but Ilva three hundred, the island rich in unexhausted
mines of steel. Third Asilas, interpreter between men
and gods, master of the entrails of beasts and the stars in
heaven, of speech of birds and ominous lightning flashes,
draws a thousand men after him in serried lines bristling
with spears, bidden to his command from Pisa city, of
Alphaean birth on Etruscan soil. Astyr follows, excellent
in beauty, Astyr, confident in his horse and glancing arms.
Three hundred more—all have one heart to follow—come
from the householders of Caere and the fields of Minio, and
ancient Pyrgi, and fever-stricken Graviscae.

Let me not pass thee by, O Cinyras, bravest in war of
Ligurian captains, and thee, Cupavo, with thy scant company, from whose crest rise the swan plumes, fault, O
Love, of thee and thine, and blazonment of his father's
form. For they tell that Cycnus, in grief for his beloved
Phaëthon, while he sings and soothes his woeful love with
music amid the shady sisterhood of poplar boughs, drew
over him the soft plumage of white old age, and left earth
and passed crying through the sky. His son, followed on
shipboard with a band of like age, sweeps the huge Centaur
forward with his oars; he leans over the water, and

threatens the waves with a vast rock he holds on high, and furrows the deep seas with his length of keel.

He too calls a train from his native coasts, Ocnus, son of prophetic Manto and the river of Tuscany, who gave thee, O Mantua, ramparts and his mother's name ; Mantua, rich in ancestry, yet not all of one blood, a threefold race, and under each race four cantons ; herself she is the cantons' head, and her strength is of Tuscan blood. From her likewise hath Mezentius five hundred in arms against him, whom Mincius, child of Benacus, draped in gray reeds, led to battle in his advancing pine. Aulestes moves on heavily, smiting the waves with the swinging forest of an hundred oars ; the channels foam as they sweep the sea-floor. He sails in the vast Triton, who amazes the blue waterways with his shell, and swims on with shaggy front, in human show from the flank upward ; his belly ends in a dragon ; beneath the monster's breast the wave gurgles into foam. So many were the chosen princes who went in thirty ships to aid Troy, and cut the salt plains with brazen prow.

And now day had faded from the sky, and gracious Phoebe trod mid-heaven in the chariot of her nightly wandering : Aeneas, for his charge allows not rest to his limbs, himself sits guiding the tiller and managing the sails. And lo, in middle course a band of his own fellow-voyagers meets him, the nymphs whom bountiful Cybele had bidden be gods of the sea, and turn to nymphs from ships ; they swam on in even order, and cleft the flood, as many as erewhile, brazen-plated prows, had anchored on the beach. From far they know their king, and wheel their bands about him, and Cymodocea, their readiest in speech, comes up behind, catching the stern with her right hand : her back rises out, and her left hand oars her passage through the silent water. Then she thus accosts her amazed lord : 'Wakest thou, seed of gods, Aeneas ? wake, and loosen the sheets of thy sails. We are thy fleet, Idaean pines from the holy hill, now nymphs of the sea. When the treacherous Rutulian urged us head-long with sword and fire, unwillingly we broke thy bonds, and we search for thee over ocean. This new guise our Lady made for us in pity, and granted us to be goddesses and spend our life under the waves. But thy boy Ascanius is held within wall and trench among the Latin weapons and the rough edge of war. Already the Arcadian cavalry and the brave Etruscan together hold the appointed ground. Turnus' plan is fixed to bar their way with his squadrons, that they may not reach the camp. Up and arise, and ere the coming of the Dawn bid thy crews be called to arms ; and take thou the shield which the Lord of Fire forged for victory and rimmed about with gold. To-morrow's daylight, if thou deem not my words vain, shall see Rutulians heaped high in slaughter.' She ended, . and, as she went, pushed the tall ship on with her hand wisely and well ; the ship shoots through the water fleeter than javelin or windswift arrow. Thereat the rest quicken their speed. The son of Anchises of Troy is himself deep in bewilderment ; yet the omen cheers his courage. Then looking on the heavenly vault, he briefly prays : 'O gracious upon Ida, mother of gods, whose delight is in Dindy-mus and turreted cities and lions coupled to thy rein, do thou lead me in battle, do thou meetly prosper thine augury, and draw nigh thy Phrygians, goddess, with favour-able feet.' Thus much he spoke ; and meanwhile the broad light of returning day now began to pour in, and chased away the night. First he commands his comrades to follow his signals, brace their courage to arms and prepare for battle. And now his Trojans and his camp are in his sight as he stands high astern, when next he lifts the

blazing shield on his left arm. The Dardanians on the
walls raise a shout to the sky.   Hope comes to kindle
wrath ; they hurl their missiles strongly; even as under
black clouds cranes from the Strymon utter their signal
notes and sail clamouring across the sky, and noisily stream
down the gale. But this seemed marvellous to the
Rutulian king and the captains of Ausonia, till looking
back they see the ships steering for the beach, and all the
sea as a single fleet sailing in.   His helmet-spike blazes,
flame pours from the cresting plumes, and the golden
shield-boss spouts floods of fire; even as when in trans-
parent night comets glow blood-red and drear, or the
splendour of Sirius, that brings drought and sicknesses on
wretched men, rises and saddens the sky with malignant
beams.

Yet gallant Turnus in unfailing confidence will prevent
them on the shore and repel their approach to land.
'What your prayers have sought is given, the sweep of the
sword-arm.   The god of battles is in the hands of men.
Now remember each his wife and home : now recall the
high deeds of our fathers' honour.   Let us challenge meeting at the water's edge, while they waver and their feet yet
slip as they disembark.   Fortune aids daring. . . .' So
speaks he, and counsels inly whom he shall lead to meet
them, whom leave in charge of the leaguered walls.

Meanwhile Aeneas lands his allies by gangways from the
high ships.   Many watch the retreat and slack of the sea,
and leap boldly into the shoal water; others slide down the
oars.   Tarchon, marking the shore where the shallows do
not seethe and plash with broken water, but the sea glides
up and spreads its tide unbroken, suddenly turns his bows
to land and implores his comrades : 'Now, O chosen crew,
bend strongly to your oars; lift your ships, make them go ;
let the prows cleave this hostile land and the keel plough

herself a furrow.   I will let my vessel break up on such
harbourage if once she takes the land.'   When Tarchon
had spoken in such wise, his comrades rise on their oar-
blades and carry their ships in foam towards the Latin
fields, till the prows are fast on dry land and all the keels
are aground unhurt.   But not thy galley, Tarchon ; for she
dashes on a shoal, and swings long swaying on the cruel
bank, pitching and slapping the flood, then breaks up,
and lands her crew among the waves.   Broken oars and
floating thwarts entangle them, and the ebbing wave sucks
their feet away.

Nor does Turnus keep idly dallying, but swiftly hurries
his whole array against the Trojans and ranges it to face
the beach.   The trumpets blow.   At once Aeneas charges
and confounds the rustic squadrons of the Latins, and slays
Theron for omen of battle.   The giant advances to challenge
Aeneas ; but through sewed plates of brass and tunic
rough with gold the sword plunges in his open side.   Next
he strikes Lichas, cut from his mother already dead, and
consecrated, Phoebus, to thee, since his infancy was
granted escape from the perilous steel.   Near thereby he
struck dead brawny Cisseus and vast Gyas, whose clubs
were mowing down whole files : naught availed them the
arms of Hercules and their strength of hand, nor Melampus
their father, ever of Alcides' company while earth yielded
him sore travail.   Lo ! while Pharus utters weak vaunts the
hurled javelin strikes on his shouting mouth.   Thou too,
while thou followest thy new delight, Clytius, whose cheeks
are golden with youthful down—thou, luckless Cydon, struck
down by the Dardanian hand, wert lying past thought, ah
pitiable ! of the young loves that were ever thine, did not
the close array of thy brethren interpose, the children of
Phorcus, seven in number, and send a sevenfold shower of
darts.   Some glance ineffectual from helmet and shield ;

some Venus the bountiful turned aside as they grazed his body. Aeneas calls to trusty Achates : ' Give me store of weapons ; none that hath been planted in Grecian body on the plains of Ilium shall my hand hurl at Rutulian in vain.' Then he catches and throws his great spear ; the spear flies grinding through the brass of Maeon's shield, and breaks through corslet and through breast. His brother Alcanor runs up and sustains with his right arm his sinking brother ; through his arm the spear passes speeding straight on its message, and holds its bloody way, and the hand dangles by the sinews lifeless from the shoulder. Then Numitor, seizing his dead brother's javelin, aims at Aeneas, but might not fairly pierce him, and grazed tall Achates on the thigh. Here Clausus of Cures comes confident in his pride of strength, and with a long reach strikes Dryops under the chin, and, urging the stiff spear-shaft home, stops the accents of his speech and his life together, piercing the throat ; but he strikes the earth with his forehead, and vomits clots of blood. Three Thracians likewise of Boreas' sovereign race, and three sent by their father Idas from their native Ismarus, fall in divers wise before him. Halesus and his Auruncan troops hasten thither ; Messapus too, seed of Neptune, comes up charioted. This side and that strive to hurl back the enemy, and fight hard on the very edge of Ausonia. As when in the depth of air adverse winds rise in battle with equal spirit and strength ; not they, not clouds nor sea, yield one to another ; long the battle is doubtful ; all stands locked in counterpoise : even thus clash the ranks of Troy and ranks of Latium, foot fast on foot, and man crowded up on man.

But in another quarter, where a torrent had driven a wide path of rolling stones and bushes torn away from the banks, Pallas saw his Arcadians, unaccustomed to move as infantry, giving back before the Latin pursuit, when the

roughness of the ground bade them dismount. This only
was left in his strait, to kindle them to valour, now by
entreaties, now by taunts: ' Whither flee you, comrades ?
by your deeds of bravery, by your leader Evander's name,
by your triumphant campaigns, and my hope that now rises
to rival my father's honour, trust not to flight. Our swords
must hew a way through the enemy. Where yonder mass
of men presses thickest, there your proud country calls you
with Pallas at your head. No gods are they who bear us
down; mortals, we feel the pressure of a mortal foe; we
have as many lives and hands as he. Lo, the deep shuts
us in with vast sea barrier; even now land fails our flight;
shall we make ocean or Troy our goal ? '

So speaks he, and bursts amid the serried foe. First
Lagus meets him, drawn thither by malign destiny; him, as
he tugs at a ponderous stone, hurling his spear where the
spine ran dissevering the ribs, he pierces and wrenches out
the spear where it stuck fast in the bone. Nor does Hisbo
catch him stooping, for all that he hoped it; for Pallas, as
he rushes unguarded on, furious at his comrade's cruel
death, receives him on his sword and buries it in his dis-
tended lungs. Next he attacks Sthenius, and Anchemolus
of Rhoetus' ancient family, who dared to violate the bridal
chamber of his stepmother. You, too, the twins Larides
and Thymber, fell on the Rutulian fields, children of
Daucus, indistinguishable for likeness and a sweet perplexity to your parents. But now Pallas made cruel
difference between you; for thy head, Thymber, is swept
off by Evander's sword; thy right hand, Larides, severed,
seeks its master, and the dying fingers jerk and clutch at
the sword. Fired by his encouragement, and beholding
his noble deeds, the Arcadians advance in wrath and
shame to meet the enemy in arms. Then Pallas pierces
Rhoeteus as he flies past in his chariot. This space, this

much of respite was given to Ilus; for at Ilus he had
aimed the strong spear from afar, and Rhœteus intercepts
its passage, in flight from thee, noble Teuthras and Tyres
thy brother; he rolls from the chariot in death, and his
heels strike the Rutulian fields. And as the shepherd,
when summer winds have risen to his desire, kindles the
woods dispersedly; on a sudden the mid spaces catch,
and a single flickering line of fire spreads wide over the
plain; he sits looking down on his conquest and the revel
of the flames; even so, Pallas, do thy brave comrades
gather close to sustain thee. But warrior Halesus advances
full on them, gathering himself behind his armour; he
slays Ladon, Pheres, Demodocus; his gleaming sword shears
off Strymonius' hand as it rises to his throat; he strikes
Thoas on the face with a stone, and drives the bones
asunder in a shattered mass of blood and brains. Halesus
had his father the soothsayer kept hidden in the woodland : when the old man's glazing eyes sank to death, the
Fates laid hand on him and devoted him to the arms of
Evander. Pallas aims at him, first praying thus : 'Grant
now, lord Tiber, to the steel I poise and hurl, a prosperous
way through brawny Halesus' breast ; thine oak shall bear
these arms and the dress he wore.' The god heard it ;
while Halesus covers Imaon, he leaves, alas! his breast
unarmed to the Arcadian's weapon. Yet at his grievous
death Lausus, himself a great arm of the war, lets not his
columns be dismayed ; at once he meets and cuts down
Abas, the check and stay of their battle. The men of
Arcadia go down before him ; down go the Etruscans,
and you, O Teucrians, invincible by Greece. The armies
close, matched in strength and in captains ; the rear ranks
crowd in ; weapons and hands are locked in the press.
Here Pallas strains and pushes on, here Lausus opposite,
nearly matched in age, excellent in beauty ; but fortune

had denied both return to their own land. Yet that they
should meet face to face the sovereign of high Olympus
allowed not; an early fate awaits them beneath a mightier
foe.

Meanwhile Turnus' gracious sister bids him take
Lausus' room, and his fleet chariot parts the ranks. When
he saw his comrades, 'It is time,' he cried, 'to stay from
battle. I alone must assail Pallas; to me and none other
Pallas is due; I would his father himself were here to
see.' So speaks he, and his Rutulians draw back from a
level space at his bidding. But then as they withdrew, he,
wondering at the haughty command, stands in amaze at
Turnus, his eyes scanning the vast frame, and his fierce
glance perusing him from afar. And with these words he
returns the words of the monarch: 'For me, my praise
shall even now be in the lordly spoils I win, or in illustrious
death: my father will bear calmly either lot: away with
menaces.' He speaks, and advances into the level ring.
The Arcadians' blood gathers chill about their hearts.
Turnus leaps from his chariot and prepares to close with
him. And as a lion sees from some lofty outlook a bull
stand far off on the plain revolving battle, and flies at him,
even such to see is Turnus' coming. When Pallas deemed
him within reach of a spear-throw, he advances, if so
chance may assist the daring of his overmatched strength,
and thus cries into the depth of sky: 'By my father's hospitality and the board whereto thou camest a wanderer, on
thee I call, Alcides; be favourable to my high emprise;
let Turnus even in death discern me stripping his blood-
stained armour, and his swooning eyes endure the sight
of his conqueror.' Alcides heard him, and deep in his
heart he stifled a heavy sigh, and let idle tears fall.
Then with kindly words the father accosts his son:
'Each hath his own appointed day; short and irrecoverable

is the span of life for all : but to spread renown by deeds
is the task of valour.   Under high Troy town many and
many a god's son fell; nay, mine own child Sarpedon likewise perished.   Turnus too his own fate summons, and his
allotted period hath reached the goal.'   So speaks he, and
turns his eyes away from the Rutulian fields.   But Pallas
hurls his spear with all his strength, and pulls his sword
flashing out of the hollow scabbard.   The flying spear lights
where the armour rises high above the shoulder, and, forcing
a way through the shield's rim, ceased not till it drew blood
from mighty Turnus.   At this Turnus long poises the spear-
shaft with its sharp steel head, and hurls it on Pallas with
these words : *See thou if our weapon have not a keener point.*
He ended ; but for all the shield's plating of iron and brass,
for all the bull-hide that covers it round about, the quivering
spear-head smashes it fair through and through, passes the
guard of the corslet, and pierces the breast with a gaping
hole.   He tears the warm weapon from the wound ; in
vain ; together and at once life-blood and sense follow it.
He falls heavily on the ground, his armour clashes over
him, and his bloodstained face sinks in death on the hostile
soil.   And Turnus standing over him . . . : 'Arcadians,' he
cries, 'remember these my words, and bear them to Evander.
I send him back his Pallas as was due.   All the meed of
the tomb, all the solace of sepulture, I give freely.   Dearly
must he pay his welcome to Aeneas.'   And with these
words, planting his left foot on the dead, he tore away the
broad heavy sword-belt engraven with a tale of crime, the
array of grooms foully slain together on their bridal night,
and the nuptial chambers dabbled with blood, which Clonus,
son of Eurytus, had wrought richly in gold.   Now Turnus
exults in spoiling him of it, and rejoices at his prize.   Ah
spirit of man, ignorant of fate and the allotted future, or to
keep bounds when elate with prosperity !—the day will

come when Turnus shall desire to have bought Pallas' safety at a great ransom, and curse the spoils of this fatal day.   But with many moans and tears Pallas' comrades lay him on his shield and bear him away amid their ranks.   O grief and glory and grace of the father to whom thou shalt return !   This one day sent thee first to war, this one day takes thee away, while yet thou leavest heaped high thy Rutulian dead.

And now no rumour of the dreadful loss, but a surer messenger flies to Aeneas, telling him his troops are on the thin edge of doom; it is time to succour the routed Teucrians.   He mows down all that meets him, and hews a broad path through their columns with furious sword, as he seeks thee, O Turnus, in thy fresh pride of slaughter. Pallas, Evander, all flash before his eyes ; the board whereto but then he had first come a wanderer, and the clasped hands.   Here four of Sulmo's children, as many more of Ufens' nurture, are taken by him alive to slaughter in sacrifice to the shade below, and slake the flames of the pyre with captive blood.   Next he levelled his spear full on Magus from far.   He stoops cunningly; the spear flies quivering over him ; and, clasping his knees, he speaks thus beseechingly : ' By thy father's ghost, by Iülus thy growing hope, I entreat thee, save this life for a child and a parent. My house is stately ; deep in it lies buried wealth of engraven silver ; I have masses of wrought and unwrought gold.   The victory of Troy does not turn on this, nor will a single life make so great a difference.'   He ended; to him Aeneas thus returns answer : ' All the wealth of silver and gold thou tellest of, spare thou for thy children.   Turnus hath broken off this thy trafficking in war, even then when Pallas fell.   Thus judges the ghost of my father Anchises, thus Iülus.'   So speaking, he grasps his helmet with his left hand, and, bending back his neck, drives his

sword up to the hilt in the suppliant. Hard by is Hae-
monides, priest of Phoebus and Trivia, his temples wound
with the holy ribboned chaplet, all glittering in white-robed
array. Him he meets and chases down the plain, and,
standing over his fallen foe, slaughters him and wraps him
in great darkness ; Serestus gathers the armour and carries
it away on his shoulders, a trophy, King Gradivus, to thee.
Caeculus, born of Vulcan's race, and Umbro, who comes
from the Marsian hills, fill up the line. The Dardanian
rushes full on them. His sword had hewn off Anxur's left
arm, with all the circle of the shield—he had uttered brave
words and deemed his prowess would second his vaunts,
and perchance with spirit lifted up had promised himself
hoar age and length of years—when Tarquitus in the pride
of his glittering arms met his fiery course, whom the nymph
Dryope had borne to Faunus, haunter of the woodland.
Drawing back his spear, he pins the ponderous shield to
the corslet ; then, as he vainly pleaded and would say
many a thing, strikes his head to the ground, and, rolling
away the warm body, cries thus over his enemy : ' Lie there
now, terrible one I no mother's love shall lay thee in the
sod, or place thy limbs beneath thine heavy ancestral tomb.
To birds of prey shalt thou be left, or borne down sunk in
the eddying water, where hungry fish shall suck thy wounds.'
Next he sweeps on Antaeus and Lucas, the first of Turnus'
train, and brave Numa and tawny-haired Camers, born of
noble Volscens, who was wealthiest in land of the Ausonians,
and reigned in silent Amyclae. Even as Aegaeon, who, men
say, had an hundred arms, an hundred hands, fifty mouths
and breasts ablaze with fire, and arrayed against Jove's
thunders as many clashing shields and drawn swords : so
Aeneas, when once his sword's point grew warm, rages
victorious over all the field. Nay, lo I he darts full in face
on Niphaeus' four-horse chariot ; before his long strides

and dreadful cry they turned in terror and dashed back,
throwing out their driver and tearing the chariot down
the beach.   Meanwhile the brothers Lucagus and Liger
drive up with their pair of white horses.   Lucagus valiantly
waves his drawn sword, while his brother wheels his horses
with the rein.   Aeneas, wrathful at their mad onslaught,
rushes on them, towering high with levelled spear.   To him
Liger . . . 'Not Diomede's horses dost thou discern, nor
Achilles' chariot, nor the plains of Phrygia : now on this
soil of ours the war and thy life shall end together.'
Thus fly mad Liger's random words.   But not in words
does the Trojan hero frame his reply : for he hurls his
javelin at the foe.   As Lucagus spurred on his horses,
bending forward over the whip, with left foot advanced
ready for battle, the spear passes through the lower rim
of his shining shield and pierces his left groin, knocks
him out of the chariot, and stretches him in death on
the fields.   To him good Aeneas speaks in bitter words:
' Lucagus, no slackness in thy coursers' flight hath betrayed
thee, or vain shadow of the foe turned them back ; thyself
thou leapest off the harnessed wheels.'   In such wise he
spoke, and caught the horses.   His brother, slipping down
from the chariot, pitiably outstretched helpless hands : 'Ah,
by the parents who gave thee birth, great Trojan, spare this
life and pity my prayer.'   More he was pleading; but
Aeneas : ' Not such were the words thou wert uttering.
Die, and be brother undivided from brother.'   With that
his sword's point pierces the breast where the life lies hid.
Thus the Dardanian captain dealt death over the plain,
like some raging torrent stream or black whirlwind.   At
last the boy Ascanius and his troops burst through the ineffectual leaguer and issue from the camp.

Meanwhile Jupiter breaks silence to accost Juno : ' O
sister and wife best beloved, it is Venus, as thou deemedst,

nor is thy judgment astray, who sustains the forces of Troy;
not their own valour of hand in war, and untamable spirit
and endurance in peril.' To whom Juno beseechingly:

'Why, fair my lord, vexest thou one sick at heart and
trembling at thy bitter words? If that force were in my
love that once was, and that was well, never had thine
omnipotence denied me leave to withdraw Turnus from
battle and preserve him for his father Daunus in safety.
Now let him perish, and pay forfeit to the Trojans of his
innocent blood. Yet he traces his birth from our name,
and Pilumnus was his father in the fourth generation, and
oft and again his bountiful hand hath heaped thy courts
with gifts.'

To her the king of high heaven thus briefly spoke: 'If
thy prayer for him is delay of present death and respite from
his fall, and thou dost understand that I ordain it thus, re-
move thy Turnus in flight, and snatch him from the fate
that is upon him. For so much indulgence there is room.
But if any ampler grace mask itself in these thy prayers,
and thou dreamest of change in the whole movement of
the war, idle is the hope thou nursest.'

And Juno, weeping: 'Ah yet, if thy mind were gracious
where thy lips are stern, and this gift of life might remain
confirmed to Turnus! Now his portion is bitter and
guiltless death, or I wander idly from the truth. Yet, oh
that I rather deluded myself with false alarms, and thou
who canst wouldst bend thy course to better counsels.'

These words uttered, she darted through the air straight
from high heaven, cloud-girt in driving tempest, and
sought the Ilian ranks and camp of Laurentum. Then the
goddess, strange and ominous to see, fashions into the
likeness of Aeneas a thin and pithless shade of hollow mist,
decks it with Dardanian weapons, and gives it the mimicry
of shield and divine helmet plume, gives unsubstantial

words and senseless utterance, and the mould and motion
of his tread : like shapes rumoured to flit when death is
past, or dreams that delude the slumbering senses. But in
front of the battle-ranks the phantom dances rejoicingly,
and with arms and mocking accents provokes the foe.
Turnus hastens up and sends his spear whistling from far
on it ; it gives back and turns its footsteps. Then indeed
Turnus, when he believed Aeneas turned and fled from
him, and his spirit madly drank in the illusive hope :
'Whither fliest thou, Aeneas? forsake not thy plighted
bridal chamber. This hand shall give thee the land thou
hast sought overseas.' So clamouring he pursues, and
brandishes his drawn sword, and sees not that his rejoicing
is drifting with the winds. The ship lay haply moored to a
high ledge of rock, with ladders run out and gangway ready,
wherein king Osinius sailed from the coasts of Clusium.
Here the fluttering phantom of flying Aeneas darts and
hides itself. Nor is Turnus slack to follow ; he overleaps
the barriers and springs across the high gangways. Scarcely
had he lighted on the prow ; the daughter of Saturn snaps
the hawser, and the ship, parted from her cable, runs out
on the ebbing tide. And him Aeneas seeks for battle and
finds not, and sends many a man that meets him to death.
Then the light phantom seeks not yet any further hiding-
place, but, flitting aloft, melts in a dark cloud ; and a blast
comes down meanwhile and sweeps Turnus through the
seas. He looks back, witless of his case and thankless for
his salvation, and, wailing, stretches both hands to heaven :
'Father omnipotent, was I so guilty in thine eyes, and is
this the punishment thou hast ordained? Whither am I
borne? whence came I? what flight is this, or in what guise
do I return? Shall I look again on the camp or walls of
Laurentum? What of that array of men who followed me
to arms? whom—oh horrible !—I have abandoned all amid

a dreadful death; and now I see the stragglers and catch
the groans of those who fall. What do I? or how may
earth ever yawn for me deep enough? Do you rather, O
winds, be pitiful, carry my bark on rock or reef; it is I,
Turnus, who desire and implore you; or drive me on the
cruel shoals of the Syrtis, where no Rutulian may follow
nor rumour know my name.' Thus speaking, he wavers
in mind this way and that: maddened by the shame, shall
he plunge on his sword's harsh point and drive it through
his side, or fling himself among the waves, and seek by
swimming to gain the winding shore, again to return on
the Trojan arms? Thrice he essayed either way; thrice
queenly Juno checked and restrained him in pity of heart.
Cleaving the deep, he floats with the tide down the flood,
and is borne on to his father Daunus' ancient city.

But meanwhile at Jove's prompting fiery Mezentius
takes his place in the battle and assails the triumphant
Teucrians. The Tyrrhene ranks gather round him, and all
at once in unison shower their darts down on the hated
foe. As a cliff that juts into the waste of waves, meeting the raging winds and breasting the deep, endures all
the threatening force of sky and sea, itself fixed im-
movable, so he dashes to earth Hebrus son of Dolichaon,
and with him Latagus, and Palmus as he fled; catching
Latagus full front in the face with a vast fragment of mountain rock, while Palmus he hamstrings, and leaves him rolling helpless; his armour he gives Lausus to wear on his
shoulders, and the plumes to fix on his crest. With them
fall Evanthes the Phrygian, and Mimas, fellow and birthmate of Paris; for on one night Theano bore him to his father
Amycus, and the queen, Cisseus' daughter, was delivered of
Paris the firebrand; he sleeps in his fathers' city; Mimas
lies a stranger on the Laurentian coast. And as the boar
driven by snapping hounds from the mountain heights,

many a year hidden by Vesulus in his pines, many an one
fed in the Laurentian marsh among the reedy forest, once
come among the nets, halts and snorts savagely, with
shoulders bristling up, and none of them dare be wrathful
or draw closer, but they shower from a safe distance their
darts and cries; even thus none of those whose anger is
righteous against Mezentius have courage to meet him with
drawn weapon: far off they provoke him with missiles and
huge clamour, and he turns slow and fearless round about,
grinding his teeth as he shakes the spears off his shield.
From the bounds of ancient Corythus Acron the Greek
had come, leaving for exile a bride half won. Seeing him
afar dealing confusion amid the ranks, in crimson plumes
and his plighted wife's purple,—as an unpastured lion often
ranging the deep coverts, for madness of hunger urges him,
if he haply catches sight of a timorous roe or high-antlered
stag, he gapes hugely for joy, and, with mane on end, clings
crouching over its flesh, his cruel mouth bathed in reeking
gore. . . . so Mezentius darts lightly among the thick of
the enemy. Hapless Acron goes down, and, spurning the
dark ground, gasps out his life, and covers the broken javelin with his blood. But the victor deigned not to bring
down Orodes with the blind wound of his flying lance as
he fled; full face to face he meets him, and engages man
with man, conqueror not by stealth but armed valour.
Then, as with planted foot, he thrust him off the spear: ' O
men,' he cries, 'Orodes lies low, no slight arm of the war.'
His comrades shout after him the glad battle chant. And
the dying man: 'Not unavenged nor long, whoso thou art,
shalt thou be glad in victory: thee too an equal fate marks
down, and in these fields thou shalt soon lie.' And smiling on him half wrathfully, Mezentius: 'Now die thou.
But of me let the father of gods and king of men take
counsel.' So saying, he drew the weapon out of his body.

Grim rest and iron slumber seal his eyes; his lids close
on everlasting night. Caedicus slays Alcathoüs, Sacrator
Hydaspes, Rapo Parthenius and the grim strength of Orses,
Messapus Clonius and Erichaetes son of Lycaon, the one
when his reinless horse stumbling had flung him to the
ground, the other as they met on foot. And Agis the
Lycian advanced only to be struck from horseback by
Valerus, brave as his ancestry; and Thronius by Salius,
and Salius by Nealces with treacherous arrow-shot that stole
from far.

Now the heavy hand of war dealt equal woe and
counterchange of death; in even balance conquerors and
conquered slew and fell; nor one nor other knows of retreat. The gods in Jove's house pity the vain rage of
either and all the agonising of mortals. From one side
Venus, from one opposite Juno, daughter of Saturn, looks
on; pale Tisiphone rages among the many thousand men.
But now, brandishing his huge spear, Mezentius strides
glooming over the plain, vast as Orion when, with planted
foot, he cleaves his way through the vast pools of mid-ocean
and his shoulder overtops the waves, or carrying an ancient
mountain-ash from the hilltops, paces the ground and hides
his head among the clouds: so moves Mezentius, huge in
arms. Aeneas, espying him in the deep columns, makes
on to meet him. He remains, unterrified, awaiting his
noble foe, steady in his own bulk, and measures with his
eye the fair range for a spear. 'This right hand's divinity,
and the weapon I poise and hurl, now be favourable I thee,
Lausus, I vow for the live trophy of Aeneas, dressed in the
spoils stripped from the pirate's body.' He ends, and
throws the spear whistling from far; it flies on, glancing
from the shield, and pierces illustrious Antores hard by him
sidelong in the flank; Antores, companion of Hercules,
who, sent thither from Argos, had stayed by Evander, and

settled in an Italian town. Hapless he goes down with a
wound not his own, and in death gazes on the sky, and
Argos is sweet in his remembrance. Then good Aeneas
throws his spear; through the sheltering circle of threefold
brass, through the canvas lining and fabric of triple-sewn
bull-hide it went, and sank deep in his groin; yet carried
not its strength home. Quickly Aeneas, joyful at the sight
of the Tyrrhenian's blood, snatches his sword from his thigh
and presses hotly on his struggling enemy. Lausus saw,
and groaned deeply for love of his dear father, and tears
rolled over his face. Here will I not keep silence of thy
hard death-doom and thine excellent deeds (if in any wise
things wrought in the old time may win belief), nor of thyself, O fitly remembered! He, helpless and trammelled,
withdrew backward, the deadly spear-shaft trailing from his
shield. The youth broke forward and plunged into the
fight; and even as Aeneas' hand rose to bring down the
blow, he caught up his point and held him in delay. His
comrades follow up with loud cries, so the father may withdraw in shelter of his son's shield, while they shower their
darts and bear back the enemy with missiles from a distance.
Aeneas wrathfully keeps covered. And as when storm-
clouds pour down in streaming hail, all the ploughmen and
country-folk scatter off the fields, and the wayfarer cowers
safe in his fortress, a stream's bank or deep arch of rock,
while the rain falls, that they may do their day's labour
when sunlight reappears; thus under the circling storm
of weapons Aeneas sustains the cloud of war till it
thunders itself all away, and calls on Lausus, on Lausus,
with chiding and menace: 'Whither runnest thou on
thy death, with daring beyond thy strength? thine affection betrays thee into rashness.' But none the less he
leaps madly on; and now wrath rises higher and fiercer
in the Dardanian captain, and the Fates pass Lausus' last

threads through their hand; for Aeneas drives the sword
strongly right through him up all its length: the point
pierced the light shield that armed his assailant, and the
tunic sewn by his mother with flexible gold: blood filled
his breast, and the life left the body and passed mourning
through the air to the under world. But when Anchises'
son saw the look on the dying face, the face pale in
wonderful wise, he sighed deeply in pity, and reached forth
his hand, as the likeness of his own filial affection flashed
across his soul. 'What now shall good Aeneas give thee,
what, O poor boy, for this thy praise, for guerdon of a nature
so noble? Keep for thine own the armour thou didst
delight in; and I restore thee, if that matters aught at all,
to the ghosts and ashes of thy parents. Yet thou shalt
have this sad comfort in thy piteous death, thou fallest
by great Aeneas' hand.' Then, chiding his hesitating
comrades, he lifts him from the ground, dabbling the
comely-ranged tresses with blood.

Meanwhile his father, by the wave of the Tiber river,
stanched his wound with water, and rested his body against
a tree-trunk. Hard by his brazen helmet hangs from the
boughs, and the heavy armour lies quietly on the meadow.
Chosen men stand round; he, sick and panting, leans his
neck and lets his beard spread down over his chest. Many
a time he asks for Lausus, and sends many an one to call
him back and carry a parent's sad commands. But Lausus
his weeping comrades were bearing lifeless on his armour,
mighty and mightily wounded to death. Afar the soul
prophetic of ill knew their lamentation: he soils his gray
hairs plenteously with dust, and stretches both hands on
high, and clings on the dead. 'Was life's hold on me so
sweet, O my son, that I let him I bore receive the hostile
stroke in my room? Am I, thy father, saved by these
wounds of thine, and living by thy death? Alas and woe!

now at last exile is bitter! now the wound is driven deep!
And I, even I, O my son, stained thy name with crime,
driven in hatred from the throne and sceptre of my fathers.
I owed vengeance to my country and my people's resent-
ment; might mine own guilty life but have paid it by every
form of death! Now I live, and leave not yet man and
day; but I will.' As he speaks thus he raises himself
painfully on his thigh, and though the violence of the
deep wound cripples him, yet unbroken he bids his horse be
brought, his beauty, his comfort, that ever had carried him
victorious out of war, and says these words to the grieving
beast: 'Rhoebus, we have lived long, if aught at all lasts
long with mortals. This day wilt thou either bring back in
triumph the gory head and spoils of Aeneas, and we will
avenge Lausus' agonies; or if no force opens a way, thou
wilt die with me: for I deem not, bravest, thou wilt deign
to bear an alien rule and a Teucrian lord.' He spoke, and
took his welcome seat on the back he knew, loading both
hands with keen javelins, his head sheathed in glittering
brass and shaggy horse-hair plumes. Thus he galloped in.
Through his heart sweep together the vast tides of shame
and mingling madness and grief. And with that he thrice
loudly calls Aeneas. Aeneas knew the call, and makes
glad invocation: 'So the father of gods speed me, so
Apollo on high: do thou essay to close hand to hand. . . .'
Thus much he utters, and moves up to meet him with
levelled spear. And he: 'Why seek to frighten me, fierce
man, now my son is gone? this was thy one road to my
ruin. We shrink not from death, nor relent before any of
thy gods. Cease; for I come to my death, first carrying
these gifts for thee.' He spoke, and hurled a weapon at
his enemy; then plants another and yet another as he darts
round in a wide circle; but they are stayed on the boss of
gold. Thrice he rode wheeling close round him by the

left, and sent his weapons strongly in; thrice the Trojan hero turns round, taking the grim forest on his brazen guard. Then, weary of lingering in delay on delay, and plucking out spear-head after spear-head, and hard pressed in the uneven match of battle, with much counselling of spirit now at last he bursts forth, and sends his spear at the war-horse between the hollows of the temples. The creature raises itself erect, beating the air with its feet, throws its rider, and coming down after him in an entangled mass, slips its shoulder as it tumbles forward. The cries of Trojans and Latins kindle the sky. Aeneas rushes up, drawing his sword from the scabbard, and thus above him: 'Where now is gallant Mezentius and all his fierce spirit?' Thereto the Tyrrhenian, as he came to himself and gazing up drank the air of heaven: 'Bitter foe, why these taunts and menaces of death? Naught forbids my slaughter; neither on such terms came I to battle, nor did my Lausus make treaty for this between me and thee. This one thing I beseech thee, by whatsoever grace a vanquished enemy may claim: allow my body sepulture. I know I am girt by the bitter hatred of my people. Stay, I implore, their fury, and grant me and my son union in the tomb.' So speaks he, and takes the sword in his throat unfalteringly, and the lifeblood spreads in a wave over his armour.

BOOK ELEVENTH

THE COUNCIL OF THE LATINS, AND THE LIFE AND DEATH OF CAMILLA

MEANWHILE Dawn arose forth of Ocean. Aeneas, though the charge presses to give a space for burial of his comrades, and his mind is in the tumult of death, began to pay the gods his vows of victory with the breaking of the East. He plants on a mound a mighty oak with boughs lopped away on every hand, and arrays it in the gleaming arms stripped from Mezentius the captain, a trophy to thee, mighty Lord of War; he fixes on it the plumes dripping with blood, the broken spears, and the corslet struck and pierced in twelve places; he ties the shield of brass on his left hand, and hangs from his neck the ivory sword. Then among his joyous comrades (for all the throng of his captains girt him close about) he begins in these words of cheer:

'The greatest deed is done, O men ; be all fear gone for what remains. These are the spoils of a haughty king, the first-fruits won from him ; my hands have set Mezentius here. Now our way lies to the walls of the Latin king. Prepare your arms in courage, and let your hopes anticipate the war ; let no ignorant delay hinder or tardy thoughts of fear keep us back, so soon as heaven grant us to pluck up the standards and lead our army from the camp. Mean-

while let us commit to earth the unburied bodies of our
comrades, since deep in Acheron this honour is left alone.
Go,' says he, 'grace with the last gifts those noble souls
whose blood won us this land for ours; and first let Pallas
be sent to Evander's mourning city, he whose valour failed
not when the day of darkness took him, and the bitter
wave of death.'

So speaks he weeping, and retraces his steps to the
door, where aged Acoetes watched Pallas' lifeless body laid
out for burial; once armour-bearer to Evander in Parrhasia,
but now gone forth with darker omens, appointed attendant
to his darling foster-child. Around is the whole train of
servants, with a crowd of Trojans, and the Ilian women
with hair unbound in mourning after their fashion. When
Aeneas entered at the high doorway they beat their breasts
and raise a loud wail aloft, and the palace moans to their
grievous lamentation. Himself, when he saw the pillowed
head and fair face of Pallas, and on his smooth breast the
gaping wound of the Ausonian spear-head, speaks thus with
welling tears:

'Did Fortune in her joyous coming,' he cries, 'O luckless boy, grudge thee the sight of our realm, and a triumphal entry to thy father's dwelling? Not this promise of
thee had I given to Evander thy sire at my departure, when
he embraced me as I went and bade me speed to a wide
empire, and yet warned me in fear that the men were
valiant, the people obstinate in battle. And now he, fast
ensnared by empty hope, perchance offers vows and heaps
gifts on his altars; we, a mourning train, go in hollow
honour by his corpse, who now owes no more to aught
in heaven. Unhappy! thou wilt see thy son cruelly slain;
is this our triumphal return awaited? is this my strong
assurance? Ah me, what a shield is lost, mine Iülus, to
Ausonia and to thee!'

This lament done, he bids raise the piteous body, and
sends a thousand men chosen from all his army for the last
honour of escort, to mingle in the father's tears ; a small
comfort in a great sorrow, yet the unhappy parent's due.
Others quickly plait a soft wicker bier of arbutus rods and
oak shoots, and shadow the heaped pillows with a leafy
covering. Here they lay him, high on their rustic strew-
ing; even as some tender violet or drooping hyacinth-
blossom plucked by a maiden's finger, whose sheen and
whose grace is not yet departed, but no more does Earth
the mother feed it or lend it strength.   Then Aeneas bore
forth two purple garments stiff with gold, that Sidonian
Dido's own hands, happy over their work, had once wrought
for him, and shot the warp with delicate gold. One of
these he sadly folds round him, a last honour, and veils in
its covering the tresses destined to the fire ; and heaps up
besides many a Laurentine battle-prize, and bids his spoils
pass forth in long train; with them the horses and arms
whereof he had stripped the enemy, and those, with hands
tied behind their back, whom he would send as nether
offering to his ghost, and sprinkle the blood of their slaying
on the flame.   Also he bids his captains carry stems dressed
in the armour of the foe, and fix on them the hostile names.
Unhappy Acoetes is led along, outworn with age , he smites
his breast and rends his face, and flings himself forward all
along the ground.   Likewise they lead forth the chariot
bathed in Rutulian blood ; behind goes weeping Aethon
the war-horse, his trappings laid away, and big drops wet his
face.   Others bear his spear and helmet, for all else is
Turnus' prize.   Then follow in mourning array the Teucrians
and all the Tyrrhenians, and the Arcadians with arms reversed.   When the whole long escorting file had taken its
way, Aeneas stopped, and sighing deep, pursued thus: 'Once
again war's dreadful destiny calls us hence to other tears:

hail thou for evermore, O princely Pallas, and for evermore
farewell.' And without more words he bent his way to the
high walls and advanced towards his camp.

And now envoys were there from the Latin city with
wreathed boughs of olive, praying him of his grace to restore
the dead that lay strewn by the sword over the plain, and
let them go to their earthy grave: no war lasts with men
conquered and bereft of breath; let this indulgence be
given to men once called friends and fathers of their brides.
To them Aeneas grants leave in kind and courteous wise,
spurning not their prayer, and goes on in these words:
'What spite of fortune, O Latins, hath entangled you in the
toils of war, and made you fly our friendship? Plead you
for peace to the lifeless bodies that the battle-lot hath
slain? I would fain grant it even to the living. Neither
have I come but because destiny had given me this place
to dwell in; nor wage I war with your people; your king
it is who hath broken our covenant and preferred to trust
himself to Turnus' arms. Fitter it were Turnus had faced
death to-day. If he will fight out the war and expel the
Teucrians, it had been well to meet me here in arms; so
had he lived to whom life were granted of heaven or his
own right hand. Now go, and kindle the fire beneath your
hapless countrymen.' Aeneas ended: they stood dumb in
silence, with faces bent steadfastly in mutual gaze. Then
aged Drances, ever young Turnus' assailant in hatred and
accusation, with the words of his mouth thus answers him
again:

'O Trojan, great in renown, yet greater in arms, with
what praises may I extol thy divine goodness? Shall thy
righteousness first wake my wonder, or thy toils in war?
We indeed will gratefully carry these words to our fathers'
city, and, if fortune grant a way, will make thee at one with
King Latinus. Let Turnus seek his own alliances. Nay,

it will be our delight to rear the massy walls of destiny and
stoop our shoulders under the stones of Troy.'

He ended thus, and all with one voice murmured
assent. Twelve days' truce is struck, and in mediation of
the peace Teucrians and Latins stray mingling unharmed on
the forest heights. The tall ash echoes to the axe's strokes;
they overturn pines that soar into the sky, and busily cleave
oaken logs and scented cedar with wedges, and drag mountain-ashes on their groaning waggons.

And now flying Rumour, harbinger of the heavy woe,
fills Evander and Evander's house and city with the same
voice that but now told of Pallas victorious over Latium.
The Arcadians stream to the gates, snatching funeral torches
after their ancient use; the road gleams with the long line
of flame, and parts the fields with a broad pathway of light;
the arriving crowd of Phrygians meets them and mingles in
mourning array. When the matrons saw all the train
approach their dwellings they kindle the town with loud
wailing. But no force may withhold Evander; he comes
amid them; the bier is set down; he flings himself on
Pallas, and clasps him with tears and sighs, and scarcely
at last does grief leave his voice's utterance free. 'Other
than this, O Pallas! was thy promise to thy father, that
thou wouldst not plunge recklessly into the fury of battle.
I knew well how strong was the fresh pride of arms and the
sweetness of honour in a first battle. Ah, unhappy first-
fruits of his youth and bitter prelude of the war upon our
borders! ah, vows and prayers of mine that no god heard!
and thou, pure crown of wifehood, happy that thou art
dead and not spared for this sorrow! But I have outgone
my destiny in living, to stay here the survivor of my child.
Would I had followed the allied arms of Troy, to be overwhelmed by Rutulian weapons! Would my life had been
given, and I and not my Pallas were borne home in this

procession ! I would not blame you, O Teucrians, nor our
treaty and the friendly hands we clasped : our old age had
that appointed debt to pay. Yet if untimely death awaited
my son, it will be good to think he fell leading the Teucrians
into Latium, and slew his Volscian thousands before he
fell. Nay, no other funeral than this would I deem thy
due, my Pallas, than good Aeneas does, than the mighty
Phrygians, than the Tyrrhene captains and all the army of
Tyrrhenia. Great are the trophies they bring on whom
thine hand deals death ; thou also, Turnus, wert standing
now a great trunk dressed in arms, had his age and his
strength of years equalled thine. But why, unhappy, do I
delay the Trojan arms ? Go, and forget not to carry this
message to your king : Thine hand it is that keeps me
lingering in a life that is hateful since Pallas fell, and
Turnus is the debt thou seest son and father claim : for
thy virtue and thy fortune this scope àlone is left. I ask
not joy in life ; I may not ; but to carry this to my son
deep in the under world.'

Meanwhile Dawn had raised her gracious light on weary
men, bringing back task and toil : now lord Aeneas, now
Tarchon, have built the pyres on the winding shore. Hither
in ancestral fashion hath each borne the bodies of his kin ;
the dark fire is lit beneath, and the vapour hides high
heaven in gloom. Thrice, girt in glittering arms, they have
marched about the blazing piles, thrice compassed on
horseback the sad fire of death, and uttered their wail.
Tears fall fast upon earth and armour ; cries of men and
blare of trumpets roll skyward. Then some fling on the
fire Latin spoils stripped from the slain, helmets and
shapely swords, bridles and glowing chariot wheels ; others
familiar gifts, the very shields and luckless weapons of the
dead. Around are slain in sacrifice oxen many in number,
and bristly swine and cattle gathered out of all the country

are slaughtered over the flames. Then, crowding the shore, they gaze on their burning comrades, and guard the embers of the pyres, and cannot tear themselves away till dewy Night wheels on the star-spangled glittering sky.

Therewithal the unhappy Latins far apart build count-less pyres and bury many bodies of men in the ground ; and many more they lift and bear away to the neighbouring country, or send them back to the city ; the rest, a vast heap of undistinguishable slaughter, they burn uncounted and unhonoured ; on all sides the broad fields gleam with crowded rivalry of fires. The third Dawn had rolled away the chill shadow from the sky ; mournfully they piled high the ashes and mingled bones from the embers, and heaped a load of warm earth above them. Now in the dwellings of rich Latinus' city the noise is loudest and most the long wail. Here mothers and their sons' unhappy brides, here beloved sisters sad-hearted and orphaned boys curse the disastrous war and Turnus' bridal, and bid him his own self arm and decide the issue with the sword, since he claims for himself the first rank and the lordship of Italy. Drances fiercely embitters their cry, and vouches that Turnus alone is called, alone is claimed for battle. Yet therewith many a diverse-worded counsel is for Turnus, and the great name of the queen overshadows him, and he rises high in renown of trophies fitly won.

Among their stir, and while confusion is fiercest, lo ! to crown all, the envoys from great Diomede's city bring their gloomy message : nothing is come of all the toil and labour spent ; gifts and gold and strong entreaties have been of no avail ; Latium must seek other arms, or sue for peace to the Trojan king. For heavy grief King Latinus himself swoons away. The wrath of heaven and the fresh graves before his eyes warn him that Aeneas is borne on by fate's evident will. So he sends imperial summons to

his high council, the foremost of his people, and gathers
them within his lofty courts. They assemble, and stream
up the crowded streets to the royal dwelling. Latinus,
eldest in years and first in royalty, sits amid them with
cheerless brow, and bids the envoys sent back from the
Aetolian city tell the news they bring, and demands a full
and ordered reply. Then tongues are hushed; and Venulus,
obeying his word, thus begins to speak :

‘ We have seen, O citizens, Diomede in his Argive camp,
and outsped our way and passed all its dangers, and touched
the hand whereunder the land of Ilium fell. He was
founding a town, named Argyripa after his ancestral people,
on the conquered fields of Iapygian Garganus. After we
entered in, and licence of open speech was given, we lay forth
our gifts, we instruct him of our name and country, who
are its invaders, and why we are drawn to Arpi. He heard
us, and replied thus with face unstirred :

‘ “ O fortunate races, realm of Saturn, Ausonians of old,
how doth fortune vex your quiet and woo you to tempt wars
you know not ? We that have drawn sword on the fields of
Ilium—I forbear to tell the drains of war beneath her high
walls, the men sunken in yonder Simoïs—have all over the
world paid to the full our punishment and the reward of
guilt, a crew Priam's self might pity ; as Minerva's baleful
star knows, and the Euboïc reefs and Caphereus' revenge.
From that warfaring driven to alien shores, Menelaus son
of Atreus is in exile far as Proteus' Pillars, Ulysses hath seen
the Cyclopes of Aetna. Shall I make mention of the
realm of Neoptolemus, and Idomeneus' household gods
overthrown ? or of the Locrians who dwell on the Libyan
beach ? Even the lord of Mycenae, the mighty Achaeans'
general, sank on his own threshold edge under his accursed
wife's hand, where the adulterer crouched over conquered
Asia. Aye, or that the gods grudged it me to return to

my ancestral altars, to see the bride of my desire, and lovely
Calydon ! Now likewise sights of appalling presage pursue
me ; my comrades, lost to me, have soared winging into the
sky, and flit birds about the rivers—ah me, dread punishment of my people !—and fill the cliffs with their melancholy cries.   This it was I had to look for even from the
time when I madly assailed celestial limbs with steel, and
sullied the hand of Venus with a wound.   Do not, ah, do
not urge me to such battles.   Neither have I any war with
Troy since her towers are overthrown, nor do I remember
with delight the woes of old.   Turn to Aeneas with the
gifts you bear to me from your ancestral borders.   We
have stood to face his grim weapons, and met him hand to
hand ; believe one who hath proved it, how mightily he
rises over his shield, in what a whirlwind he hurls his spear.
Had the land of Ida borne two more like him, Dardanus
had marched to attack the towns of Inachus, and Greece
were mourning fate's reverse.   In all our delay before that
obstinate Trojan city, it was Hector and Aeneas whose hand
stayed the Grecian victory and bore back its advance to
the tenth year.   Both were splendid in courage, both eminent in arms ; Aeneas was first in duty.   Let your hands join
in treaty as they may ; but beware that your weapons close
not with his."

'Thou hast heard, most gracious king, at once what
is the king's answer, and what his counsel for our great
struggle.'

Scarcely thus the envoys, when a diverse murmur ran
through the troubled lips of the Ausonians ; even as, when
rocks delay some running river, it plashes in the barred
pool, and the banks murmur nigh to the babbling wave.
So soon as their minds were quieted, and their hurrying
lips hushed, the king, first calling on the gods, begins from
his lofty throne :

' Ere now could I wish, O Latins, we had determined
our course of state, and it had been better thus; not to
meet in council at such a time as now, with the enemy
seated before our walls. We wage an ill-timed war, fellow-
citizens, with a divine race, invincible, unbroken in battle,
who brook not even when conquered to drop the sword.
If you had hope in appeal to Aetolian arms, abandon it ;
though each man's hope is his own, you discern how narrow
a path it is. Beyond that you see with your eyes and handle
with your hands the total ruin of our fortunes. I blame
no one ; what valour's utmost could do is done ; we have
fought with our whole kingdom's strength. Now I will
unfold what I doubtfully advise and purpose, and with your
attention instruct you of it in brief. There is an ancient
land of mine bordering the Tuscan river, stretching far
westward beyond the Sicanian borders. Auruncans and
Rutulians sow on it, work the stiff hills with the ploughshare, and pasture them where they are roughest. Let all
this tract, with a pine-clad belt of mountain height, pass to
the Teucrians in friendship; let us name fair terms of
treaty, and invite them as allies to our realm; let them
settle, if they desire it so, and found a city. But if they
have a mind to try other coasts and another people, and
can abide to leave our soil, let us build twice ten ships of
Italian oak, or as many more as they can man ; timber lies
at the water's edge for all ; let them assign the number and
fashion of the vessels, and we will supply brass, labour,
dockyards. Further, it is our will that an hundred ambassadors of the highest rank in Latium shall go to bear our
words and ratify the treaty, holding forth in their hands the
boughs of peace, and carrying for gifts weight of gold and
ivory, and the chair and striped robe, our royal array. Give
counsel openly, and succour our exhausted state.'

Then Drances again, he whose jealous ill-will was

wrought to anger and stung with bitterness by Turnus' fame,
lavish of wealth and quick of tongue though his hand was
cold in war, held no empty counsellor and potent in faction
—his mother's rank ennobled a lineage whose paternal
source was obscure—rises, and with these words heaps and
heightens their passion :

'Dark to no man and needing no voice of ours, O
gracious king, is that whereon thou takest counsel. All
confess they know how our nation's fortune sways ; but their
words are choked. Let him grant freedom of speech and
abate his breath, he by whose disastrous government and
perverse way (I will speak out, though he menace me with
arms and death) we see so many stars of battle gone down and
all our city sunk in mourning ; while he, confident in flight,
assails the Trojan camp and makes heaven quail before his
arms. Add yet one to those gifts of thine, to all the riches
thou bidst us send or promise to the Dardanians, most
gracious of kings, but one ; let no man's passion overbear
thee from giving thine own daughter to an illustrious son
and a worthy marriage, and binding this peace by perpetual
treaty. Yet if we are thus terror-stricken heart and soul,
let us implore him in person, in person plead him of his
grace to give way, to restore king and country their proper
right. Why again and again hurlest thou these unhappy
citizens on peril so evident, O source and spring of Latium's
woes ? In war is no safety ; peace we all implore of thee,
O Turnus, and the one pledge that makes peace inviolable.
I the first, I whom thou picturest thine enemy, as I care
not if I am, see, I bow at thy feet. Pity thine allies ; relent, and retire before thy conqueror. Enough have we
seen of rout and death, and desolation over our broad lands.
Or if glory stir thee, if such strength kindle in thy breast,
and if a palace so delight thee for thy dower, be bold, and
advance stout-hearted upon the foe. We verily, that Turnus

may have his royal bride, must lie scattered on the plains,
worthless lives, a crowd unburied and unwept. Do thou
also, if thou hast aught of might, if the War-god be
in thee as in thy fathers, look him in the face who chal-
lenges. . . .'

At these words Turnus' passion blazed out. He utters
a groan, and breaks forth thus in deep accents:

'Copious indeed, Drances, and fluent is ever thy speech
at the moment war calls for action; and when the fathers
are summoned thou art there the first. But we need no
words to fill our senate-house, safely as thou wingest them
while the mounded walls keep off the enemy, and the trenches
swim not yet with blood. Thunder on in rhetoric, thy
wonted way: accuse thou me of fear, Drances, since thine
hand hath heaped so many Teucrians in slaughter, and thy
glorious trophies dot the fields. Trial is open of what live
valour can do; nor indeed is our foe far to seek; on all
sides they surround our walls. Are we going to meet them?
Why linger? Will thy bravery ever be in that windy tongue
and those timorous feet of thine? . . . *My conqueror!* Shall
any justly flout me as conquered, who sees Tiber swoln
fuller with Ilian blood, and all the house and people of
Evander laid low, and the Arcadians stripped of their
armour? Not such did Bitias and huge Pandarus prove
me, and the thousand men whom on one day my conquering hand sent down to hell, shut as I was in their walls and
closed in the enemy's ramparts. *In war is no safety.* Fool!
be thy boding on the Dardanian's head and thine own fortunes. Go on; cease not to throw all into confusion with
thy terrors, to exalt the strength of a twice vanquished race,
and abase the arms of Latinus before it. Now the princes
of the Myrmidons tremble before Phrygian arms, now
Tydeus' son and Achilles of Larissa, and Aufidus river recoils from the Adriatic wave. Or when the scheming villain

pretends to shrink at my abuse, and sharpens calumny by
terror! never shall this hand—keep quiet!—rob thee of
such a soul ; with thee let it abide, and dwell in that breast
of thine.   Now I return to thee, my lord, and thy weighty
resolves.   If thou dost repose no further hope in our arms,
if all hath indeed left us, and one repulse been our utter
ruin, and our fortune is beyond recovery, let us plead for
peace and stretch forth unarmed hands.   Yet ah! had we
aught of our wonted manhood, his toil beyond all other is
blessed and his spirit eminent, who rather than see it thus,
hath fallen prone in death and once bitten the ground.   But
if we have yet resources and an army still unbroken, and
cities and peoples of Italy remain for our aid ; but if even
the Trojans have won their glory at great cost of blood
(they too have their deaths, and the storm fell equally on all),
why do we shamefully faint even on the threshold?   Why
does a shudder seize our limbs before the trumpet sound?
Often do the Days and the varying change of toiling Time
restore prosperity ; often Fortune in broken visits makes
man her sport and again establishes him.   The Aetolian of
Arpi will not help us ; but Messapus will, and Tolumnius
the fortunate, and the captains sent by many a nation ; nor
will fame be scant to follow the flower of Latium and the
Laurentine land.   Camilla the Volscian too is with us,
leading her train of cavalry, squadrons splendid in brass.
But if I only am claimed by the Teucrians for combat, if
that is your pleasure, and I am the barrier to the public
good, Victory does not so hate and shun my hands that I
should renounce any enterprise for so great a hope.   I shall
meet him in courage, did he outmatch great Achilles and
wear arms like his forged by Vulcan's hands.   To you and
to my father Latinus I Turnus, unexcelled in bravery by
any of old, consecrate my life.   *Aeneas calls on him alone :*
let him, I implore : let not Drances rather appease with his

s

life this wrath of heaven, if such it be, or win the renown of valour.'

Thus they one with another strove together in uncertainty; Aeneas moved from his camp to battle. Lo, a messenger rushes spreading confusion through the royal house, and fills the town with great alarms : the Teucrians, ranged in battle-line with the Tyrrhene forces, are marching down by the Tiber river and filling the plain. Immediately spirits are stirred and hearts shaken and wrath roused in fierce excitement among the crowd. Hurrying hands grasp at arms; for arms their young men clamour; the fathers shed tears and mutter gloomily. With that a great noise rises aloft in diverse contention, even as when flocks of birds haply settle on a lofty grove, or swans utter their hoarse cry among the vocal pools on the fish-filled river of Padusa. 'Yes, citizens !' cries Turnus, seizing his time : 'gather in council and sit praising peace, while they rush on dominion in arms !' Without more words he sprung up and issued swiftly from the high halls. 'Thou, Volusus,' he cries, 'bid the Volscian battalions arm, and lead out the Rutulians. Messapus, and Coras with thy brother, spread your armed cavalry widely over the plain. Let a division entrench the city gates and man the towers : the rest of our array attack with me where I command.' The whole town goes rushing to the walls; lord Latinus himself, dismayed by the woeful emergency, quits the council and puts off his high designs, and chides himself sorely for not having given Aeneas unasked welcome, and made him son and bulwark of the city. Some entrench the gates, or bring up supply of stones and poles. The hoarse clarion utters the ensanguined note of war. A motley ring of boys and matrons girdle the walls. Therewithal the queen with a crowd of mothers ascends bearing gifts to Pallas' towered temple, and by her side goes maiden Lavinia, source of all that woe,

her beautiful eyes cast down. The mothers enter in, and
while the temple steams with their incense, pour from the
high doorway their mournful cry: 'Maiden armipotent,
Tritonian, sovereign of war, break with thine hand the spear
of the Phrygian plunderer, hurl him prone to earth and
dash him down beneath our lofty gates.' Turnus arrays
himself in hot haste for battle, and even now hath done
on his sparkling breastplate with its flickering scales of
brass, and clasped his golden greaves, his brows yet bare
and his sword buckled to his side; he runs down from the
fortress height glittering in gold, and exultantly anticipates
the foe. Thus when a horse snaps his tether, and, free at
last, rushes from the stalls and gains the open plain, he
either darts towards the pastures of the herded mares, or
bathing, as is his wont, in the familiar river waters, dashes
out and neighs with neck stretched high, glorying, and his
mane tosses over collar and shoulder. Camilla with her
Volscian array meets him face to face in the gateway; the
princess leaps from her horse, and all her squadron at her
example slide from horseback to the ground. Then she
speaks thus:

'Turnus, if bravery hath any just self-confidence, I dare
and promise to engage Aeneas' cavalry, and advance to
meet the Tyrrhene horse. Permit my hand to try war's
first perils: do thou on foot keep by the walls and guard
the city.'

To this Turnus, with eyes fixed on the terrible maiden:

'O maiden flower of Italy, how may I essay to express,
how to prove my gratitude? But now, since that spirit of
thine excels all praise, share thou the toil with me.
Aeneas, as the report of the scouts I sent assures, hath
sent on his light-armed horse to annoy us and scour the
plains; himself he marches on the city across the lonely
ridge of the mountain steep. I am arranging a stratagem of

war in his pathway on the wooded slope, to block a gorge
on the highroad with armed troops. Do thou receive
and join battle with the Tyrrhene cavalry; with thee shall
be gallant Messapus, the Latin squadrons, and Tiburtus'
division : do thou likewise assume a captain's charge.'

So speaks he, and with like words heartens Messapus
and the allied captains to battle, and advances towards the
enemy. There is a sweeping curve of glen, made for ambushes and devices of arms. Dark thick foliage hems it in
on either hand, and into it a bare footpath leads by a
narrow gorge and difficult entrance. Right above it on
the watch-towers of the hill-top lies an unexpected level,
hidden away in shelter, whether one would charge from
right and left or stand on the ridge and roll down heavy
stones. Hither he passes by a line of way he knew, and,
seizing his ground, occupies the treacherous woods.

Meanwhile in the heavenly dwellings Latona's daughter
addressed fleet Opis, one of her maiden fellowship and
sacred band, and sadly uttered these accents : 'Camilla
moves to fierce war, O maiden, and vainly girds on our
arms, dear as she is beyond others to me. For her love of
Diana is not newly born, nor her spirit stirred by sudden
affection. Driven from his kingdom through jealousy of
his haughty power, Metabus left ancient Privernum town,
and bore his infant with him in his flight through war and
battle, the companion of his exile, and called her by her
mother Casmilla's name, with a little change, Camilla.
Carrying her before him on his breast, he sought a long
ridge of lonely woodland; on all sides angry weapons
pressed on him, and Volscian soldiery spread hurrying
round about. Lo, in mid flight swoln Amasenus ran
foaming with banks abrim, so heavily had the clouds burst
in rain. He would swim it; but love of the infant holds
him back in alarm for so dear a burden. Inly revolving

all, he settled reluctantly on a sudden resolve: the great
spear that the warrior haply carried in his stout hand, of
hard-knotted and seasoned oak, to it he ties his daughter
swathed in cork-tree bark of the woodland, and binds her
balanced round the middle of the spear; poising it in his
great right hand he thus cries aloft: "Gracious one, haunter
of the woodland, maiden daughter of Latona, a father devotes this babe to thy service; thine is this weapon she holds,
thine infant suppliant, flying through the air from her enemies.
Accept her, I implore, O goddess, for thine own, whom now
I entrust to the chance of air." He spoke, and drawing
back his arm, darts the spinning spear-shaft: the waters
roar: over the racing river poor Camilla shoots on the
whistling weapon. But Metabus, as a strong band now
presses nigher, plunges into the river, and triumphantly
pulls spear and girl, his gift to Trivia, from the grassy turf.
No cities ever received him within house or rampart, nor
had his savagery submitted to it; he led his life on the
lonely pastoral hills. Here he nursed his daughter in the
underwood among tangled coverts, on the milk of a wild
brood-mare's teats, squeezing the udder into her tender
lips. And so soon as the baby stood and went straight on
her feet, he armed her hands with a sharp javelin, and hung
quiver and bow from her little shoulders. Instead of gold
to clasp her tresses, instead of the long skirted gown, a
tiger's spoils hang down her back. Even then her tender
hand hurled childish darts, and whirled about her head the
twisted thong of her sling, and struck down the crane
from Strymon or the milk-white swan. Many a mother
among Tyrrhenian towns destined her for their sons in
vain; content with Diana alone, she keeps unsoiled for
ever the love of her darts and maidenhood. Would she
had not plunged thus into warfare and provoked the Trojans
by attack! so were she now dear to me and one of my

company. But since bitter doom is upon her, up, glide
from heaven, O Nymph, and seek the Latin borders, where
under evil omen they join in baleful battle. Take these,
and draw from the quiver an avenging shaft; by it shall he
pay me forfeit of his blood, whoso, Trojan or Italian alike,
shall sully her sacred body with a wound. Thereafter will
I in a sheltering cloud bear body and armour of the hapless
girl unspoiled to the tomb, and lay them in her native
land.' She spoke; but the other sped lightly down the
aery sky, girt about with dark whirlwind on her echoing
way.

But meanwhile the Trojan force nears the walls, with
the Etruscan captains and their whole cavalry arrayed in
ordered squadrons. Their horses' trampling hoofs thunder
on all the field, as, swerving this way and that, they chafe at
the reins' pressure; the iron field bristles wide with spears,
and the plain is aflame with uplifted arms. Likewise
Messapus and the Latin horse, and Coras and his brother,
and maiden Camilla's squadron, come forth against them on
the plain, and draw back their hands and level the flickering
points of their long lances, in a fire of neighing horses and
advancing men. And now each had drawn within javelin-
cast of each, and drew up; with a sudden shout they dart
forth, and urge on their furious horses; from all sides at
once weapons shower thick like snow, and veil the sky with
their shadow. In a moment Tyrrhenus and fiery Aconteus
charge violently with crossing spears, and are the first to
fall; they go down with a heavy crash, and their beasts
break and shatter chest upon chest. Aconteus, hurled off
like a thunderbolt or some mass slung from an engine, is
dashed away, and scatters his life in air. Immediately the
lines waver, and the Latins wheeling about throw their
shields behind them and turn their horses towards the
town. The Trojans pursue; Asilas heads and leads on

their squadrons. And now they drew nigh the gates, and
again the Latins raise a shout and wheel their supple necks
about; the pursuers fly, and gallop right back with loosened
rein: as when the sea, running up in ebb and flow, now
rushes shoreward and strikes over the cliffs in a wave of
foam, drenching the edge of the sand in its curving sweep;
now runs swirling back, and the surge sucks the rolling
stones away. Twice the Tuscans turn and drive the
Rutulians towards the town; twice they are repelled, and
look back behind them from cover of their shields. But
when now meeting in a third encounter, the lines are locked
together all their length, and man singles out his man;
then indeed, amid groans of the dying, deep in blood roll
armour and bodies, and horses half slain mixed up with
slaughtered men. The battle swells fierce. Orsilochus
hurled his spear at the horse of Remulus, whom himself he
shrank to meet, and left the steel in it under the ear; at
the stroke the charger rears madly, and, mastered by the
wound, lifts his chest and flings up his legs: the rider is
thrown and rolls over on the ground. Catillus strikes down
Iollas, and Herminius mighty in courage, mighty in limbs
and arms, bareheaded, tawny-haired, bare-shouldered;
undismayed by wounds, he leaves his vast body open
against arms. Through his broad shoulders the quivering
spear runs piercing him through, and doubles him up with
pain. Everywhere the dark blood flows; they deal death
with the sword in battle, and seek a noble death by
wounds.

But amid the slaughter Camilla rages, a quivered
Amazon, with one side stripped for battle, and now sends
tough javelins showering from her hand, now snatches the
strong battle-axe in her unwearying grasp; the golden bow,
the armour of Diana, clashes on her shoulders; and even
when forced backward in retreat, she turns in flight and

aims darts from her bow. But around her are her chosen
comrades, maiden Larina, Tulla, Tarpeia brandishing an
axe inlaid with bronze, girls of Italy, whom Camilla the
bright chose for her own escort, good at service in peace
and war : even as Thracian Amazons when the streams of
Thermodon clash beneath them as they go to war in
painted arms, whether around Hippolyte, or while martial
Penthesilea returns in her chariot, and the crescent-shielded
columns of women dance with loud confused cry. Whom
first, whom last, fierce maiden, does thy dart strike down ?
First Euneus, son of Clytius ; for as he meets her the long
fir shaft crashes through his open breast. He falls spouting
streams of blood, and bites the gory ground, and dying
writhes himself upon his wound. Then Liris and Pagasus
above him ; who fall headlong and together, the one thrown
as he reins up his horse stabbed under him, the other while
he runs forward and stretches his unarmed hand to stay his
fall. To these she joins Amastrus, son of Hippotas, and
follows from far with her spear Tereus and Harpalycus and
Demophoön and Chromis : and as many darts as the
maiden sends whirling from her hand, so many Phrygians
fall. Ornytus the hunter rides near in strange arms on his
Iapygian horse, his broad warrior's shoulders swathed in
the hide stripped from a bullock, his head covered by a
wolf's wide-grinning mouth and white-tusked jaws; a rustic
pike arms his hand ; himself he moves amid the squadrons
a full head over all. Catching him up (for that was easy
amid the rout), she runs him through, and thus cries above
her enemy : 'Thou wert hunting wild beasts in the forest,
thoughtest thou, Tyrrhenian ? the day is come for a woman's
arms to refute thy words. Yet no light fame shalt thou carry
to thy fathers' ghosts, to have fallen under the weapon of
Camilla.' Next Orsilochus and Butes, the two mightiest
of mould among the Teucrians ; Butes she pierces in the

back with her spear-point between corslet and helmet,
where the neck shews as he sits, and the shield hangs from
his left shoulder ; Orsilochus she flies, and darting in a wide
circle, slips into the inner ring and pursues her pursuer ;
then rising her full height, she drives the strong axe deep
through armour and bone, as he pleads and makes much
entreaty ; warm brain from the wound splashes his face.
One met her thus and hung startled by the sudden sight,
the warrior son of Aunus haunter of the Apennine, not the
meanest in Liguria while fate allowed him to deceive.
And he, when he discerns that no fleetness of foot may
now save him from battle or turn the princess from pursuit,
essays to wind a subtle device of treachery, and thus begins :
‘How hast thou glory, if a woman trust in her horse's
strength ? Debar retreat ; trust thyself to level ground at
close quarters with me, and prepare to fight on foot. Soon
wilt thou know how windy boasting brings one to harm.’
He spoke ; but she, furious and stung with fiery indignation,
hands her horse to an attendant, and takes her stand in
equal arms on foot and undismayed, with naked sword and
shield unemblazoned. But he, thinking his craft had won
the day, himself flies off on the instant, and turning his
rein, darts off in flight, pricking his beast to speed with iron-
armed heel. ‘False Ligurian, in vain elated in thy pride !
for naught hast thou attempted thy slippery native arts, nor
will thy craft bring thee home unhurt to treacherous
Aunus.’ So speaks the maiden, and with running feet
swift as fire crosses his horse, and catching the bridle, meets
him in front and takes her vengeance in her enemy's blood :
as lightly as the falcon, bird of bale, swoops down from
aloft on a pigeon high in a cloud, and pounces on and
holds her, and disembowels her with taloned feet, while
blood and torn feathers flutter down the sky.

But the creator of men and gods sits high on Olympus’

summit watching this, not with eyes unseeing : he kindles
Tyrrhenian Tarchon to the fierce battle, and sharply goads
him on to wrath. So Tarchon gallops amid the slaughter
where his squadrons retreat, and urges his troops in
changing tones, calling man on man by name, and rallies
the fliers to fight. 'What terror, what utter cowardice
hath fallen on your spirits, O never to be stung to shame,
O slack alway ? a woman drives you in disorder and routs
our ranks ! Why wear we steel? for what are these idle
weapons in our hands ? Yet not slack in Venus' service
and wars by night, or, when the curving flute proclaims
Bacchus' revels, to look forward to the feast and the cups
on the loaded board (this your passion, this your desire !)
till the soothsayer pronounce the offering favourable, and
the fatted victim invite you to the deep groves.' So
speaking, he spurs his horse into the midmost, ready himself to die, and bears violently down full on Venulus ; and
tearing him from horseback, grasps his enemy and carries
him away with him on the saddle-bow by main force. A
cry rises up, and all the Latins turn their eyes. Tarchon
flies like fire over the plain, carrying the armed man, and
breaks off the steel head from his own spear and searches
the uncovered places, trying where he may deal the mortal
blow ; the other struggling against him keeps his hand off
his throat, and strongly parries his attack. And, as when
a golden eagle snatches and soars with a serpent in his
clutch, and his feet are fast in it, and his talons cling ; but
the wounded snake writhes in coiling spires, and its scales
rise and roughen, and its mouth hisses as it towers upward ;
the bird none the less attacks his struggling prize with
crooked beak, while his vans beat the air : even so Tarchon carries Tiburtus out of the ranks, triumphant in his
prize. Following their captain's example and issue the
men of Maeonia charge in.   Then Arruns, due to his

doom, circles in advance of fleet Camilla with artful javelin, and tries how fortune may be easiest. Where the maiden darts furious amid the ranks, there Arruns slips up and silently tracks her footsteps; where she returns victorious and retires from amid the enemy, there he stealthily bends his rapid reins. Here he approaches, and here again he approaches, and strays all round and about, and untiringly shakes his certain spear. Haply Chloreus, sacred to Cybele and once her priest, glittered afar, splendid in Phrygian armour; a skin feathered with brazen scales and clasped with gold clothed the horse that foamed under his spur; himself he shone in foreign blue and scarlet, with fleet Gortynian shafts and a Lycian horn; a golden bow was on his shoulder, and the soothsayer's helmet was of gold; red gold knotted up his yellow scarf with its rustling lawny folds; his tunics and barbarian trousers were wrought in needlework. Him, whether that she might nail armour of Troy on her temples, or herself move in captive gold, the maiden pursued in blind chase alone of all the battle conflict, and down the whole line, reckless and fired by a woman's passion for spoils and plunder: when at last out of his ambush Arruns chooses his time and darts his javelin, praying thus aloud to heaven: ' Apollo, most high of gods, holy Soracte's warder, to whom we beyond all do worship, for whom the blaze of the pinewood heap is fed, where we thy worshippers in pious faith print our steps amid the deep embers of the fire, grant, O Lord omnipotent, that our arms wipe off this disgrace. I seek not the dress the maiden wore, nor trophy or any spoil of victory; other deeds shall bring me praise; let but this dread scourge fall stricken beneath my wound, I will return inglorious to my native towns.' Phoebus heard, and inly granted half his vow to prosper, half he shred into the flying breezes. To surprise and strike down Camilla in sudden death, this he yielded to his prayer; that his high home might see his return he gave not, and a gust swept off his accents on the gale. So, when the spear sped from his hand hurtled through the air, all the Volscians marked it well and turned their eyes on the queen; and she alone knew not wind or sound of the weapon on its aery path, till the spear passed home and sank where her breast met it, and, driven deep, drank her maiden blood. Her companions run hastily up and catch their sinking mistress. Arruns takes to flight more alarmed than all, in mingled fear and exultation, and no longer dares to trust his spear or face the maiden's weapons. And as the wolf, some shepherd or great bullock slain, plunges at once among the trackless mountain heights ere hostile darts are in pursuit, and knows how reckless he hath been, and drooping his tail lays it quivering under his belly, and seeks the woods; even so does Arruns withdraw from sight in dismay, and, satisfied to escape, mingles in the throng of arms. The dying woman pulls at the weapon with her hand; but the iron head is fixed deep in the wound up between the rib-bones. She swoons away with loss of blood; chilling in death her eyes swoon away; the once lustrous colour leaves her face. Then gasping, she thus accosts Acca, one of her birthmates, who alone before all was true to Camilla, with whom her cares were divided; and even so she speaks: 'Thus far, Acca my sister, have I availed; now the bitter wound overmasters me, and all about me darkens in haze. Haste away, and carry to Turnus my last message; to take my place in battle, and repel the Trojans from the town. And now goodbye.' Even with the words she dropped the reins and slid to ground unconscious. Then the unnerving chill overspread her, her neck slackened, her head sank overpowered by death, and her arms fell, and with a moan the life fled indignant into the dark. Then indeed an

infinite cry rises and smites the golden stars; the battle
grows bloodier now Camilla is down; at once in serried
ranks all the Teucrian forces pour in, with the Tyrrhene
captains and Evander's Arcadian squadrons.

But Opis, Trivia's sentinel, long ere now sits high on the
hill-tops, gazing on the battle undismayed. And when afar
amid the din of angry men she espied Camilla done woefully to death, she sighed and uttered forth a deep cry:
'Ah too, too cruel, O maiden, the forfeit thou hast paid
for daring armed attack on the Teucrians! and nothing
hath availed thee thy lonely following of Diana in the
woodlands, nor wearing our quiver on thy shoulder.   Yet
thy Queen hath not left thee unhonoured now thy latter
end is come; nor will this thy death be unnamed among
the nations, nor shalt thou bear the fame of one unavenged;
for whosoever hath sullied thy body with a wound shall
pay death for due.'   Under the mountain height was a great
earthen mound, tomb of Dercennus, a Laurentine king of
old, shrouded in shadowy ilex.   Hither the goddess most
beautiful first swoops down, and marks Arruns from the
mounded height.   As she saw him glittering in arms and
idly exultant: 'Why,' she cries, 'wanderest thou away?
hitherward direct thy steps; come hither to thy doom, to
receive thy fit reward for Camilla.   Shalt thou die, and
by Diana's weapons?'   The Thracian spoke, and slid out
a fleet arrow from her gilded quiver, and stretched it level
on the bow, and drew it far, till the curving tips met one
another, and now her hands touched in counterpoise, the
left the steel edge, the string in the right her breast.   At
once and in a moment Arruns heard the whistle of the
dart and the resounding air, as the steel sank in his
body.   His comrades leave him forgotten on the unknown
dust of the plain, moaning his last and gasping his life
away; Opis wings her flight to the skyey heaven.

At once the light squadron of Camilla retreat now they
have lost their mistress; the Rutulians retreat in confusion,
brave Atinas retreats. Scattered captains and thinned com-
panies make for safety, and turn their horses backward to
the town. Nor does any avail to make stand against the
swarming death-dealing Teucrians, or bear their shock in
arms; but their unstrung bows droop on their shoulders,
and the four-footed galloping horse-hoof shakes the crumbling plain. The eddying dust rolls up thick and black
towards the walls, and on the watch-towers mothers beat
their breasts and the cries of women rise up to heaven.
On such as first in the rout broke in at the open gates the
mingling hostile throng follows hard; nor do they escape
death, alas! but in the very gateway, within their native
city and amid their sheltering homes, they are pierced
through and gasp out their life. Some shut the gates, and
dare not open to their pleading comrades nor receive them
in the town; and a most pitiful slaughter begins between
armed men who guard the entry and others who rush upon
their arms. Barred out before their weeping parents' eyes
and faces, some, swept on by the rout, roll headlong into
the trenches; some, blindly rushing with loosened rein,
batter at the gates and stiffly-bolted doorway. The very
mothers from the walls in eager heat (true love of country
points the way, when they see Camilla) dart weapons with
shaking hand, and eagerly make hard stocks of wood and
fire-hardened poles serve for steel, and burn to die among
the foremost for their city's sake.

Meanwhile among the forests the terrible news pours
in on Turnus, and Acca brings him news of the mighty
invasion; the Volscian lines are destroyed; Camilla is
fallen; the enemy thicken and press on, and have swept
all before them down the tide of battle. Raging he
leaves the hills he had beset—Jove's stern will ordains it

so—and quits the rough woodland. Scarcely had he marched out of sight and gained the plain when lord Aeneas enters the open defiles, surmounts the ridge, and issues from the dim forest. So both advance swiftly to the town with all their columns, no long march apart, and at once Aeneas descried afar the plains all smoking with dust, and saw the Laurentine columns, and Turnus knew Aeneas terrible in arms, and heard the advancing feet and the neighing of the horses. And straightway would they join battle and essay the conflict, but that ruddy Phoebus even now dips his weary coursers in the Iberian flood, and night draws on over the fading day. They encamp before the city, and draw their trenches round the walls.

THE SLAYING OF TURNUS

WHEN Turnus sees the Latins broken and fainting in the thwart issue of war, his promise claimed for fulfilment, and men's eyes pointed on him, his own spirit rises in unappeasable flame. As the lion in Phoenician fields, his breast heavily wounded by the huntsmen, at last starts into arms, and shakes out the shaggy masses from his exultant neck, and undismayed snaps the brigand's planted weapon, roaring with blood-stained mouth; even so Turnus kindles and swells in passion. Then he thus addresses the king, and so furiously begins:

'Turnus stops not the way; there is no excuse for the coward Aeneadae to take back their words or renounce their compact. I join battle; bring the holy things, my lord, and swear the treaty. Either this hand shall hurl to hell the Dardanian who skulks from Asia, and the Latins sit and see my single sword wipe out the nation's reproach; or let him rule his conquest, and Lavinia pass to his espousal.'

To him Latinus calmly replied: 'O excellent young man! the more thy hot valour abounds, the more intently must I counsel, and weigh fearfully what may befall. Thou hast thy father Daunus' realm, hast many towns taken by

thine hand, nor is Latinus lacking in gold and goodwill.
There are other maidens unwedded in Latium and
Laurentine fields, and of no mean birth. Let me unfold
this hard saying in all sincerity: and do thou drink it into
thy soul. I might not ally my daughter to any of her old
wooers ; such was the universal oracle of gods and men.
Overborne by love for thee, overborne by kinship of blood
and my weeping wife's complaint, I broke all fetters, I
severed the maiden from her promised husband, I took up
unrighteous arms. Since then, Turnus, thou seest what
calamities, what wars pursue me, what woes thyself before
all dost suffer. Twice vanquished in pitched battle, we
scarce guard in our city walls the hopes of Italy : the streams
of Tiber yet run warm with our blood, and our bones whiten
the boundless plain. Why fall I away again and again ?
what madness bends my purpose ? if I am ready to take
them into alliance after Turnus' destruction, why do I not
rather bar the strife while he lives ? What will thy
Rutulian kinsmen, will all Italy say, if thy death—Fortune
make void the word !—comes by my betrayal, while thou
suest for our daughter in marriage ? Cast a glance on war's
changing fortune ; pity thine aged father, who now far away
sits sad in his native Ardea.'

In nowise do the words bend Turnus' passion : he
rages the more fiercely, and sickens of the cure. So soon
as he found speech he thus made utterance :

'The care thou hast for me, most gracious lord, for me
lay down, I implore thee, and let me purchase honour with
death. Our hand too rains weapons, our steel is strong ;
and our wounds too draw blood. The goddess his mother
will be far from him to cover his flight, woman-like, in a
cloud and an empty phantom's hiding.'

But the queen, dismayed by the new terms of battle,
wept, and clung to her fiery son as one ready to die :

'Turnus, by these tears, by Amata's regard, if that touches thee at all—thou art now the one hope, the repose of mine unhappy age ; in thine hand is Latinus' honour and empire, on thee is the weight of all our sinking house—one thing I beseech thee ; forbear to join battle with the Teucrians. What fate soever awaits thee in the strife thou seekest, it awaits me, Turnus, too : with thee will I leave the hateful light, nor shall my captive eyes see Aeneas my daughter's lord.' Lavinia tearfully heard her mother's words with cheeks all aflame, as deep blushes set her face on fire and ran hotly over it. Even as Indian ivory, if one stain it with sanguine dye, or where white lilies are red with many a rose amid : such colour came on the maiden's face. Love throws him into tumult, and stays his countenance on the girl : he burns fiercer for arms, and briefly answers Amata :

'Do not, I pray thee, do not weep for me, neither pursue me thus ominously as I go to the stern shock of war. Turnus is not free to dally with death. Thou, Idmon, bear my message to the Phrygian monarch in this harsh wording : So soon as to-morrow's Dawn rises in the sky blushing on her crimson wheels, let him not loose Teucrian or Rutulian : let Teucrian and Rutulian arms have rest, and our blood decide the war ; on that field let Lavinia be sought in marriage.'

These words uttered, withdrawing swiftly homeward, he orders out his horses, and rejoicingly beholds them snorting before his face : those that Orithyia's self gave to grace Pilumnus, such as would excel the snows in whiteness and the gales in speed. The eager charioteers stand round and pat their chests with clapping hollowed hands, and comb their tressed manes. Himself next he girds on his shoulders the corslet stiff with gold and pale mountain-bronze, and buckles on the sword and shield and scarlet-

plumed helmet-spikes : that sword the divine Lord of Fire
had himself forged for his father Daunus and dipped glowing in the Stygian wave.   Next, where it stood amid his
dwelling leaning on a massy pillar, he strongly seizes his
stout spear, the spoil of Actor the Auruncan, and brandishes
it quivering, and cries aloud : ' Now, O spear that never
hast failed at my call, now the time is come ; thee princely
Actor once, thee Turnus now wields in his grasp.   Grant
this strong hand to strike down the effeminate Phrygian, to
rend and shatter the corslet, and defile in dust the locks
curled with hot iron and wet with myrrh.'   Thus madly he
runs on : sparkles leap out from all his blazing face, and
his keen eyes flash fire : even as the bull when before his
first fight he bellows awfully, and drives against a tree's
trunk to make trial of his angry horns, and buffets the air
with blows or scatters the sand in prelude of battle.

And therewithal Aeneas, terrible in his mother's armour,
kindles for warfare and awakes into wrath, rejoicing that
offer of treaty stays the war.   Comforting his comrades and
sorrowing Iülus' fear, he instructs them of destiny, and bids
bear answer of assurance to King Latinus, and name the
laws of peace.

Scarcely did the morrow shed on the mountain-tops the
beams of risen day, as the horses of the sun begin to rise
from the deep flood and breathe light from their lifted
nostrils ; Rutulian and Teucrian men measured out and
made ready a field of battle under the great city's ramparts,
and midway in it hearth-fires and grassy altars to the gods
of both peoples ; while others bore spring water and fire,
draped in priestly dress and their brows bound with grass
of the field.   The Ausonian army issue forth, and crowd
through the gates in streaming serried columns.   On this
side all the Trojan and Tyrrhenian host pour in diverse
armament, girt with iron even as though the harsh battle-

strife called them forth. Therewith amid their thousands
the captains dart up and down, splendid in gold and purple,
Mnestheus, seed of Assaracus, and brave Asilas, and Messapus, tamer of horses, brood of Neptune : then each on signal
given retired to his own ground ; they plant their spears in
the earth and lean their shields against them. Mothers in
eager abandonment, and the unarmed crowd and feeble
elders beset towers and house-roofs, or stand at the lofty
gates.

But Juno, on the summit that is now called the Alban—
then the mountain had neither name nor fame or honour—
looked forth from the hill and surveyed the plain and double
lines of Laurentine and Trojan, and Latinus' town. Straightway spoke she thus to Turnus' sister, goddess to goddess,
lady of pools and noisy rivers : such worship did Jupiter
the high king of air consecrate to her for her stolen
virginity :

'Nymph, grace of rivers, best beloved of our soul, thou
knowest how out of all the Latin women that ever rose to
high-hearted Jove's thankless bed, thee only have I preferred and gladly given part and place in heaven. Learn
thy woe, that thou blame not me for it, Juturna. Where
fortune seemed to allow and the Destinies granted Latinus'
estate to prosper, I shielded Turnus and thy city. Now I
see him joining battle with unequal fates, and the day of
doom and deadly force draws nigh. Mine eyes cannot look
on this battle and treaty : thou, if thou darest aught of more
present help for the brother of thy blood, go on ; it befits
thee. Haply relief shall follow misery.'

Scarcely thus : when Juturna's eyes overbrimmed with
tears, and thrice and again she smote her hand on her
gracious breast. 'This is not time for tears,' cries Juno,
daughter of Saturn : 'hasten and snatch thy brother, if it
may be, from his death ; or do thou waken war, and make

the treaty abortive. I encourage thee to dare.' With such urgence she left her, doubting and dismayed, and grievously wounded in soul.

Meanwhile the kings go forth; Latinus in mighty pomp rides in his four-horse chariot; twelve gilded rays go glittering round his brows, symbol of the Sun his ancestor; Turnus moves behind a white pair, clenching in his hand two broad-headed spears. On this side lord Aeneas, fount of the Roman race, ablaze in starlike shield and celestial arms, and close by Ascanius, second hope of mighty Rome, issue from the camp; and the priest, in spotless raiment, hath brought the young of a bristly sow and an unshorn sheep of two years old, and set his beasts by the blazing altars. They, turning their eyes towards the sunrising, scatter salted corn from their hands and clip the beasts with steel over the temples, and pour cups on the altars. Then Aeneas the good, with sword drawn, thus makes invocation:

'Be the Sun now witness, and this Earth to my call, for whose sake I have borne to suffer so sore travail, and the Lord omnipotent, and thou his wife, at last, divine daughter of Saturn, at last I pray more favourable; and thou, mighty Mavors, who wieldest all warfare in lordship beneath thy sway; and on the Springs and Rivers I call, and the Dread of high heaven, and the divinities of the blue seas: if haply victory fall to Turnus the Ausonian, the vanquished make covenant to withdraw to Evander's city; Iülus shall quit the soil; nor ever hereafter shall the Aeneadae return in arms to renew warfare, or attack this realm with the sword. But if Victory grant battle to us and ours (as I think the rather, and so the rather may the gods seal their will), I will not bid Italy obey my Teucrians, nor do I claim the realm for mine; let both nations, un-conquered, join treaty for ever under equal law. Gods and worship shall be of my giving : my father Latinus shall bear the sword, and have a father's prescribed command. For me my Teucrians shall establish a city, and Lavinia give the town her name.'

Thus Aeneas first : thereon Latinus thus follows :

' By these same I swear, O Aeneas, by Earth, Sea, Sky, and the twin brood of Latona and Janus the double-facing, and the might of nether gods and grim Pluto's shrine ; this let our Father hear, who seals treaties with his thunderbolt. I touch the altars, I take to witness the fires and the gods between us ; no time shall break this peace and truce in Italy, howsoever fortune fall; nor shall any force turn my will aside, not if it dissolve land into water in turmoil of deluge, or melt heaven in hell : so surely as this sceptre ' (for haply he bore a sceptre in his hand) 'shall never burgeon into thin leafage and shady shoot, since once in the forest cut down right to the stem it lost its mother, and the steel lopped away its tressed arms : a tree of old : now the craftsman's hand hath bound it in adornment of brass and given it to our Latin fathers' bearing.'

With such words they sealed mutual treaty midway in sight of the princes. Then they duly slay the consecrated beasts over the flames, and tear out their live entrails, and pile the altars with laden chargers.

But long ere this the Rutulians deemed the battle unequal, and their hearts are stirred in changeful motion ; and now the more, as they discern nigher that in ill-matched strength . . . . heightened by Turnus, as advancing with noiseless pace he humbly worships at the altar with downcast eye, by his wasted cheeks and the pallor on his youthful frame. Soon as Juturna his sister saw this talk spread, and the people's mind waver in uncertainty, into the mid ranks, in feigned form of Camertus— his family was high in long ancestry, and his father's name

for valour renowned, and himself most valiant in arms—
into the mid ranks she glides, not ignorant of her task, and
scatters diverse rumours, saying thus: 'Shame, O Rutulians!
shall we set one life in the breach for so many such as
these? are we unequal in numbers or bravery? See, Troy
and Arcadia is all they bring, and those fate-bound bands
that Etruria hurls on Turnus. Scarce is there an enemy to
meet every other man of ours. He indeed will ascend to
the gods for whose altars he devotes himself, and move
living in the lips of men: we, our country lost, shall bow
to the haughty rigour of our lords, if we now sit slackly on
the field.'

By such words the soldiers' counsel was kindled yet
higher and higher, and a murmur crept through their
columns; the very Laurentines, the very Latins are
changed; and they who but now hoped for rest from battle
and rescue of fortune now desire arms and pray the treaty
were undone, and pity Turnus' cruel lot. To this Juturna
adds a yet stronger impulse, and high in heaven shews a
sign more potent than any to confuse Italian souls with
delusive augury. For on the crimsoned sky Jove's tawny
bird flew chasing, in a screaming crowd, fowl of the shore
that winged their column; then suddenly stooping to the
water, pounces on a noble swan with merciless crooked
talons. The startled Italians watch, while all the birds
together clamorously wheel round from flight, wonderful to
see, and dim the sky with their pinions, and in thickening
cloud urge their foe through air, till, conquered by their
attack and his heavy prey, he yielded and dropped it from
his talons into the river, and winged his way deep into the
clouds. Then indeed the Rutulians clamorously greet the
omen, and their hands flash out. And Tolumnius the
augur cries before them all: 'This it was, this, that my
vows often have sought; I welcome and know a deity;

follow me, follow, snatch up the sword, O hapless people
whom the greedy alien frightens with his arms like silly
birds, and with strong hand ravages your shores. He too
will take to flight, and spread his sails afar over ocean.
Do you with one heart close up your squadrons, and defend
in battle your lost king.' He spoke, and darting forward,
hurled a weapon full on the enemy ; the whistling cornel-
shaft sings, and unerringly cleaves the air. At once and
with it a vast shout goes up, and all their rows are amazed,
and their hearts hotly stirred. The spear flies on ; where
haply stood opposite in ninefold brotherhood all the beautiful sons of one faithful Tyrrhene wife, borne of her to
Gylippus the Arcadian, one of them, midway where
the sewn belt rubs on the flank and the clasp bites the
fastenings of the side, one of them, excellent in beauty
and glittering in arms, it pierces clean through the ribs
and stretches on the yellow sand. But of his banded
brethren, their courage fired by grief, some grasp and draw
their swords, some snatch weapons to throw, and rush
blindly forward. The Laurentine columns rush forth against
them ; again from the other side Trojans and Agyllines and
Arcadians in painted armour flood thickly in : so hath one
passion seized all to make decision by the sword. They
pull the altars to pieces ; through all the air goes a thick
storm of weapons, and faster falls the iron rain. Bowls and
hearth-fires are carried off ; Latinus himself retreats, bearing
the outraged gods of the broken treaty. The others harness
their chariots, or vault upon their horses and come up with
swords drawn. Messapus, eager to shatter the treaty, rides
menacingly down on Aulestes the Tyrrhenian, a king in a
king's array. Retreating hastily, and tripped on the altars
that meet him behind, the hapless man goes down on his
head and shoulders. But Messapus flies up with wrathful
spear, and strikes him, as he pleads sore, a deep down-

ward blow from horseback with his beam-like spear, saying
thus : *That for him : the high gods take this better victim.*
The Italians crowd in and strip his warm limbs. Corynaeus
seizes a charred brand from the altar, and meeting Ebysus
as he advances to strike, darts the flame in his face ; his
heavy beard flamed up, and gave out a scorched smell.
Following up his enemy's confusion, the other seizes him
with his left hand by the hair, and bears him to earth with
a thrust of his planted knee, and there drives the unyielding
sword into his side. Podalirius pursues and overhangs
with naked sword the shepherd Alsus as he rushes amid
the foremost line of weapons ; Alsus swings back his axe,
and severs brow and chin full in front, wetting his armour
all over with spattered blood. Grim rest and iron slumber
seal his eyes ; his lids close on everlasting night.

But good Aeneas, his head bared, kept stretching his
unarmed hand and calling loudly to his men : ' Whither
run you ? What is this strife that so spreads and swells ?
Ah, restrain your wrath ! truce is already stricken, and all
its laws ordained ; mine alone is the right of battle.
Leave me alone, and my hand shall confirm the treaty ;
these rites already make Turnus mine.' Amid these accents,
amid words like these, lo ! a whistling arrow winged its
way to him, sped from what hand or driven by what god,
none knows, or what chance or deity brought such honour
to the Rutulians ; the renown of the high deed was buried,
nor did any boast to have dealt Aeneas' wound. Turnus,
when he saw Aeneas retreating from the ranks and his
captains in dismay, burns hot with sudden hope. At once
he calls for his horses and armour, and with a bound leaps
proudly into his chariot and handles the reins. He darts
on, dealing many a brave man's body to death ; many an
one he rolls half-slain, or crushes whole files under his
chariot, or seizes and showers spears on the fugitives. As

when by the streams of icy Hebrus Mavors kindles to
bloodshed and clashes on his shield, and stirs war and
speeds his furious coursers; they outwing south winds
and west on the open plain; utmost Thrace groans under
their hoof-beats; and around in the god's train rush the
faces of dark Terror, and Wraths and Ambushes; even so
amid the battle Turnus briskly lashes on his reeking
horses, trampling on the foes that lie piteously slain; the
galloping hoof scatters bloody dew, and spurns mingled
gore and sand. And now hath he dealt Sthenelus to
death, and Thamyrus and Pholus, him and him at close
quarters, the other from afar; from afar both the sons of
Imbrasus, Glaucus and Lades, whom Imbrasus himself
had nurtured in Lycia and equipped in equal arms,
whether to meet hand to hand or to outstrip the winds
on horseback. Elsewhere Eumedes advances amid the
fray, ancient Dolon's brood, illustrious in war, renewing
his grandfather's name, his father's courage and strength
of hand, who of old dared to claim Pelides' chariot as his
price if he went to spy out the Grecian camp; to him the
son of Tydeus told out another price for his venture, and
he dreams no more of Achilles' horses. Him Turnus
descried far on the open plain, and first following him
with light javelin through long space of air, stops his
double-harnessed horses and leaps from the chariot, and
descends on his fallen half-lifeless foe, and, planting his
foot on his neck, wrests the blade out of his hand and dyes
its glitter deep in his throat, adding these words withal:
'Behold, thou liest, Trojan, meting out those Hesperian
fields thou didst seek in war. Such guerdon is theirs who
dare to tempt my sword; thus do they found their city.'
Then with a spear-cast he sends Asbutes to follow him, and
Chloreus and Sybaris, Dares and Thersilochus, and Thymoetes fallen flung over his horse's neck. And as when

the Edonian North wind's wrath roars on the deep Aegean,
and the wave follows it shoreward; where the blast comes
down, the clouds race over the sky; so, wheresoever
Turnus cleaves his way, columns retreat and lines turn and
run; his own speed bears him on, and his flying plume
tosses as his chariot meets the breeze. Phegeus brooked
not his proud approach; he faced the chariot, and caught
and twisted away in his right hand the mouths of his
horses, spurred into speed and foaming on the bit. Dragged
along and hanging by the yoke he is left uncovered; the
broad lance-head reaches him, pins and pierces the double-
woven breastplate, and lightly wounds the surface of his
body. Yet turning, he advanced on the enemy behind his
shield, and sought succour in the naked point; when the
wheel running forward on its swift axle struck him headlong
and flung him to ground, and Turnus' sword following it
smote off his head between the helmet-rim and the upper
border of the breastplate, and left the body on the sand.

And while Turnus thus victoriously deals death over
the plains, Mnestheus meantime and faithful Achates, and
Ascanius by their side, set down Aeneas in the camp,
dabbled with blood and leaning every other step on his
long spear. He storms, and tries hard to pull out the dart
where the reed had broken, and calls for the nearest way
of remedy, to cut open the wound with broad blade, and
tear apart the weapon's lurking-place, and so send him back
to battle. And now Iapix son of Iasus came, beloved
beyond others of Phoebus, to whom once of old, smitten
with sharp desire, Apollo gladly offered his own arts
and gifts, augury and the lyre and swift arrows: he, to
lengthen out the destiny of a parent given over to die,
chose rather to know the potency of herbs and the practice
of healing, and deal in a silent art unrenowned. Aeneas
stood chafing bitterly, propped on his vast spear, mourning

Iülus and a great crowd of men around, unstirred by their tears. The aged man, with garment drawn back and girt about him in Paeonian fashion, makes many a hurried effort with healing hand and the potent herbs of Phoebus, all in vain; in vain his hand solicits the arrow-head, and his pincers' grasp pulls at the steel. Fortune leads him forward in nowise; Apollo aids not with counsel; and more and more the fierce clash swells over the plains, and the havoc draws nigher on. Already they see the sky a mass of dust, the cavalry approaching, and shafts falling thickly amid the camp; the dismal cry uprises of warriors fighting and falling under the War-god's heavy hand. At this, stirred deep by her son's cruel pain, Venus his mother plucked from Cretan Ida a stalk of dittamy with downy leaves and bright-tressed flowers, the plant not unknown to wild goats when winged arrows are fast in their body. This Venus bore down, her shape girt in a dim halo; this she steeps with secret healing in the river-water poured out and sparkling abrim, and sprinkles life-giving juice of ambrosia and scented balm. With that water aged Iapix washed the wound, unwitting; and suddenly, lo! all the pain left his body, all the blood in the deep wound was stanched. And now following his hand the arrow fell out with no force, and strength returned afresh as of old. 'Hasten! arms for him quickly! why stand you?' cries Iapix aloud, and begins to kindle their courage against the enemy; 'this comes not by human resource or schooling of art, nor does my hand save thee, Aeneas: a higher god is at work, and sends thee back to higher deeds.' He, eager for battle, had already clasped on the greaves of gold right and left, and scorning delay, brandishes his spear. When the shield is adjusted by his side and the corslet on his back, he clasps Ascanius in his armed embrace, and lightly kissing him through the helmet, cries: 'Learn of me, O boy, valour

and toil indeed, fortune of others. Now mine hand shall
give thee defence in war, and lead thee to great reward : do
thou, when hereafter thine age ripens to fulness, keep this
in remembrance, and as thou recallest the pattern of thy
kindred, let thy spirit rise to thy father Aeneas, thine uncle
Hector.'

These words uttered, he issued towering from the gates,
brandishing his mighty spear : with him in serried column
rush Antheus and Mnestheus, and all the throng streams
forth of the camp. The field drifts with blinding dust, and
the startled earth trembles under the tramp of feet. From
his earthworks opposite Turnus saw and the Ausonians saw
them come, and an icy shudder ran deep through their
frame ; first and before all the Latins Juturna heard and
knew the sound, and in terror fled away. He flies on, and
hurries his dark column over the open plain. As when in
fierce weather a storm-cloud moves over mid sea to land,
with presaging heart, ah me, the hapless husbandmen
shudder from afar ; it will deal havoc to their trees and
destruction to their crops, and make a broad path of ruin ;
the winds fly before it, and bear its roar to the beach ; so
the Rhoeteian captain drives his army full on the foe ; one
and all they close up in wedges, and mass their serried ranks.
Thymbraeus smites massive Osiris with the sword, Mnestheus slays Arcetius, Achates Epulo, Gyas Ufens : Tolumnius the augur himself goes down, he who had hurled the
first weapon against the foe. Their cry rises to heaven, and
in turn the routed Rutulians give backward in flight over
the dusty fields. Himself he deigns not to cut down the
fugitives, nor pursue such as meet him fair on foot or
approach in arms : Turnus alone he tracks and searches in
the thick haze, alone calls him to conflict. Then panic-
stricken the warrior maiden flings Turnus' charioteer out
over his reins, and leaving him far where he slips from the

chariot-pole, herself succeeds and turns the wavy reins, tones and limbs and armour all of Metiscus' wearing. As when a black swallow flits through some rich lord's spacious house, and circles in flight the lofty halls, gathering her tiny food for sustenance to her twittering nestlings, and now swoops down the spacious colonnades, now round the wet ponds; in like wise dart Juturna's horses amid the enemy, and her fleet chariot passes flying over all the field. And now here and now here she displays her triumphant brother, nor yet allows him to close, but flies far and away. None the less does Aeneas thread the circling maze to meet him, and tracks his man, and with loud cry cries on him through the scattered ranks. Often as he cast eyes on his enemy and essayed to outrun the speed of the flying-footed horses, so often Juturna wheeled her team away. Alas, what can he do? Vainly he tosses on the ebb and flow, and in his spirit diverse cares make conflicting call; when Messapus, who haply bore in his left hand two tough spear-shafts topped with steel, runs lightly up and aims and hurls one of them upon him with unerring stroke. Aeneas stood still, and gathered himself behind his armour, sinking on bended knee; yet the rushing spear bore off his helmet-spike, and dashed the helmet-plume from the crest. Then indeed his wrath swells; and forced to it by their treachery, while chariot and horses disappear, he calls Jove oft and again to witness, and the altars of the violated treaty, and now at last plunges amid their lines. Sweeping terrible down the tide of battle he wakens fierce indiscriminate carnage, and flings loose all the reins of wrath.

What god may now unfold for me in verse so many woes, so many diverse slaughters and death of captains whom now Turnus, now again the Trojan hero, drives over all the field? Was it well, O God, that nations destined to everlasting peace should clash in so vast a shock? Aeneas

meets Sucro the Rutulian; the combat stayed the first rush
of the Teucrians, but delayed them not long; he catches
him on the side, and, when fate comes quickest, drives the
harsh sword clean through the ribs where they fence the
breast. Turnus brings down Amycus from horseback with
his brother Diores, and meets them on foot; him he strikes
with his long spear as he comes, him with his sword-point,
and hangs both severed heads on his chariot and carries
them off dripping with blood. The one sends to death
Talos and Tanaïs and brave Cethegus, three at one meeting, and gloomy Onites, of Echionian name, and Peridia the
mother that bore him; the other those brethren sent from
Lycia and Apollo's fields, and Menoetes the Arcadian, him
who loathed warfare in vain; who once had his art and
humble home about the river-fisheries of Lerna, and knew
not the courts of the great, but his father was tenant of the
land he tilled. And as fires kindled dispersedly in a dry
forest and rustling laurel-thickets, or foaming rivers where
they leap swift and loud from high hills, and speed to sea
each in his own path of havoc; as fiercely the two, Aeneas
and Turnus, dash amid the battle; now, now wrath surges
within them, and unconquerable hearts are torn; now in all
their might they rush upon wounds. The one dashes
Murranus down and stretches him on the soil with a vast
whirling mass of rock, as he cries the names of his fathers
and forefathers of old, a whole line drawn through Latin
kings; under traces and yoke the wheels spurned him, and
the fast-beating hoofs of his rushing horses trample down
their forgotten lord. The other meets Hyllus rushing on
in gigantic pride, and hurls his weapon at his gold-bound
temples; the spear pierced through the helmet and stood
fast in the brain. Neither did thy right hand save thee
from Turnus, O Cretheus, bravest of the Greeks; nor did
his gods shield Cupencus when Aeneas came; he gave his

breast full to the steel, nor, alas! was the brazen shield's
delay aught of avail. Thee likewise, Aeolus, the Laurentine
plains saw sink backward and cover a wide space of earth;
thou fallest, whom Argive battalions could not lay low, nor
Achilles the destroyer of Priam's realm. Here was thy goal
of death; thine high house was under Ida, at Lyrnesus
thine high house, on Laurentine soil thy tomb. The whole
battle-lines gather up, all Latium and all Dardania, Mnestheus and valiant Serestus, with Messapus, tamer of horses,
and brave Asilas, the Tuscan battalion and Evander's
Arcadian squadrons; man by man they struggle with all
their might; no rest nor pause in the vast strain of conflict.

At this Aeneas' mother most beautiful inspired him to
advance on the walls, directing his columns on the town and
dismaying the Latins with sudden and swift disaster. As in
search for Turnus he bent his glance this way and that round
the separate ranks, he descries the city free from all this warfare, unpunished and unstirred. Straightway he kindles at
the view of a greater battle; he summons Mnestheus and
Sergestus and brave Serestus his captains, and mounts a
hillock; there the rest of the Teucrian army gathers
thickly, still grasping shield and spear. Standing on the
high mound amid them, he speaks: 'Be there no delay to
my words; Jupiter is with us; neither let any be slower to
move that the design is sudden. This city to-day, the
source of war, the royal seat of Latinus, unless they yield
them to receive our yoke and obey their conquerors, will I
raze to ground, and lay her smoking roofs level with the
dust. Must I wait forsooth till Turnus please to stoop to
combat, and choose again to face his conqueror? This, O
citizens,· is the fountain-head and crown of the accursed
war. Bring brands speedily, and reclaim the treaty in fire.'
He ended; all with spirit alike emulous form a wedge and
advance in serried masses to the walls. Ladders are run

up, and fire leaps sudden to sight. Some rush to the
separate gates, and cut down the guards of the entry, others
hurl their steel and darken the sky with weapons. Aeneas
himself among the foremost, upstretching his hand to the city
walls, loudly reproaches Latinus, and takes the gods to witness
that he is again forced into battle, that twice now do the
Italians choose warfare and break a second treaty. Discord
rises among the alarmed citizens : some bid unbar the town
and fling wide their gates to the Dardanians, and pull the
king himself towards the ramparts ; others bring arms and
hasten to defend the walls : as when a shepherd tracks bees
to their retreat in a recessed rock, and fills it with stinging
smoke, they within run uneasily up and down their waxen
fortress, and hum louder in rising wrath ; the smell rolls in
darkness along their dwelling, and a blind murmur echoes
within the rock as the smoke issues to the empty air.

   This fortune likewise befell the despairing Latins, this
woe shook the whole city to her base. The queen espies
from her roof the enemy's approach, the walls scaled and
firebrands flying on the houses ; and nowhere Rutulian
ranks, none of Turnus' columns to meet them ; alas ! she
deems him destroyed in the shock of battle, and, distracted
by sudden anguish, shrieks that she is the source of guilt,
the spring of ill, and with many a mad utterance of frenzied
grief rends her purple attire with dying hand, and ties
from a lofty beam the ghastly noose of death. And when
the unhappy Latin women knew this calamity, first her
daughter Lavinia tears her flower-like tresses and roseate
cheeks, and all the train around her madden in her suit ;
the wide palace echoes to their wailing, and from it the
sorrowful rumour spreads abroad throughout the town. All
hearts sink ; Latinus goes with torn raiment, in dismay at his
wife's doom and his city's downfall, defiling his hoary hair
with soilure of sprinkled dust.

U

Meanwhile on the skirts of the field Turnus chases
scattered stragglers, ever slacker to battle, ever less and less
exultant in his coursers' victorious speed. The confused
cry came to him borne in blind terror down the breeze,
and his startled ears caught the echoing tumult and disastrous
murmur of the town. 'Ah me! what agony shakes the
city? or what is this cry that fleets so loud from the distant
town?' So speaks he, and distractedly checks the reins.
And to him his sister, as changed into his charioteer
Metiscus' likeness she swayed horses and chariot-reins, thus
rejoined: 'This way, Turnus, let us pursue the brood of
Troy, where victory opens her nearest way; there are others
whose hands can protect their dwellings. Aeneas falls
fiercer on the Italians, and closes in conflict; let our hand
too deal pitiless death on his Teucrians. Neither in tale of
dead nor in glory of battle shalt thou retire outdone.'
Thereat Turnus : . . .

'Ah my sister, long ere now I knew thee, when first
thine arts shattered the treaty, and thou didst mingle in the
strife; and now thy godhead conceals itself in vain. But
who hath bidden thee descend from heaven to bear this
sore travail? was it that thou mightest see thy hapless
brother cruelly slain? for what do I, or what fortune yet
gives promise of safety? Before my very eyes, calling
aloud on me, I saw Murranus, than whom none other
is left me more dear, sink huge to earth, borne down by as
huge a wound. Hapless Ufens is fallen, not to see our
shame; corpse and armour are in Teucrian hands. The
destruction of their households, this was the one thing yet
lacking; shall I suffer it? Shall my hand not refute
Drances' jeers? shall I turn my back, and this land see
Turnus a fugitive? Is Death all so bitter? Do you, O
Shades, be gracious to me, since the powers of heaven are
estranged; to you shall I go down, a pure spirit and

ignorant of your blame, never once unworthy of my mighty fathers of old.'

Scarce had he spoken thus; lo! Saces, borne flying on his foaming horse through the thickest of the foe, an arrow-wound right in his face, darts, beseeching Turnus by his name. 'Turnus, in thee is our last safety; pity thy people. Aeneas thunders in arms, and threatens to overthrow and hurl to destruction the high Italian fortress; and already fire-brands are flying on our roofs. On thee, on thee the Latins turn their gazing eyes; King Latinus himself mutters in doubt, whom he is to call his sons, to whom he shall incline in union. Moreover the queen, thy surest stay, hath fallen by her own hand and in dismay fled the light. Alone in front of the gates Messapus and valiant Atinas sustain the battle-line. Round about them to right and left the armies stand locked and the iron field shivers with naked points; thou wheelest thy chariot on the sward alone.' At the distracting picture of his fortune Turnus froze in horror and stood in dumb gaze; together in his heart sweep the vast mingling tides of shame and maddened grief, and love stung to frenzy and resolved valour. So soon as the dark-ness cleared and light returned to his soul, he fiercely turned his blazing eyeballs towards the ramparts, and gazed back from his wheels on the great city. And lo! a spire of flame wreathing through the floors wavered up sky-ward and held a turret fast, a turret that he himself had reared of mortised planks and set on rollers and laid with high gangways. 'Now, O my sister, now fate prevails: cease to hinder; let us follow where deity and stern fortune call. I am resolved to face Aeneas, resolved to bear what bitterness there is in death; nor shalt thou longer see me shamed, sister of mine. Let me be mad, I pray thee, with this madness before the end.' He spoke, and leapt swiftly from his chariot to the field, and darting through weapons

and through enemies, leaves his sorrowing sister, and bursts
in rapid course amid their columns. And as when a rock
rushes headlong from some mountain peak, torn away by
the blast, or if the rushing rain washes it away, or the
stealing years loosen its ancient hold ; the reckless mountain mass goes sheer and impetuous, and leaps along the
ground, hurling with it forests and herds and men ; thus
through the scattering columns Turnus rushes to the city
walls, where the earth is wettest with bloodshed and the air
sings with spears ; and beckons with his hand, and thus
begins aloud : ' Forbear now, O Rutulians, and you, Latins,
stay your weapons. Whatsoever fortune is left is mine : I
singly must expiate the treaty for you all, and make decision
with the sword.' All drew aside and left him room.

But lord Aeneas, hearing Turnus' name, abandons the
walls, abandons the fortress height, and in exultant joy
flings aside all hindrance, breaks off all work, and clashes
his armour terribly, vast as Athos, or as Eryx, or as the lord
of Apennine when he roars with his tossing ilex woods
and rears his snowy crest rejoicing into air. Now indeed
Rutulians and Trojans and all Italy turned in emulous
gaze, and they who held the high city, and they whose ram
was battering the foundations of the wall, and unarmed
their shoulders. Latinus himself stands in amaze at the
mighty men, born in distant quarters of the world, met and
making decision with the sword. And they, in the empty
level field that cleared for them, darted swiftly forward, and
hurling their spears from far, close in battle shock with
clangour of brazen shields. Earth utters a moan ; the
sword-strokes fall thick and fast, chance and valour joining
in one. And as in broad Sila or high on Taburnus, when
two bulls rush to deadly battle forehead to forehead, the
herdsmen retire in terror, all the herd stands dumb in
dismay, and the heifers murmur in doubt which shall be

lord in the woodland, which all the cattle must follow;
they violently deal many a mutual wound, and gore with
their stubborn horns, bathing their necks and shoulders in
abundant blood; all the woodland moans back their
bellowing : even thus Aeneas of Troy and the Daunian
hero rush together shield to shield; the mighty crash fills
the sky. Jupiter himself holds up the two scales in even
balance, and lays in them the different fates of both, trying
which shall pay forfeit of the strife, whose weight shall sink
in death. Turnus darts out, thinking it secure, and rises
with his whole reach of body on his uplifted sword ; then
strikes ; Trojans and Latins cry out in excitement, and
both armies strain their gaze. But the treacherous sword
shivers, and in mid stroke deserts its eager lord. If flight
aid him not now! He flies swifter than the wind, when
once he descries a strange hilt in his weaponless hand.
Rumour is that in his headlong hurry, when mounting
behind his yoked horses to begin the battle, he left his
father's sword behind and caught up his charioteer Metiscus'
weapon; and that served him long, while Teucrian
stragglers turned their backs; when it met the divine
Vulcanian armour, the mortal blade like brittle ice snapped
in the stroke ; the shards lie glittering upon the yellow
sand. So in distracted flight Turnus darts afar over the
plain, and now this way and now that crosses in wavering
circles; for on all hands the Teucrians locked him in
crowded ring, and the dreary marsh on this side, on this
the steep city ramparts hem him in.

  Therewith Aeneas pursues, though ever and anon his
knees, disabled by the arrow, hinder and stay his speed ;
and foot hard on foot presses hotly on his hurrying enemy :
as when a hunter courses with a fleet barking hound some
stag caught in a river-loop or girt by the crimson-feathered
toils, and he, in terror of the snares and the high river-bank,

darts back and forward in a thousand ways; but the keen
Umbrian clings agape, and just catches at him, and as
though he caught him snaps his jaws while the baffled
teeth close on vacancy.   Then indeed a cry goes up, and
banks and pools answer round about, and all the sky
echoes the din.   He, even as he flies, chides all his
Rutulians, calling each by name, and shrieks for the sword
he knew.   But Aeneas denounces death and instant doom
if one of them draw nigh, and doubles their terror with
threats of their city's destruction, and though wounded
presses on.   Five circles they cover at full speed, and
unwind as many this way and that; for not light nor slight
is the prize they seek, but Turnus' very lifeblood is at
issue.   Here there haply had stood a bitter-leaved wild
olive, sacred to Faunus, a tree worshipped by mariners of
old; on it, when rescued from the waves, they were wont to
fix their gifts to the god of Laurentum and hang their
votive raiment; but the Teucrians, unregarding, had
cleared away the sacred stem, that they might meet on
unimpeded lists.   Here stood Aeneas' spear; hither borne
by its own speed it was held fast stuck in the tough root.
The Dardanian stooped over it, and would wrench away
the steel, to follow with the weapon him whom he could
not catch in running.   Then indeed Turnus cries in frantic
terror: 'Faunus, have pity, I beseech thee! and thou, most
gracious Earth, keep thy hold on the steel, as I ever have
kept your worship, and the Aeneadae again have polluted
it in war.'   He spoke, and called the god to aid in vows
that fell not fruitless.   For all Aeneas' strength, his long
struggling and delay over the tough stem availed not to
unclose the hard grip of the wood.   While he strains and
pulls hard, the Daunian goddess, changing once more into
the charioteer Metiscus' likeness, runs forward and passes
her brother his sword.   But Venus, indignant that the

Nymph might be so bold, drew nigh and wrenched away
the spear where it stuck deep in the root. Erect in fresh
courage and arms, he with his faithful sword, he towering
fierce over his spear, they face one another panting in the
battle shock.

Meanwhile the King of Heaven's omnipotence accosts
Juno as she gazes on the battle from a sunlit cloud. 'What
yet shall be the end, O wife? what remains at the last?
Heaven claims Aeneas as his country's god, thou thyself
knowest and avowest to know, and fate lifts him to the
stars. With what device or in what hope hangest thou
chill in cloudland? Was it well that a deity should be
sullied by a mortal's wound? or that the lost sword—for
what without thee could Juturna avail?—should be restored
to Turnus and swell the force of the vanquished? Forbear now, I pray, and bend to our entreaties; let not the
pain thus devour thee in silence, and distress so often flood
back on me from thy sweet lips. The end is come. Thou
hast had power to hunt the Trojans over land or wave, to
kindle accursed war, to put the house in mourning, and
plunge the bridal in grief: further attempt I forbid thee.'
Thus Jupiter began: thus the goddess, daughter of Saturn,
returned with looks cast down :

'Even because this thy will, great Jupiter, is known to
me for thine, have I left, though loth, Turnus alone on
earth; nor else wouldst thou see me now, alone on this
skyey seat, enduring good and bad; but girt in flame I
were standing by their very lines, and dragging the Teucrians
into the deadly battle. I counselled Juturna, I confess it,
to succour her hapless brother, and for his life's sake
favoured a greater daring; yet not the arrow-shot, not the
bending of the bow, I swear by the merciless well-head of
the Stygian spring, the single ordained dread of the gods in
heaven. And now I retire, and leave the battle in loathing.

This thing I beseech thee, that is bound by no fatal law,
for Latium and for the majesty of thy kindred.   When
now they shall plight peace with prosperous marriages (be
it so!), when now they shall join in laws and treaties, bid
thou not the native Latins change their name of old, nor
become Trojans and take the Teucrian name, or change
their language, or alter their attire: let Latium be, let
Alban kings endure through ages, let Italian valour be
potent in the race of Rome.   Troy is fallen; let her and
her name lie where they fell.'
      To her smilingly the designer of men and things :
      ' Jove's own sister thou art, and second seed of Saturn,
such surge of wrath tosses within thy breast !   But come,
allay this madness so vainly stirred.   I give thee thy will,
and yield thee ungrudged victory.   Ausonia shall keep her
native speech and usage, and as her name is, it shall be.
The Trojans shall sink mingling into their blood; I will
add their sacred law and ritual, and make all Latins and
of a single speech.   Hence shall spring a race of tempered
Ausonian blood, whom thou shalt see outdo men and gods
in duty; nor shall any nation so observe thy worship.'   To
this Juno assented, and in gladness withdrew her purpose ;
meanwhile she quits her cloud, and retires out of the sky.
      This done, the Father revolves inly another counsel,
and prepares to separate Juturna from her brother's arms.
Twin monsters there are, called the Dirae by their name,
whom with infernal Megaera the dead of night bore at one
single birth, and wreathed them in like serpent coils, and
clothed them in windy wings.   They appear at Jove's
throne and in the courts of the grim king, and quicken the
terrors of wretched men whensoever the lord of heaven
deals sicknesses and dreadful death, or sends terror of war
upon guilty cities.   One of these Jupiter sent swiftly down
from heaven's height, and bade her meet Juturna for a

sign. She wings her way, and darts in a whirlwind to earth.
Even as an arrow through a cloud, darting from the string
when Parthian hath poisoned it with bitter gall, Parthian or
Cydonian, and sped the immedicable shaft, leaps through
the swift shadow whistling and unknown; so sprung and
swept to earth the daughter of Night. When she espies the
Ilian ranks and Turnus' columns, suddenly shrinking to the
shape of a small bird that often sits late by night on tombs
or ruinous roofs, and vexes the darkness with her cry, in
such change of likeness the monster shrilly passes and
repasses before Turnus' face, and her wings beat restlessly
on his shield. A strange numbing terror unnerves his
limbs, his hair thrills up, and the accents falter on his
tongue. But when his hapless sister knew afar the whistling wings of the Fury, Juturna unbinds and tears her
tresses, with rent face and smitten bosom. ' How, O
Turnus, can thine own sister help thee now? or what more
is there if I break not under this? What art of mine can
lengthen out thy day? can I contend with this ominous
thing? Now, now I quit the field. Dismay not my
terrors, disastrous birds; I know these beating wings, and
the sound of death, nor do I miss high-hearted Jove's
haughty ordinance. Is this his repayment for my maidenhood? what good is his gift of life for ever? why have I
forfeited a mortal's lot? Now assuredly could I make all
this pain cease, and go with my unhappy brother side by
side into the dark. Alas mine immortality! will aught of
mine be sweet to me without thee, my brother? Ah, how
may Earth yawn deep enough for me, and plunge my godhead in the under world!'

So spoke she, and wrapping her head in her gray vesture,
the goddess moaning sore sank in the river depth.

But Aeneas presses on, brandishing his vast tree-like
spear, and fiercely speaks thus: ' What more delay is there

now? or why, Turnus, dost thou yet shrink away? Not in speed of foot, in grim arms, hand to hand, must be the conflict. Transform thyself as thou wilt, and collect what strength of courage or skill is thine ; pray that thou mayest wing thy flight to the stars on high, or that sheltering earth may shut thee in.' The other, shaking his head : ' Thy fierce words dismay me not, insolent I the gods dismay me, and Jupiter's enmity.' And no more said, his eyes light on a vast stone, a stone ancient and vast that haply lay upon the plain, set for a landmark to divide contested fields : scarcely might twelve chosen men lift it on their shoulders, of such frame as now earth brings to birth : then the hero caught it up with trembling hand and whirled it at the foe, rising higher and quickening his speed. But he knows not his own self running nor going nor lifting his hands or moving the mighty stone ; his knees totter, his blood freezes cold ; the very stone he hurls, spinning through the empty void, neither wholly reached its distance nor carried its blow home. And as in sleep, when nightly rest weighs down our languorous eyes, we seem vainly to will to run eagerly on, and sink faint amidst our struggles; the tongue is powerless, the familiar strength fails the body, nor will words or utterance follow : so the disastrous goddess brings to naught all Turnus' valour as he presses on. His heart wavers in shifting emotion ; he gazes on his Rutulians and on the city, and falters in terror, and shudders at the imminent spear; neither sees he whither he may escape nor how rush violently on the enemy, and nowhere his chariot or his sister at the reins. As he wavers Aeneas poises the deadly weapon, and, marking his chance, hurls it in from afar with all his strength of body. Never with such a roar are stones hurled from some engine on ramparts, nor does the thunder burst in so loud a peal. Carrying grim death with it, the spear flies in fashion of some dark whirlwind, and opens the rim of the corslet and the utmost circles of the sevenfold shield. Right through the thigh it passes hurtling on; under the blow Turnus falls huge to earth with his leg doubled under him. The Rutulians start up with a groan, and all the hill echoes round about, and the width of high woodland returns their cry. Lifting up beseechingly his humbled eyes and suppliant hand: 'I have deserved it,' he says, 'nor do I ask for mercy; use thy fortune. If an unhappy parent's distress may at all touch thee, this I pray; even such a father was Anchises to thee; pity Daunus' old age, and restore to my kindred which thou wilt, me or my body bereft of day. Thou art conqueror, and Ausonia hath seen me stretch conquered hands. Lavinia is thine in marriage; press not thy hatred farther.'

Aeneas stood wrathful in arms, with rolling eyes, and lowered his hand; and now and now yet more the speech began to bend him to waver: when high on his shoulder appeared the sword-belt with the shining bosses that he knew, the luckless belt of the boy Pallas, whom Turnus had struck down with mastering wound, and wore on his shoulders the fatal ornament. The other, as his eyes drank in the plundered record of his fierce grief, kindles to fury, and cries terrible in anger: 'Mayest thou, thou clad in the spoils of my dearest, escape mine hands? Pallas it is, Pallas who now strikes the sacrifice, and exacts vengeance in thy guilty blood.' So saying, he fiercely plunges the steel full in his breast. But his limbs grow slack and chill, and the life with a moan flies indignantly into the dark.

THE END.

NOTES

Book First

l. 123—*Accipiunt inimicum imbrem*. Inimica non tantum hostilia sed perniciosa.—Serv. on ix. 315. The word often has this latter sense in Virgil.

l. 396—*Aut capere aut captas iam despectare videntur*. Henry seems unquestionably right in explaining *captas despectare* of the swans rising and hovering over the place where they had settled, this action being more fully expressed in the next two lines. The parallelism between ll. 396 and 400 exists, but it is inverted, *capere* corresponding to *subit*, *captas despectare* to *tenet*.

l. 427—*lata theatris* with the balance of MS. authority.

l. 550—*Arvaque* after Med. and Pal. ; *armaque* Con.

l. 636—*Munera laetitiamque die* ('ut multi legunt,' says Serv.), though it has little MS. authority, has been adopted because it is strongly probable on internal grounds, as giving a basis for the other two readings, *dei* and *dii*.

l. 722—*The long-since-unstirred spirit*.
And weep afresh love's long-since-cancell'd woe.
                                SHAKESPEARE, Sonnet XXX.

l. 726—*dependent lychni laquearibus aureis*. Serv. on viii. 25, *summique ferit laquearia tecti*, says 'multi lacuaria legunt. nam lacus dicuntur: unde est . . . lacunar. non enim a laqueis dicitur.' As Prof. Nettleship has pointed out, this seems to indicate that there are two words, *laquear* from *laqueus*, meaning chain or network, and *lacuar* or *lacunar* from *lacus*, meaning sunk work.

Book Second

l. 30—*Classibus hic locus.* Ad equites referre debemus.—Serv. Cf. also vii. 716.

L 76—Omitted with the best MSS.

L 234—*moenia pandimus urbis.* Moenia cetera urbis tecta vel aedes accipiendum.—Serv. This is the sense which the word generally has in Virgil : it is often used in contrast with *muri*, or as a synonym of *urbs ;* and in most cases *city* is its nearest English equivalent.

l. 381—*caerula colla tumentem.* Caerulum est viride cum nigro.—Serv. on vii. 198. Cf. iii. 208, where it is used of the colour of the sea after a storm.

l. 616—*nimbo effulgens.* est fulgidum lumen quo deorum capita cinguntur. sic etiam pingi solet.—Serv. Cf. xii. 416.

Book Third

l. 127—*freta concita terris* with all the best MSS. ; *consita* Con.

l. 152—*qua se Plena per insertas fundebat Luna fenestras.* The usual explanation, which makes *insertas* an epithet transferred by a sort of hypallage from *Luna* to *fenestras,* is extremely violent, and makes the word little more than a repetition of *se fundebat.* Servius mentions two other interpretations ; *non seratas, quasi insertatas,* and *clatratas ;* the last has been adopted in the translation.

In the passage of Lucretius (ii. 114) which Virgil has imitated here,

Contemplator enim cum solis lumina . . .

Inserti fundunt radii per opaca domorum,

it is possible that *clatris* may be the lost word.

l. 684—*Contra iussa monent Heleni, Scyllam atque Charybdim Inter, utramque viam leti discrimine parvo Ni teneant cursus.*

In this difficult passage it is probably best to take *cursus* as the subject to teneant (*cursus teneant,* id est agantur.—Serv. Cf. also l. 454 above, *quamvis vi cursus in altum Vela vocet*), *viam* being either the direct object of *teneant,* or in loose apposition to *Scyllam atque Charybdim.*

l. 708—*tempestatibus actis* with Rom. and Pal.; *actus* Con. after Med.

BOOK FOURTH

Totus hic liber . . . in consiliis et subtilitatibus est. nam paene comicus stilus est. nec mirum, ubi de amore tractatur. —Serv.

l. 273—Omitted with the best MSS.

l. 528—Omitted with the best MSS.

BOOK FIFTH

l. 595—*iuduntque per undas*, omitted with the preponderance of MS. authority.

BOOK SIXTH

l. 242—Omitted with the balance of MS. authority.

l. 806—*virtutem extendere factis* with Med.; *virtute extendere vires* Con.

BOOK EIGHTH

l. 46—Omitted with the majority of the best MSS.

l. 383—*Arma rogo. Genetrix nato te filia Nerei.*

Arma rogo. hic distinguendum, ut cui petat non dicat, sed relinquat intellegi . . . *Genetrix nato te filia Nerei.* hoc est, soles hoc praestare matribus.—Serv.

BOOK NINTH

l. 29—Omitted with all the best MSS.

l. 122—Omitted with all the best MSS.

l. 281—   *Me nulla dies tam fortibus ausis*
             Dissimilem arguerit tantum, Fortuna secunda
             Aut adversa cadat.

With some hesitation I have adopted this reading as the one open to least objection, though the balance of authority is decidedly in favour of *haud adversa.* For the position of *tantum* cf. Ecl. x. 46, according to the 'subtilior explicatio' now generally adopted.

l. 412—*Et venit adversi in tergum Sulmonis ibique*
Frangitur, et fisso transit praecordia ligno.
   The phrase *in tergum* occurs twice elsewhere : ix. 764—meaning 'on the back'; and xi. 653—meaning 'backward'; and in x. 718 the uncertainty about the order of the lines makes it possible that *tergo decutit hastas* was meant to refer to the boar, not to Mezentius. But the passages quoted by the editors there shew that the word might be used in the sense of 'shield'; and this being so we are scarcely justified in reading *aversi* against all the good MSS.

l. 529—Omitted with most MSS.

Book Tenth

l. 278—Omitted with the best MSS.

l. 754—*Insidiis, iaculo et longe fallente sagitta.* The MS. authority is decidedly in favour of this, the more difficult reading ; and the hendiadys is not more violent than those in Georg. ii. 192, Aen. iii. 223.

Book Twelfth

l. 218—*Tum magis, ut propius cernunt non viribus aequis.*
   With Ribbeck I believe that there is a gap in the sense here, and have marked one in the translation.

l. 520—*Limina* with Med. *Numera* Con.

ll. 612, 613—Omitted with the best MSS.

l. 751—*Venator cursu canis et latratibus instat.* I take *cursu canis* as equivalent to *currente cane*, as in i. 324, *spumantis apri cursum clamore prementem.*

www.ingramcontent.com/pod-product-compliance
Lightning Source LLC
Chambersburg PA
CBHW031405270326
41929CB00010BA/1329